FREE Study Skills DVD

Dear Customer,

Thank you for your purchase from Mometrix! We consider it an honor and privilege that you have purchased our product and want to ensure your satisfaction.

As a way of showing our appreciation and to help us better serve you, we have developed a Study Skills DVD that we would like to give you for <u>FREE</u>. **This DVD covers our "best practices" for studying for your exam, from using our study materials to preparing for the day of the test.**

All that we ask is that you email us your feedback that would describe your experience so far with our product. Good, bad or indifferent, we want to know what you think!

To get your **FREE Study Skills DVD**, email <u>freedvd@mometrix.com</u> with "FREE STUDY SKILLS DVD" in the subject line and the following information in the body of the email:

    a. The name of the product you purchased.

    b. Your product rating on a scale of 1-5, with 5 being the highest rating.

    c. Your feedback. It can be long, short, or anything in-between, just your impressions and experience so far with our product. Good feedback might include how our study material met your needs and will highlight features of the product that you found helpful.

    d. Your full name and shipping address where you would like us to send your free DVD.

If you have any questions or concerns, please don't hesitate to contact me directly.

Thanks again!

Sincerely,

Jay Willis
Vice President
<u>jay.willis@mometrix.com</u>
1-800-673-8175

FTCE

Prekindergarten/Primary PK–3

SECRETS

Study Guide
Your Key to Exam Success

FTCE Test Review for the
Florida Teacher Certification Examinations

Published by
Mometrix Test Preparation
FTCE Exam Secrets Test Prep Team

Copyright © 2017 by Mometrix Media LLC

All rights reserved. This product, or parts thereof, may not be reproduced, stored in a retrieval system, or transmitted in any form or by any means—electronic, mechanical, photocopy, recording, scanning, or other—except for brief quotations in critical reviews or articles, without the prior written permission of the publisher.

Written and edited by the FTCE Exam Secrets Test Prep Staff

Printed in the United States of America

This paper meets the requirements of ANSI/NISO Z39.48-1992 (Permanence of Paper).

Mometrix offers volume discount pricing to institutions. For more information or a price quote, please contact our sales department at sales@mometrix.com or 888-248-1219.

Mometrix Media LLC is not affiliated with or endorsed by any official testing organization. All organizational and test names are trademarks of their respective owners.

ISBN 13: 978-1-60971-755-1
ISBN 10:1-60971-755-4

Dear Future Exam Success Story:

Congratulations on your purchase of our study guide. Our goal in writing our study guide was to cover the content on the test, as well as provide insight into typical test taking mistakes and how to overcome them.

Standardized tests are a key component of being successful, which only increases the importance of doing well in the high-pressure high-stakes environment of test day. How well you do on this test will have a significant impact on your future, and we have the research and practical advice to help you execute on test day.

The product you're reading now is designed to exploit weaknesses in the test itself, and help you avoid the most common errors test takers frequently make.

How to use this study guide

We don't want to waste your time. Our study guide is fast-paced and fluff-free. We suggest going through it a number of times, as repetition is an important part of learning new information and concepts.

First, read through the study guide completely to get a feel for the content and organization. Read the general success strategies first, and then proceed to the content sections. Each tip has been carefully selected for its effectiveness.

Second, read through the study guide again, and take notes in the margins and highlight those sections where you may have a particular weakness.

Finally, bring the manual with you on test day and study it before the exam begins.

Your success is our success

We would be delighted to hear about your success. Send us an email and tell us your story. Thanks for your business and we wish you continued success.

Sincerely,

Mometrix Test Preparation Team

Need more help? Check out our flashcards at: http://MometrixFlashcards.com/FTCE

TABLE OF CONTENTS

Top 20 Test Taking Tips

1. Carefully follow all the test registration procedures
2. Know the test directions, duration, topics, question types, how many questions
3. Setup a flexible study schedule at least 3-4 weeks before test day
4. Study during the time of day you are most alert, relaxed, and stress free
5. Maximize your learning style; visual learner use visual study aids, auditory learner use auditory study aids
6. Focus on your weakest knowledge base
7. Find a study partner to review with and help clarify questions
8. Practice, practice, practice
9. Get a good night's sleep; don't try to cram the night before the test
10. Eat a well balanced meal
11. Know the exact physical location of the testing site; drive the route to the site prior to test day
12. Bring a set of ear plugs; the testing center could be noisy
13. Wear comfortable, loose fitting, layered clothing to the testing center; prepare for it to be either cold or hot during the test
14. Bring at least 2 current forms of ID to the testing center
15. Arrive to the test early; be prepared to wait and be patient
16. Eliminate the obviously wrong answer choices, then guess the first remaining choice
17. Pace yourself; don't rush, but keep working and move on if you get stuck
18. Maintain a positive attitude even if the test is going poorly
19. Keep your first answer unless you are positive it is wrong
20. Check your work, don't make a careless mistake

Copyright © Mometrix Media. You have been licensed one copy of this document for personal use only. Any other reproduction or redistribution is strictly prohibited. All rights reserved.

Child Growth and Development

Sensorimotor period of cognitive development

From birth to 1 month old, infants learn to comprehend their environment through their inborn reflexes, such as the sucking reflex and the reflex of looking at their surroundings. From 1–4 months old, babies begin to coordinate their physical sensations with new schemas, i.e. mental constructs/concepts they form to represent elements of reality. For example, an infant might suck her thumb by chance and feel pleasure from the activity; in the future, she will repeat thumb-sucking because the pleasure is rewarding. Piaget called this second substage "Primary Circular Reactions." In the third substage, around 4–8 months, which he called "Secondary Circular Reactions," children also repeat rewarding actions, but now they are focused on things in the environment that they can affect, rather than just the child's own person. For example, once a baby learns to pick up an object and mouth it, s/he will repeat this. Thus, babies learn an early method of environmental exploration through their mouths, an extension of their initial sucking reflex.

According to Piaget, babies about 8–12 months are in the "Coordination of Reactions" substage of the Sensorimotor stage. Having begun repeating actions purposely to achieve environmental effects during the previous substage of Secondary Circular Reactions, in Coordination of Reactions, infants begin further exploring their surroundings. They frequently imitate others' observed behaviors. They more obviously demonstrate intentional behaviors. They become able to combine schemas (mental constructs) to attain certain results. They develop object permanence, the understanding that unseen objects still exist. They learn to associate certain objects with their properties. For example, once a baby realizes a rattle makes a noise when shaken, s/he will deliberately shake it to produce the sound. In "Tertiary Circular Reactions," at about 12–18 months, children begin experimenting through trial-and-error. For instance, a child might test various actions or sounds for getting parents' attention. From 18–24 months, in the substage of "Early Representational Thought," children begin representing objects and events with symbols. They begin to understand the world via not only actions, but mental operations.

From birth until about 2 years of age, infants are in what Piaget termed the Sensorimotor stage of cognitive development. They learn through environmental input they receive through their senses; motor actions they engage in; and through feedback they receive from their bodies and the environment about their actions. For example, a baby kicks his legs, sees his feet moving, and reaches for them. He sees objects, reaches for them, and grasps them. Eventually, babies learn they can make some objects move by touching or hitting them. They learn through repeated experiences that when they throw objects out of their cribs, their parents retrieve them. They will seem to make a game of this, not to annoy parents, but as a way of learning rules of cause and effect by repeating actions to see the same results. They also enjoy their ability to be causal agents and their power to achieve effects through their actions.

Object permanence

One of the landmarks of infant cognitive development is learning that concrete objects are not "out of sight, out of mind"; in other words, things still continue to exist even when they are out of our sight. Babies generally develop this realization around 8–9 months old, though some may be earlier or later. Some researchers after Piaget have found object permanence in babies as young as 3 1/2 months. Younger infants typically attend to an object of interest only when they can see it; if it is

Copyright © Mometrix Media. You have been licensed one copy of this document for personal use only. Any other reproduction or redistribution is strictly prohibited. All rights reserved.

removed or hidden, they are upset/confused at its disappearance and/or shift their attention to something else. A sign that they have developed object permanence is if they search for the object after it is moved or hidden. Babies only become interested in "hide and seek" types of games once they have developed this understanding that the existence of objects and people persist beyond their immediate vision or proximity. Another example of emerging object permanence is the delight babies begin to take in "peek-a-boo" games.

Schema

Piaget proposed we form mental constructs or concepts that he called schemata, representing elements of the environment, beginning in infancy. A schema does not represent an individual object, but a category or class of things. For example, a baby might form a schema representing "things to suck on," initially including her bottle, her thumb, and her pacifier. Piaget said assimilation is when we can fit something new into an existing schema: the child in this example assimilates "Daddy's knee" into her schema of things she can suck on when she discovers this action. When something new cannot be assimilated into an existing schema, we either modify that schema or form a new schema, which both constitute accommodation. The baby in our example, becoming a toddler, might modify her schema of things to suck to include straws, which require a different sucking technique. Piaget said assimilation and accommodation combined constitute the process of adaptation, i.e. adjusting, to our environment through interacting with it.

Example 1: A toddler on an airplane sees a nearby stranger who is male, about 5'8", with white hair and eyeglasses. Both of his grandfathers have these same general appearances. He murmurs to himself, "Hi, Granddaddy."

The toddler in this example did not actually mistake a complete stranger for either one of his grandfathers. Notice that he did not directly address the stranger as "Granddaddy" with conversational loudness, but murmured it to himself. He recognized this man was not someone he knew. However, he recognized common elements with his grandfathers in the man's appearance. According to Piaget's theory of cognitive development, the explanation for this is that the child had formed a schema, i.e. a mental construct, to represent men about 5'8" with white hair and eyeglasses, based initially on his early knowledge of two such men he knew, his grandfathers, and then extending to include other similar-appearing men, through the process of assimilation of new information into an existing schema. His description did not mean he thought the stranger was named "Granddaddy." Rather, the word "Granddaddy" was not only the name he called one grandfather, but also the word he used to label his schema for all men who appeared to fit into this category.

Example 2: A toddler sees a large, brown dog through the window and says, "Moo."

Piaget found that forming schemas, or mental constructs to represent objects and actions, is how babies and children learn about themselves and the world through their interactions with their bodies and the environment. If they can fit a new experience into an existing schema, they assimilate it; or when necessary, they change an existing schema or form a new one to accommodate a new stimulus. Therefore, in this example, the toddler had seen cows in picture books, photos, or on a farm, and learned to associate the sound "Moo" with cows, reinforced by the teaching of toys, books, and adults. She had formed a schema for large, brown, four-legged, furry animals. Because the dog she saw fit these properties, she assimilated the dog into her cow schema. If she were then told this was a dog that says "Bow-wow," she would either form a new schema for

Copyright © Mometrix Media. You have been licensed one copy of this document for personal use only. Any other reproduction or redistribution is strictly prohibited. All rights reserved.

dogs; or, if she had previously only seen smaller dogs, accommodate (modify) her existing dog schema to include larger dogs.

Conservation

Conservation is the cognitive ability to understand that objects or substances retain their properties of numbers or amounts even when their appearance, shape, or configuration changes. Piaget found from his experiments with children that this ability develops around the age of five years. He also found children develop conservation of number, length, mass, weight, volume, and quantity respectively at slightly different ages. One example of a conservation experiment is with liquid volume: the experimenter pours the same amount of liquid into a short, wide container and a tall, thin one. Children who have not developed conservation of liquid volume typically say one container has more liquid, even though they saw both amounts were equal, based on one container's looking fuller. Similarly, children who have not developed conservation of number, shown equal numbers of beads, usually say a group arranged in a long row has more beads than a group clustered together. Children having developed conservation recognize the amounts are the same regardless of appearance.

Piaget

Piaget's Preoperational stage of cognitive development
Children between (roughly) two and six years old are in Piaget's Preoperational stage of cognitive development. Having begun to use objects to represent other things, i.e. symbolic representation, near the end of the previous Sensorimotor stage, children now further develop this ability during pretend/make-believe play. They may pretend a broom is a guitar or a horse; or talk using a block as a phone. Toddlers begin to play "house," pretending they and their playmates are the mommy, the daddy, the mailman, the doctor, etc. The reason Piaget called this stage Preoperational is that children are not yet capable of performing mental "operations," including following concrete logic or manipulating information mentally. Their thinking is intuitive rather than following logical steps. Piaget termed Preoperational children "egocentric" in that they literally cannot adopt another's point of view, even concretely: in experiments, after seeing pictures of a scene as viewed from different positions, children could not match a picture to another person's position, selecting the picture showing the scene from their own viewpoint.

Piaget's Preoperational vs. Concrete Operational stages of cognitive development
The different thinking found between Piaget's Preoperational and Concrete Operations stages is exemplified in experiments he and others conducted to prove his theory. For example, the absence/presence of ability to conserve liquid volume across shape/appearance has been shown in experiments with differently aged children. A preschooler is shown a tall, thin beaker and a short, wide one. The experimenter also shows the child two identically sized and shaped containers with identical amounts of liquid in each. The experimenter then pours the equal amounts of liquid into the two differently shaped beakers. The preschooler will say either the thin beaker holds more liquid because it is taller or the short beaker holds more because it is wider. Piaget termed this "centration"—focusing on only one property at a time. An older child "decentrates," can "conserve" the amount, and knows both beakers hold identical amounts. Older children also use reversibility and logic, e.g. "I know they are still equal, because I just saw you pour the same amount into each beaker."

Piaget called the stage of most children aged 2–6 years Preoperational because children these ages cannot yet perform mental operations, i.e. manipulate information mentally. At around 6–7 years

- 4 -

Copyright © Mometrix Media. You have been licensed one copy of this document for personal use only. Any other reproduction or redistribution is strictly prohibited. All rights reserved.

old, children begin to develop Concrete Operations. A key aspect of this stage is the ability to think logically. This ability first develops relative to concrete objects and events. Concrete Operational children still have trouble understanding abstract concepts or hypothetical situations, but they can apply logical sequences and cause and effect to things they can see, feel, and manipulate physically. For example, Concrete Operational children develop the understanding that things have the same amount or number regardless of their shape or arrangement, which Piaget termed conservation. They develop proficiency in inductive logic, i.e. drawing generalizations from specific instances. However, deductive logic, i.e. predicting specific results according to general principles, is not as well-developed until the later stage of Formal Operations involving abstract thought. Another key development of Concrete Operations is reversibility, i.e. the ability to reverse an action or operation.

Animism and magical thinking

Piaget found that children in the Preoperational stage are not yet able to perform logical mental operations. Their thinking is intuitive during the toddler and preschool years. One characteristic of the thinking of young children is animism, or assigning human qualities, feelings, and actions to inanimate objects. For example, a child seeing an autumn leaf fall off of a tree might remark, "The tree didn't like that leaf and pushed it off of its branch." Or a child with a sunburn might say, "The sun was angry at me and burned me." A related characteristic is magical thinking, which is attributing cause and effect relationships between their own feelings and thoughts and environmental events where none exists. For example, if a child says "I hate you" to another person or secretly dislikes and wishes the other gone, and something bad then happens to that person, the child is likely to believe what s/he said/felt/thought caused the other's unfortunate event. This is related to egocentrism—seeing everything as revolving around oneself.

Sensory, concrete, and centration characteristics of cognitive development

Preschool children do not think in the same ways as older children and adults do, as Piaget observed. Their thinking is strongly based upon and connected to their sensory perceptions. This means that in solving problems, they depend mainly on how things look, sound, feel, smell, and taste. Therefore, preschool children should always be given concrete objects that they can touch, explore, and experiment with in any learning experience. They are not yet capable of understanding abstract concepts or manipulating information mentally, so they must have real things to work with to understand premath concepts. For example, they will learn to count solid objects like blocks, beads, or pennies before they can count numbers in their heads. They cannot benefit from rote math memorization, or "sit still and listen" lessons. Since young children "centrate" on one characteristic/object/person/event at a time, adults can offer activities encouraging decentration/incorporating multiple aspects, e.g. not only grouping all triangles, but grouping all red triangles separately from blue triangles.

Stages of growth and development in art

Austrian and German art scholars established six stages in art. (1) The Scribble stage: from 2–4 years, children first make uncontrolled scribbles; then controlled scribbling; then progress to naming their scribbles to indicate what they represent. (2) The Preschematic stage: from ages 4–6, children begin to develop a visual schema. Schema, meaning mental representation, comes from Piaget's cognitive-developmental theory. Without complete comprehension of dimensions and sizes, children may draw people and houses the same height; they use color more emotionally than logically. They may omit or exaggerate facial features, or they might draw sizes by importance, e.g.

Copyright © Mometrix Media. You have been licensed one copy of this document for personal use only. Any other reproduction or redistribution is strictly prohibited. All rights reserved.

drawing themselves as largest among people or drawing the most important feature, e.g. the head, as the largest or only body part. (3) The Schematic stage: from 7–9 years, drawings more reflect actual physical proportions and colors. (4) Dawning Realism: from ages 9-11, drawings become increasingly representational. (5) Children aged 11–13 are in the Pseudorealistic stage, reflecting their ability to reason. (6) Children 14+ are in the Period of Decision stage, reflecting the adolescent identity crisis.

Viktor Lowenfeld

Viktor Lowenfeld (1903–1960) taught art to elementary school students and sculpture to blind students. Lowenfeld's acquaintance with Sigmund Freud, who was interested in his work with the blind, motivated Lowenfeld to pursue scientific research. He published several books on using creative arts activities therapeutically. Lowenfeld was familiar with six stages previously identified in the growth of art. He combined these with principles of human development drawn from the school of psychoanalytic psychology founded by Freud. In his adaptation, he named the six stages reflecting the development of children's art as Scribble, Preschematic, Schematic, Dawning Realism, Pseudorealistic, and Period of Decision. Lowenfeld identified adolescent learning styles as haptic, focused on physical sensations and subjective emotional experiences, and as visual, focused on appearances, each demanding corresponding instructional approaches. Lowenfeld's book Creative and Mental Growth (1947) was the most influential text in art education during the late 20th century. Lowenfeld's psychological emphasis in this text gave scientific foundations to creative and artistic expression, and identified developmentally age-appropriate art media and activities.

Music

Development of infants and young children
Long before they can speak, and before they even comprehend much speech, infants respond to the sounds of voices and to music. These responses are not only to auditory stimulation, but moreover to the emotional content in what they hear. Parents sing lullabies to babies; not only are these sounds pleasant and soothing, but they also help children develop trust in their environment as secure. Parents communicate their love to children through singing and introduce them to experiences of pleasure and excitement through music. As children grow, music progresses to be not only a medium of communication but also one of self-expression as they learn to sing/play musical sounds. Music facilitates memory, as we see through commercial jingles and mnemonic devices. Experiments find music improves spatial reasoning. Children's learning of perceptual and logical concepts like beginning/ending, sequences, cause-and-effect, balance, harmony/dissonance and mathematical number and timing concepts is reinforced by music. Music also promotes language development. Children learn about colors, counting, conceptual relationships, nature, and social skills through music.

Musical activities enhance emotional, social, aesthetic, and school readiness skills
Young children who are just learning to use spoken language often cannot express their emotions very well verbally. Music is a great aid to emotional development in that younger children can express happiness, sadness, anger, etc., through singing and/or playing music more easily than they can with words. Children of preschool ages not only listen to music and respond to what they hear, they also learn to create music through singing and playing instruments together with other children. These activities help them learn crucial social skills for their lives, like cooperating with others, collaborating, and making group or team efforts to accomplish something. When children are given guided musical experiences, they learn to make their own judgments of what is good or bad music; this provides them with the foundations for developing an aesthetic sense. Music

- 6 -

Copyright © Mometrix Media. You have been licensed one copy of this document for personal use only. Any other reproduction or redistribution is strictly prohibited. All rights reserved.

promotes preliteracy skills by enhancing phonemic awareness. As growing children develop musical appreciation and skills, these develop fundamental motor, cognitive, and social skills they need for language, school readiness, literacy, and life.

Learning activities that help young children develop cognitive abilities

As shown by Piaget, young children have difficulty reversing operations. Adults can ask them to build block structures, for example, and then dismantle them one block at a time to reverse the construction. They can ask children to retell rhymes or stories backward. They can take small groups of children for walks and ask them if they can return by the same route as they came. Young children often assume causal relationships where none exist. Adults can provide activities to produce and observe results, e.g. pouring water into different containers; knocking over bowling pins by swinging a pendulum; rolling wheeled toys down ramps; or blowing balls through mazes, and then asking them, "What happened when you did this? What would happen if you did this? What could you do to make this happen?" Young children are also often egocentric, seeing everything from their own viewpoint. Adults can help them take others' perspectives through guessing games wherein they must give each other clues to guess persons/objects and dramatic role-playing activities, where they pretend to be others.

Physical development and brain growth

Early childhood physical growth, while significant, is slower than infant growth. From birth to 2 years, children generally grow to four times their newborn weight and 2/3 their newborn length/height. From 2–3 years, however, children usually gain only about 4 lbs. and 3.5 inches. From 4–6 years, growth slows more; gains of 5–7 lbs. and 2.5 inches are typical. Due to slowing growth rates, 3- and 4-year-olds appear to eat less food, but do not; they actually just eat fewer calories per pound of body weight. Brain growth is still rapid in preschoolers: brains attain 55 percent of adult size by 2 years, and 90 percent by 6 years. The majority of brain growth is usually by 4–4.5 years, with a growth spurt around 2 years and growth rates slowing significantly between 5 and 6 years. Larger brain size indicates not more neurons, but larger sizes; differences in their organization; more glial cells nourishing and supporting neurons; and greater myelination (development of the sheath protecting nerve fibers and facilitating their efficient intercommunication).

Gender differences in motor development

On average, preschool boys have larger muscles than preschool girls, so they can run faster, climb higher, and jump farther. Boys at these ages tend to be more muscular physically. Preschool girls, while less muscular, are on the average more mature physically for their ages than boys. While boys usually exceed girls in their large-muscle, gross-motor abilities like running, jumping, and climbing, girls tend to surpass boys in small-muscle, fine-motor abilities like buttoning buttons, using scissors, and similar activities involving the manipulation of small tools, utensils, and objects. While preschool boys exhibit more strength in large-muscle, gross-motor actions, preschool girls are more advanced than preschool boys in large-muscle, gross-motor skills that do not demand strength so much as coordination, like hopping, balancing on one foot, and skipping. While these specific gender differences in preschoolers' physical and motor development have been observed consistently in research, it is also found that preschool girls' and boys' physical and motor development patterns are generally more similar than different overall.

Copyright © Mometrix Media. You have been licensed one copy of this document for personal use only. Any other reproduction or redistribution is strictly prohibited. All rights reserved.

Abilities in perceptual development that occur in infancy

In normal development, babies have usually established the ability to see, hear, smell, taste, and feel and also the ability to integrate such sensory information by the age of six months. Additional perceptual abilities, which are less obvious and more complex, continue to emerge throughout the early childhood years. For instance, young children develop increasing precision in recognizing visual concepts like size and shape. This development allows children to identify accurately the shape and size of an object no matter from what angle they perceive it. Infants have these capacities in place, but have not yet developed accuracy in using them. For example, a baby might realize that objects farther away occupy less of their visual fields than nearer objects; however, the baby has yet to learn just how much less of the visual field is taken up by the farther object. Young children attain this and similar kinds of learning by actively, energetically exploring their environments. Such activity is crucial for developing accurate perception of size, shape, and distance.

Progress in the typical motor development of young children

Genetics, physiological maturation, nutrition, and experience through practice combine to further preschoolers' motor skills development. Newborns' reflexive behaviors progress to preschoolers' voluntary activities. Also, children's perception of the size, shape, and position of the body and body parts becomes more accurate by preschool ages. In addition, increases in bilateral coordination of the body's two sides enhance preschoolers' motor skills. Motor skills development entails both learning new movements and gradually integrating previously learned movements into smooth, continuous patterns, as in learning to throw a ball with skill. Both large muscles, for gross-motor skills like climbing, running, and jumping, and small muscles, for fine-motor skills like drawing and tying knots, develop. Eye-hand coordination involves fine-motor control. Preschoolers use visual feedback, i.e. seeing whether they are making things go where and do what they want them to, in learning to manipulate small objects with their hands and fingers.

Nature-nurture interaction

The physical development of babies and young children is a product of the interactions between genetic and environmental factors. Also, a child's physical progress is equally influenced by environmental and psychological variables. For the body, brain, and nervous system to grow and develop normally, children must live in healthy environments. When the interaction of hereditary and environmental influences is not healthful, this is frequently reflected in abnormal patterns of growth. Failure to thrive syndrome is a dramatic example. When children are abused or neglected for long periods of time, they actually stop growing. The social environments of such children create psychological stress. This stress makes the child's pituitary gland stop releasing growth hormones, and growth ceases. When such environmental stress is relieved and these children are given proper care, stimulation, and affection, they begin growing again. They often grow rapidly enough to catch up on the growth they missed earlier. Normal body and brain growth—as well as psychological development—depend upon the collaboration of nature and nurture.

Interpreting pictures and eye movements

As adults, our ability to look at pictures of people and things in the environment is something we usually take for granted. Researchers have established that 3-year-old children's responses indicate their ability to recognize shading, line convergence, and other cues of depth in two-dimensional pictures. However, scientists have also found that children's sensitivity to these kinds of visual cues increases as they grow older. The eye movements and eye fixation patterns of young children affect

Copyright © Mometrix Media. You have been licensed one copy of this document for personal use only. Any other reproduction or redistribution is strictly prohibited. All rights reserved.

their ability to get the most complete and accurate information from pictorial representations of reality. When viewing pictures, adults sweep the entire picture to see it as a whole, their eye movements leaping around; to focus on specific details, adults use shorter eye movements. Preschool children differ from adults in using shorter eye movements overall, and focusing on small parts of the picture near the center or an edge. They therefore disregard, or do not see, a lot of the picture's available information.

Characteristics in art that reflects perceptual, cognitive, and motor development

Observations of young children find that while a 2 1/2-year-old can grasp a crayon and scribble with it, by the age of 4 years, s/he can draw a picture we recognize as human. The typical 4-year-old drawing of a human being is called the "tadpole person" because it has no body, a large head, and stick limbs. Between the ages of 3 and 4 years, children typically make a transition from scribbling to producing tadpole person drawings. This development is enabled by greater development in motor control and eye-hand coordination, among other variables. Between the ages of 4 and 5 years, children make another transition by progressing from drawing tadpole persons to drawing complete figures with heads and bodies. Howard Gardner, psychologist and author of the Multiple Intelligences theory, stated that children achieve a "summit of artistry" by the end of their preschool years. He describes their drawings as "characteristically colorful, balanced, rhythmic, and expressive, conveying something of the range and...vitality associated with artistic mastery." (1980)

Periods of communication development

Individual differences dictate a broad range of language development that is still normal. However, parents observing noticeably delayed language development in their children should consult professionals. Typically, babies respond to hearing their names by 6 months of age; turn their heads and eyes toward the sources of human voices they hear; and respond accordingly to friendly and angry tones of voice. By the age of 12 months, toddlers can usually understand and follow simple directions, especially when these are accompanied by physical and/or vocal cues. They can intentionally use one or more words with the correct meaning. By the age of 18 months, a normally developing child usually has acquired a vocabulary of roughly 5 to 20 words. 18-month-old children use nouns in their speech most of the time. They are very likely to repeat certain words and/or phrases over and over. At this age, children typically are able to follow simple verbal commands without needing as many visual or auditory cues as at 12 months.

By the time most children reach the age of 2 years, they have acquired a vocabulary of about 150 to 300 words. They can name various familiar objects found in their environments. They are able to use at least two prepositions in their speech, for example in, on, and/or under. 2-year-olds typically combine the words they know into short sentences. These sentences tend to be mostly noun-verb or verb-noun combinations (e.g. "Daddy work," "Watch this"). They may also include verb-preposition combinations (e.g. "Go out," "Come in"). By the age of 2 years, children use pronouns, such as I, me, and you. They typically can use at least two such pronouns correctly. A normally developing 2-year-old will respond to some commands, directions, or questions, such as "Show me your eyes" or "Where are your ears?"

By the time they are 3 years old, most normally developing children have acquired vocabularies of between 900 and 1,000 words. Typically they correctly use the pronouns I, me, and you. They use more verbs more frequently. They apply past tenses to some verbs and plurals to some nouns. 3-year-olds usually can use at least three prepositions; the most common are in, on, and under. The normally developing 3-year-old knows the major body parts and can name them. 3-year-olds

- 9 -

Copyright © Mometrix Media. You have been licensed one copy of this document for personal use only. Any other reproduction or redistribution is strictly prohibited. All rights reserved.

typically use 3-word sentences with ease. Normally, adults should find approximately 90 percent of what a 3-year-old says to be intelligible. Children this age comprehend most simple questions about their activities and environments and can answer questions about what they should do when they are thirsty, hungry, sleepy, hot, or cold. They can tell about their experiences in ways that adults can generally follow. By the age of 3 years, children should also be able to tell others their name, age, and sex.

When normally developing children are 4 years old, most know the names of animals familiar to them. They can use at least four prepositions in their speech (e.g. in, on, under, to, from, etc.). They can name familiar objects in pictures, and they know and can identify one color or more. Usually they are able to repeat four-syllable words they hear. They verbalize as they engage in their activities, which Vygotsky dubbed "private speech." Private speech helps young children think through what they are doing, solve problems, make decisions, and reinforce the correct sequences in multistep activities. When presented with contrasting items, 4-year-olds can understand comparative concepts like bigger and smaller. At this age, they are able to comply with simple commands without the target stimuli being in their sight (e.g. "Put those clothes in the hamper" [upstairs]). 4-year-old children will also frequently repeat speech sounds, syllables, words, and phrases, similar to 18-month-olds' repetitions but at higher linguistic and developmental levels.

Once most children have reached the age of 5 years, their speech has expanded from the emphasis of younger children on nouns, verbs, and a few prepositions, and is now characterized by many more descriptive words, including adjectives and adverbs. 5-year-olds understand common antonyms, e.g. big/little, heavy/light, long/short, hot/cold. They can now repeat longer sentences they hear, up to about nine words. When given three consecutive, uninterrupted commands, the typical 5-year-old can follow these without forgetting one or two. At age 5 most children have learned simple concepts of time like today, yesterday, tomorrow; day, morning, afternoon, night; and before, after, and later. 5-year-olds typically speak in relatively long sentences, and normally should be incorporating some compound sentences (with more than one independent clause) and complex sentences (with one or more independent and dependent clauses). 5-year-old children's speech is also grammatically correct most of the time.

Language and communication development depend strongly on the language a child develops within the first five years of life. During this time, three developmental periods are observed. At birth, the first period begins. This period is characterized by infant crying and gazing. Babies communicate their sensations and emotions through these behaviors, so they are expressive; however, they are not yet intentional. They indirectly indicate their needs through expressing how they feel, and when these needs are met, these communicative behaviors are reinforced. These expressions and reinforcement are the foundations for the later development of intentional communication. This becomes possible in the second developmental period, between 6 and 18 months. At this time, infants become able to coordinate their attention visually with other people relative to things and events, enabling purposeful communication with adults. During the third developmental period, from 18 months on, children come to use language as their main way of communicating and learning. Preschoolers can carry on conversations, exercise self-control through language use, and conduct verbal negotiations.

Human language abilities

Language and communication abilities are integral parts of human life that are central to learning, successful school performance, successful social interactions, and successful living. Human language ability begins before birth: the developing fetus can hear not only internal maternal

Copyright © Mometrix Media. You have been licensed one copy of this document for personal use only. Any other reproduction or redistribution is strictly prohibited. All rights reserved.

sounds, but also the mother's voice, others' voices, and other sounds outside the womb. Humans have a natural sensitivity to human sounds and languages from before they are born until they are about 4½ years old. These years are critical for developing language and communication. Babies and young children are predisposed to greater sensitivity to human sounds than other sounds, orienting them toward the language spoken around them. Children absorb their environmental language completely, including vocal tones, syntax, usage, and emphasis. This linguistic absorption occurs very rapidly. Children's first 2½ years particularly involve amazing abilities to learn language including grammatical expression.

Oral language skills achievements

Crucial oral language development skills enable children to (1) communicate by listening and responding to others' speech; (2) comprehend meanings of numerous words and concepts encountered in their listening and reading; (3) acquire information on subjects they are interested in learning about; and (4) use specific language to express their own thoughts and ideas. Research finds young children's ability to listen to, understand, and use spoken and written language is associated with their later reading, spelling, and writing literacy achievement. Infants typically begin developing oral language skills, which continue developing through life. Babies develop awareness of and attend to adult speech, and soon begin communicating their needs via gestures and speech sounds. Toddlers express emotions and ideas and solicit information via language. They start uttering simple sentences, asking questions, and giving opinions regarding their likes and dislikes. Young preschoolers expand their vocabularies from hearing others' speech and from books. They describe past and possible future events and unseen objects; tell fictional/"make-believe" stories; and use complete sentences and more complex language.

Adults' narration of child activities and actions

One oral language development technique adults can use is to narrate, i.e. describe what a child is doing as s/he does it. For example, a caregiver can say, "I see you're spreading paste on the back of your paper flower—not too much so it's lumpy, but not too little so it doesn't stick. Now you're pressing the flower onto your poster board. It sticks—good work!" Hence narration can be incorporated as prelude and segue to verbal positive reinforcement. This promotes oral language development by introducing and illustrating syntaxes. Communicating locations and directionality employs verbs and prepositions. Describing intensity and manner employs adverbs. Labeling objects/actions that are currently present/taking place with new vocabulary words serves immediately to place those words into natural contexts, facilitating more authentic comprehension of word meanings and better memory retention. Caregivers/teachers can narrate children's activities during formal instructional activities and informal situations like outdoor playtime, snack time, and cleanup time, and subsequently converse with them about what they did.

Personal narratives

Personal narratives are the way that young children relate their experiences to others by telling the stories of what happened. The narrative structure incorporates reporting components such as: who was involved; where the events took place; and what happened. Understanding and using this structure is crucial to young children for their communication; however, many young children cannot follow or apply this sequence without scaffolding (temporary support as needed) from adults. Adults can ask young children guiding questions to facilitate and advance narratives. They can also provide learning tools that engage children's visual, tactile (touch), and kinesthetic (body position and movement) senses. This reinforces narrative use, increases the depth of scaffolding,

Copyright © Mometrix Media. You have been licensed one copy of this document for personal use only. Any other reproduction or redistribution is strictly prohibited. All rights reserved.

and motivates children's participation. Children learn to play the main character; describe the setting; sequence plot actions; and use words and body language to express emotions. Topic-related action sequences or "social stories" are important for preschoolers to comprehend and express to promote daily transitions and self-regulation. Such conversational skills attainment achieves milestones in both linguistic and emotional-social development.

Play-based activities

When young children play, they often enact scenarios. Play scenarios tell stories that include who is involved, where they are, what happens, why it happens, and how the "actors" feel about it. Children engage in planning when they decide first what their playing will be about; which children are playing which roles; and who is doing what. This planning and the thought processes involved reflect narrative thinking and structure. Children who experience difficulties with planning play are more likely to avoid participating or to participate only marginally. Since playing actually requires these thought and planning processes, children who do not play spontaneously can be supported in playing by enabling them to talk about potential narratives/stories as foundations for play scenarios. When conflicts emerge during play, conversation is necessary to effect needed change. Narrative development constitutes gradual plot development; play conflicts are akin to fictional/personal narrative problems and result in changed feelings. Adults can help young children discuss problems, identify the changed feeling they cause, and discuss plans/actions for resolution.

Conversation with young children

Natural vs. intentional conversation
Children enjoy conversing with significant adults, including parents, caregivers, and teachers; and they require practice with doing so. Caregivers tend to talk with young children naturally, sometimes even automatically, throughout the day, which helps children develop significant language skills. However, caregivers can enhance young children's oral language development further through intentional conversations. One element of doing this is establishing an environment that gives the children many things to talk about and many reasons to talk. Another element of intentionally promoting oral language skills development is by engaging in shared conversations. When parents and caregivers share storybook reading with young children, this affords a particularly good springboard for shared conversations. Reading and conversing together are linguistic interactions supplying foundations for children's developing comprehension of numerous word meanings. Researchers find such abundant early word comprehension is a critical basis for later reading comprehension. Asking questions, explaining, requesting what they need, communicating feelings, and learning to listen to others talk are some important ways whereby children build listening, understanding, and speaking skills.

Elements that adults should include in their conversations with young children
Adults should converse with young children so the children get practice with: hearing and using rich and abstract vocabulary and increasingly complex sentences; using language to express ideas and ask questions for understanding; and using language to answer questions about past, future, and absent things rather than only about "here-and-now" things. To ensure they incorporate these elements in their conversations, adults can consider the following: in the home, care setting, or classroom, whose voices are heard most often and who does the most talking; the child, not the adult, should be talking at least half of the time. Adults should be using rich language with complex structures when conversing with young children. Adults should be talking with, not at children; the conversation should be shared equally rather than adults doing all the talking while children listen

Copyright © Mometrix Media. You have been licensed one copy of this document for personal use only. Any other reproduction or redistribution is strictly prohibited. All rights reserved.

to them. Adults should also ask young children questions, rather than just telling them things. Additionally, adult questions should require that children use language to formulate and communicate abstract ideas.

Benefits of adults having 1:1 conversations

When parents, caregivers, or teachers converse 1:1 with individual children, children reap benefits not as available in group conversations. Caregivers should therefore try to have such individual conversations with each child daily. In daycare and preschool settings, some good times for caregivers to do this include when children arrive and leave; during shared reading activities with one or two children; and during center time. 1:1 talk allows the adult to repeat what the child says for reinforcement. It allows the adult to extend what the child said by adding more information to it, like new vocabulary words, synonyms, meanings, or omitted details. It allows the adult to revise what the child said by restating or recasting it. It allows the child to hear his or her own ideas and thoughts reflected back to them when the adult restates them. Moreover, 1:1 conversation allows adults to contextualize the discussion accordingly with an individual child's understanding. It also allows adults to elicit children's comprehension of abstract concepts.

Extended conversations and turn-taking

When adults engage young children in extended conversations including taking many "back-and-forth" turns, these create the richest dialogues for building oral language skills. Adults make connections with and build upon children's declarations and questions. Adults model richer descriptive language by modifying/adding to children's original words with new vocabulary, adjectives, adverbs, and varying sentences with questions and statements. For example, a child shows an adult his/her new drawing, saying: "This is me and Gran in the garden," the adult can build on this/invite the child to continue: "What is your gran holding?" The child identifies what they planted: "Carrot seeds. Gran said to put them in the dirt so they don't touch." The adult can then encourage the child's use of language to express abstract thoughts: "What could happen if the seeds were touching?" The adult can then extend the conversation through discussion with the child about how plants grow or tending gardens. This introduces new concepts, builds children's linguistic knowledge, and helps them learn to verbalize their ideas.

Attaining in-depth comprehension of word meanings

To support deeper word-meaning comprehension, teachers can give multiple definitions and examples for the same word and connect new vocabulary with children's existing knowledge. For example, a teacher conducting a preschool classroom science experiment incorporates new scientific concepts with new vocabulary words and conversational practice: pouring water on a paper towel, the teacher asks children what is happening to the water. A child answers, "It's going into the paper." The teacher asks how. Another child says, "The paper's soaking it up." The teacher confirms this, teaches the word "absorb," compares the paper to a sponge, and asks how much more water will be absorbed. A child responds probably no more since water is already dripping out. The teacher pours water on a plastic lid, asking if it absorbs. Children respond, "No, it slides off." Confirming, the teacher teaches the word "repel." This teacher has introduced new science concepts and new vocabulary words; engaged the children in conversation; related new concepts and words to existing knowledge; and added information to deepen comprehension.

Copyright © Mometrix Media. You have been licensed one copy of this document for personal use only. Any other reproduction or redistribution is strictly prohibited. All rights reserved.

Topics that young children enjoy

Personal content is important with young children, who enjoy talking about themselves; e.g., what their favorite color is or where they got their new shirt; about their activities, like what they are constructing with Legos or shaping with Play-Doh; or about familiar events and things that access their knowledge, like their family activities and experiences with neighbors and friends. Here is an example of how a teacher can make use of children's conversation to reinforce it, expand it, and teach new vocabulary and grammar. The teacher asks a child what s/he is building and the child answers, "A place for sick animals." The teacher asks, "You mean an animal hospital [or vet clinic]?" and the child confirms. When a child says someone was taken to a hospital "in the siren," the teacher corrects the usage: "They took him to the hospital in the ambulance with the siren was sounding?" This recasts "siren" with the correct word choice, "ambulance." It incorporates "siren" correctly and extends the statement to a complete sentence.

Storytelling

Organize thoughts, practice new vocabulary, and exercise imagination

Young children like to communicate about their personal life experiences. When they can do this through narrative structure, it helps them use new words they are learning, organize their thoughts to express them coherently, and engage their imaginative powers. Teachers/caregivers can supply new words they need; model correct syntax for sentences by elaborating on or extending child utterances and asking them questions; and build further upon children's ideas. For example, a teacher asks a child what they did at her sister's birthday party. When the child describes the cake and makes gestures for a word she doesn't know, the teacher supplies "candles," which the child confirms and repeats. When the child then offers, "Mom says be careful with candles," the teacher asks what could happen if you're not careful, the child replies that candles can start a fire. In this way, teachers give young children models of sentence structure, teach vocabulary, and guide children in expressing their thoughts in organized sequences that listeners can follow.

Shared reading of books

When teachers share books with preschoolers, they can ask questions and discuss the content, giving great opportunities for building oral language through conversation. Books with simple text and numerous, engaging illustrations best invite preschoolers to talk about the characters and events in the pictures, and the plotlines they hear. Children's listening and speaking skills develop; they learn new information and concepts; their vocabularies increase; and their ability to define words and explain their meanings is enhanced through shared reading. Many children's books include rich varieties of words that may not occur in daily conversation, used in complete-sentence contexts. Teachers should provide preschoolers with fictional and nonfictional books; poetry and storybooks; children's reference books like picture dictionaries/encyclopedias; and "information books" covering single topics like weather, birds, reptiles, butterflies, or transportation whereby children can get answers to questions or learn topical information. Detailed illustrations, engaging content, and rich vocabulary are strong elements motivating children to develop oral language and understand how to form sentences, how to use punctuation, and how language works.

Abstract thought is stimulated by asking young children to think about things not observed and/or current. During/after sharing books, teachers can ask children what else might happen in the story; what they imagine the story's characters could be feeling or thinking—which also engages their imaginations; and ask them the meaning of the story's events using questions necessitating children's use of language to analyze this meaning. Teachers can ask younger children vocabulary

Copyright © Mometrix Media. You have been licensed one copy of this document for personal use only. Any other reproduction or redistribution is strictly prohibited. All rights reserved.

words: "What did we call this animal?" and encourage them to use language by asking them to describe story details, like "How do the firemen reach people up high in the building?" Once younger children are familiar with a story, teachers can activate and monitor their retention and recall: "Do you remember what happened to Arthur the day before that?" Teachers can ask older children to predict what they think will happen next in a story; to imagine extensions beyond the story ("What would you do if...?"); and make conclusions regarding why characters feel/behave as they do.

According to researchers' findings, the effectiveness of shared reading experiences is related to the ways that adults read with young children. Rather than merely labeling objects or events with vocabulary words, teachers should ask young children to recall the shared reading, which monitors their listening comprehension and retention abilities. They should ask children to predict what will happen next based on what already happened in a book; speculate about what could possibly happen; describe characters, actions, events, and information from the shared reading; and ask their own questions about it. Shared reading with small groups of 1–3 children permits teachers to involve each child in the book by questioning and conversing with them about the pictures and plots. To teach vocabulary, teachers can tell children word meanings; point to illustrations featuring new words; relate new words to words the children already know; give multiple, varied examples of new words; and encourage children to use new words they learn in their conversations.

Young children develop preferences for favorite books. Once they know a story's plot, they enjoy discussing their knowledge. Teachers can use this for extended conversations. They can ask children who the characters are; where the story takes place; and why characters do things and events occur. They can ask specific questions requiring children to answer how much/how many/how far a distance/how long a time, etc. Teachers can also help children via prompting to relate stories to their own real-life experiences. In a thematic approach, teachers can select several books on the same theme, like rain forests or undersea life. This affords richer extended conversations about the theme. It also allows teachers to "recycle" vocabulary by modeling and encouraging use of thematically related words, which enhances memory and in-depth comprehension of meanings. Teachers can plan activities based on book themes, like painting pictures/murals, sculpting, making collages, or constructing models, which gives children additional motivation to use the new language they learn from shared readings of books.

New experiences and information

Topics with interesting, rich content that stimulate young children's thinking are likelier to encourage them to engage in extended conversations. A teacher can base such conversations on experiences like exposure to interesting new objects/field trips. It is also a critical skill for young children to have conversations about past, future, and distant events. Their thinking is mostly concrete; getting them to discuss things that are not right here, right now, promotes their ability to think abstractly. For example, a teacher asks children what they saw visiting a construction site. One child says "a giant thing;" another supplies the word "crane;" a third specifies, "But a truck, not a bird." The teacher asks what it was doing, and one child says, "Picking up a big thing." The teacher supplies the term "I-beam," and asks, "Why do you think that's its name?" A child volunteers, "Because it looks like a big 'I'?" The teacher affirms the response and then asks the children what they think I-beams are used for in construction.

Copyright © Mometrix Media. You have been licensed one copy of this document for personal use only. Any other reproduction or redistribution is strictly prohibited. All rights reserved.

Print awareness

Even before they have learned how to read, young children develop print awareness, which constitutes children's first preparation for literacy. Children with print awareness realize that spoken language is represented by the markings on paper (or computer screens). They understand that the information in printed books adults read comes from the words, not the pictures. Children who have print awareness furthermore realize that print serves different functions within different contexts. They know that restaurant menus give information about the foods available; books tell stories or provide information; some signs show the names of stores, hotels, or restaurants, and other signs give traffic directions or danger warnings. Moreover, print awareness includes knowledge of how print is organized, e.g. that words are combinations of letters and have spaces in between them. Children with print awareness also know that [English] print is read from left to right and top to bottom; book pages are numbered; words convey ideas and meaning; and reading's purpose is to understand those ideas and acquire that meaning.

One way in which a teacher can get an idea of whether or to what extent a young child has developed print awareness is to provide the child with a storybook. Then the teacher can ask the child the following: "Show me the front of the book. Show me the back of the book. Show me the spine of the book. Where is the book's title? Where in the book are you supposed to start reading it? Show me a letter in the book. Now show me a word. Show me the first word of a sentence. Can you show me the last word of a sentence? Now will you show me the first word on a page? Please show me the last word on a page. Can you show me a punctuation mark? Can you show me a capital letter? Can you find a small letter/lowercase letter?" The teacher should also praise each correct response, supply the correct answers for incorrect responses, and review corrected answers.

Teachers should show young children the organization of books and the purpose of reading. When they read to them, they should use books with large print, which are more accessible for young children to view and begin to learn reading. Storybook text should use words familiar/predictable to young children. While reading together, teachers should point out high-frequency words like the, a, is, was, you; and specific letters, words, and punctuation marks in a story. Teachers can use index cards to label objects, areas, and centers in the classroom, pairing pictorial labels with word labels, and direct children's attention to them. They can invite preschoolers to play with printed words by making greeting cards, signs, or "writing" shopping lists and personal letters. They should point out print in calendars, posters, and signs. Also, teachers can have children narrate a story using a wordless picture book; write down their narrative on a poster; and reinforce the activity with a reward related to the story (e.g., eating pancakes after narrating the book Pancakes).

Environmental print

Street signs, traffic signs, store and restaurant names, candy wrappers, food labels, product logos, etc.—all the print we see in everyday life—are environmental print. Just as parents often play alphabetic games with children in the car ("Find something starting with A...with B..." etc.), adults can use environmental print to enhance print awareness and develop reading skills. They can ask children to find letters from their names on colorful cereal boxes. They can select one sign type, e.g. stop, one-way, or pedestrian crossing, and ask children to count how many they see during a car trip. They can have children practice reading each sign and talk about the phonemes (speech sounds) each letter represents. Adults can take photos of different signs and compile them into a little book for children to "read." By cutting familiar words from food labels, they can teach capitalized and lowercase letters; associate letters with phonemes; have children read the words; and sort words by their initial letters and by categories (signs, foods, etc.).

Copyright © Mometrix Media. You have been licensed one copy of this document for personal use only. Any other reproduction or redistribution is strictly prohibited. All rights reserved.

Reading a story aloud

Before reading a story aloud, adults should tell young children its title and the author's name. Then they can ask the children what an author does (children should respond "write stories" or something similar). Giving the illustrator's name, the adult also can then ask the children what illustrators do (children should respond "draw pictures" or something similar). Holding up the book, an adult can identify the front, spine, and back and ask the children if we start reading at the front or back (children should respond "at the front"). Adults can show young children the illustration on the front cover of the book and ask them, "From this picture, what do you think is going to happen in this story?" and remind them to answer this question in complete sentences. These exchanges before reading a story aloud activate children's fundamental knowledge regarding print and books, as well as the last example's exercising their imagination and language use.

When a teacher is reading a story aloud to young children, after reading each page aloud, s/he should have the children briefly discuss the picture illustrations on each page and how they relate to what the teacher just read aloud. After they read aloud each plot point, action, event, or page, they should ask the children open-ended (non yes/no) questions about what they just heard. This monitors and supports listening comprehension and memory retention/recall and stimulates expressive language use. When children associate something in the story with their own life experiences, teachers should have them explain the connection. As they read, teachers should stop periodically and ask the children to predict or guess what will happen next before continuing. This promotes abstract thinking, understanding of logical sequences, and also exercises the imagination. After reading the story, teachers should ask children whether they liked it and why/why not, prompting them to answer using complete sentences. This helps children to organize their thoughts and opinions and to develop clear, grammatical, complete verbal expression.

Just before reading a story aloud to young students, the teacher should identify vocabulary words in the story that s/he will need to go over with the children. The teacher can write these words on the board or on strips of paper. Discussing these words before the reading will give the children definitions for new/unfamiliar words, and help them understand word meanings within the story's context. Teachers can also give young children some open-ended questions to consider when listening to the story. They will then repeat these questions during and after the reading. Questions should NOT be ones children can answer with yes/no. When discussing vocabulary words, the teacher can also ask the children to relate words to personal life experiences. For example, with the word fish, some children may want to talk about going fishing with parents. Teachers can encourage children to tell brief personal stories, which will help them relate the story they are about to hear to their own real-life experience, making the story more meaningful.

Alphabetic principle

The alphabetic principle is the concept that letters and letter combinations represent speech sounds. Children's eventual reading fluency requires knowing these predictable relationships of letters to sounds, which they can then apply to both familiar and unfamiliar words. Young children's knowing the shapes and names of letters predicts their later reading success: knowing letter names is highly correlated with the ability to view words as letter sequences and to remember written/printed words' forms. Children must first be able to recognize and name letters to understand and apply the alphabetic principle. Young children learn letter names first, via singing the alphabet song and reciting rhymes and alphabetical jump-rope chants ("A my name is Alice, I come from Alabama, and I sell Apples; B my name is Betty..." etc.). They learn letter shapes

Copyright © Mometrix Media. You have been licensed one copy of this document for personal use only. Any other reproduction or redistribution is strictly prohibited. All rights reserved.

after names, through playing with lettered blocks, plastic/wood/cardboard letters, and alphabet books. Once they can recognize and name letters, children learn letter sounds after names and shapes and spellings after sounds.

To help young children understand that written or printed letters represent corresponding speech sounds, teachers should teach relationships between letters and sounds separately, in isolation, and should teach these directly and explicitly. They should give young children daily opportunities during lessons to practice with letter-sound relationships. These opportunities for practice should include cumulative reviews of sound-letter relationships they have already learned and new letter-sound relationships as well. Adults should begin early in providing frequent opportunities to young children for applying their increasing knowledge and understanding of sound-letter relationships to early experiences with reading. They can do this by providing English words that are spelled phonetically (i.e. spelled the same way that they sound) and have meanings that are already familiar to the young learners.

Self-concept

Self-concept development begins during early childhood. Children come to identify characteristics, abilities, values, and attitudes that they feel define them. From 18–36 months, children develop the Categorical Self. This is a concrete view of oneself, usually related to observably opposite characteristics, e.g. child versus adult, girl versus boy, short versus tall, and good versus bad. A four-year-old might say, "I'm shorter than Daddy. I have blue eyes. I can help Mommy clean house!" Young children can also describe emotional and attitudinal aspects of self-concept, e.g. "I like playing with Joshua. I'm happy today." Preschoolers do not usually integrate these aspects into a unified self-portrait, however. Also, many preschoolers do not yet realize one person can incorporate opposite qualities; a person is either good or bad to them, rather than having both good and bad qualities. The Remembered Self develops with long-term memory, including autobiographical memories and things adults have told them, to comprise one's life story. The Inner Self is the child's private feelings, desires, and thoughts.

Self-concept and self-esteem
Young children's self-concepts are founded on observable, readily defined, mainly concrete factors. Many young children also experience much adult encouragement. Because their self-concepts are more simple and concrete than those of older children and adults and because they typically receive abundant encouragement and positive reinforcement, preschoolers often have fairly high self-esteem, i.e. judgment regarding their own value. In general, young children tend to have positive, optimistic attitudes that they can learn something new, finish tasks, and succeed if they persist in their attempts. Self-esteem related specifically to one's ability to perform a given task is sometimes called "achievement-related attribution." Albert Bandura called it "self-efficacy." Young children derive self-esteem from multiple sources, including their relationships with their parents; their friendships; their abilities and achievements in tasks involving playing and helping others; their physical/athletic abilities; and their achievements in preschool/school.

Phonics instruction

Because children display individual differences in their speeds of learning sound-to-letter relationships, instruction should consider this; there is no set rate. Generally, a reasonable pace ranges from two to four sound-letter relationship per week. Relationships vary in utility: many words contain the sounds/letters m, a, t, s, p, and h, which are high-utility; but x as in box, gh as in through, ey as in they, and the sound of a as in want are lower-utility. High-utility sound-letter

Copyright © Mometrix Media. You have been licensed one copy of this document for personal use only. Any other reproduction or redistribution is strictly prohibited. All rights reserved.

relationships should be taught first. Teachers should first introduce consonant relationships using f, m, n, r, and s, which are continuous sounds children can produce in isolation with less distortion than word-initial or word-medial stops like p, b, t, d, k, and g. Teachers should also introduce similar-sounding letters like b and v or i and e, and similar-looking letters like b and d or p and g, separately to prevent confusion. Single consonants versus clusters/blends should be introduced in separate lessons. Blends should incorporate sound-letter relationships children already know.

Temperament types

Psychologists studied the behavior of infants and classified their characteristics into three types of temperaments: easy, difficult, and slow to warm up. The majority of infants are easy babies. When they cry from hunger/needing changing/being tired/feeling discomfort/needing cuddling/attention, they are easily soothed by having these needs met. They typically sleep well. While they experience normal negative emotions, their predominant mood is good. Other than normal stranger anxiety at applicable ages, they respond positively to meeting people. In contrast, difficult babies are more likely to cry longer and be much harder to soothe. It is often hard to get them to sleep, and they may sleep fitfully, with many interruptions and/or for shorter times. They are more easily frightened by strange/new people and things, and more easily upset overall. Slow to warm up babies can initially seem difficult by not being as immediately responsive to people other than their parents like easy babies. However, given some time to adjust, they eventually "warm up" to new people and situations.

Learning style

Young children with normal development learn in the same chronological sequences and learn the same types of skills. Even those with delayed development, as with intellectual disabilities, learn the same things in the same order, but simply at a slower rate and hence at later ages; and those with severe/profound impairment may never achieve certain developmental milestones. However, one aspect of learning that varies is learning style. For example, some children approach learning in a primarily visual manner. They focus on what they see and how things look. They learn best given visual stimuli, like colorful objects, pictures, and graphics. They understand abstract concepts and relationships better when these are illustrated visually. Other children approach learning in a primarily haptic or tactile way. They focus on textures and movements, learning through touch and kinesthetic senses. They learn best given concrete things to explore and manipulate, and physical activities to perform. They learn abstract concepts and relationships better through handling materials and engaging in physical movements and actions.

External and internal variables

External variables
The way young children see themselves is affected by the feedback they receive from other people. When adults like parents, caregivers, and teachers give young children positive responses to their efforts—whether they succeed initially or not—the children are more likely to develop positive self-concepts, engendering higher self-esteem, and greater self-efficacy, the belief that they have the competency to succeed at a specific task or activity. On the other hand, when adults frequently give punitive/judgmental/indifferent/otherwise negative responses to young children's efforts, children develop poorer self-images. They feel they are not valued/good/important/worthy. They develop lower self-esteem, and their self-efficacy is weaker; they come to expect failure when they attempt tasks and may not even try. Peers also affect young children's self-concepts and self-esteem.

Copyright © Mometrix Media. You have been licensed one copy of this document for personal use only. Any other reproduction or redistribution is strictly prohibited. All rights reserved.

When friends and classmates include a child in activities, this promotes a positive self-image and higher self-esteem and self-efficacy. If peers exclude, tease, or bully a young child, this can cause low self-esteem, make their self-concepts more negative, and lower their self-efficacy.

<u>Internal variable</u>
One major internal influence on self-concept is a child's basic temperament. Easy, difficult, and slow-to-warm-up temperaments in babies continue into early childhood (and throughout life). For example, children having easy temperaments are better prepared for coping with challenges and frustration. When they encounter difficulty attempting new tasks, they do not give up as easily and are more persistent. They are thus more likely to develop self-concepts of being good, valuable, and successful and hence have higher self-esteem. Since they experience more success through persistence, they develop greater self-efficacy, i.e. belief in their competence to perform specific tasks. Children with more difficult temperaments become frustrated more easily, after fewer attempts, and give up trying in discouragement or require extra help to perform new or challenging tasks. They are more at risk for believing they cannot succeed and hence are not valuable, leading to their developing lower self-esteem. This also affects self-efficacy: they are more likely to doubt their ability to perform a specific proposed task.

Locus of control

Psychologist Julian Rotter originated the term and concept of locus of control. It refers to the place (locus) where we attribute causes for outcomes we experience, either externally or internally. An external locus control is something outside of us—another person and/or his/her actions; an environmental event; or an unknown but exterior influence, like good/bad luck or random chance. An internal locus of control is something inside of us—our native ability, our motivation, or our effort. For example, blaming another for failing—"The teacher gave me something too hard/wouldn't help me/didn't tell me how to do it" or "Johnny was bothering me" are examples of external locus of control. Blaming conditions, e.g. "It was too dark/hot/cold/noisy/the sun was in my eyes" is also external. Individuals may also attribute successes externally: "The teacher helped me" or "Johnny showed me how" or "I was lucky." Blaming/crediting oneself for failure/success is internal locus of control: "I didn't study the new words" or "I'm stupid" with failures or "I worked hard"/"I'm smart" with successes.

Freud's psychoanalytic theory of personality development

Freud's orientation toward personality development was psychosexual. He believed the most important factors were the focus of erotic energy, which shifted in each developmental stage, and the child's early relationship with parents. Freud formulated five stages of development: Oral, Anal, Phallic, Latency, and Genital. He found if infants and children successfully complete each stage, they are well-adjusted; if not, they become fixated on one stage. Freud said infants from birth to 18 months are in the first Oral stage: their focus of pleasure is on the mouth as they suck to nurse. If a baby's oral need to nurse is met appropriately, s/he will progress to the following stage. However, if an infant's feeding needs are met either inadequately or excessively, s/he can develop an oral fixation. Signs of this in later life include tendencies to overeat, drink too much, smoke, bite one's nails, talk excessively, and other orally focused activities. Oral personalities either become overly dependent and gullible; or, when resisting oral compulsions, become pessimistic and aggressive to others.

Freud's theory divided personality development into five stages, each based on the corresponding erogenous zone: Oral, Anal, Phallic, Latency, and Genital. Infants 0–18 months are in the Oral stage

Copyright © Mometrix Media. You have been licensed one copy of this document for personal use only. Any other reproduction or redistribution is strictly prohibited. All rights reserved.

as the focus is on nursing. Children 18–36 months are in the second Anal stage. The focus of pleasure sensations is on the anus as they are engaged in toilet training. Society and parents demand they control retaining/expelling waste; they must learn to control anal stimulation. This can be a power struggle between child and parents. Children this age are also learning to assert their individual independence and will, mirroring the battle of wills over toileting. Success contributes to healthy development; when unsuccessful, individuals develop anal fixation. Signs of this in later life take two extremes: those who resisted parental control and asserted personal control by retaining their feces develop anal-retentive personalities, becoming rigid, controlling, and overly preoccupied with neatness and cleanliness. Conversely, those who asserted themselves by expelling their feces develop anal-expulsive personalities, with sloppy, messy, disorganized, defiant behavior.

Freud described developmental stages as focusing on particular erogenous zones. Nursing infants are in his Oral stage; toilet-training toddlers are in his Anal stage. His third stage, when children are aged 3–6 years, is the Phallic stage. Pleasure is focused on the genitals as children discover these. Freud focused his theory on males, proposing that at this age, boys develop unconscious sexual desires for their mothers and corresponding unconscious rivalries with their fathers for mother's attention. The rivalry represents aggression toward the father. Therefore they also unconsciously fear retaliation by the father in the form of castration. Freud named this the Oedipal conflict after the Greek tragic hero Oedipus, who unwittingly slew his father and married his mother. Since these unconscious impulses are socially unacceptable, boys resolve the conflict through a process Freud called "identification with the aggressor." This explains the common behavior of boys around ages 4–5, imitating and wanting to be "just like Daddy." They repress desires for mother and adopt masculine characteristics.

In his theory of personality development, Freud placed children ages 3–6 in his third Phallic stage when pleasure is focused on the genitals. He proposed that boys undergo an Oedipal conflict at this age, which he named after Greek tragedian Sophocles' Oedipus Rex, wherein the title character killed his father and married his mother. He said a boy unconsciously desires his mother, competing for her affection with his father, which equals aggression toward the father, and fears retaliation by the father through castration. He resolves these unacceptable impulses by "identifying with the aggressor," wanting to be like his father. Unsuccessful conflict resolution/fixation leads to later confusion/weakness of sexual identity, and either excessive or insufficient sexual activity. Because Freud focused only on males, later psychologists proposed a female counterpart, the Electra conflict. They pointed out how girls at the same ages become "Daddy's girls," often rejecting their mothers, and then around ages 4–5 want to be "just like Mommy," adopting feminine behaviors, paralleling male development. Freud rejected this notion.

Each of the stages in Freud's theory centered on an erogenous zone. Infants are in the Oral stage as they nurse; toddlers in the Anal stage as they are toilet-trained; preschoolers in the Phallic stage as they focus on genital discovery, unconscious sexual impulses toward their opposite-sex parent, and unconscious aggressive impulses toward their same-sex parent, and resolving conflicts over these urges. Freud labeled the stage when children are six years old to puberty the Latency stage. During this time, children begin school. They are occupied with making new friends, developing new social skills; participating in learning, developing new academic skills; and learning school rules, developing acceptable societal behaviors. Freud said that children in the Latency stage repress their sexual impulses, deferring them while developing their cognitive and social skills takes priority.

Copyright © Mometrix Media. You have been licensed one copy of this document for personal use only. Any other reproduction or redistribution is strictly prohibited. All rights reserved.

Thus sexuality is latent. From puberty on, children are in Freud's Genital stage, when sexuality reemerges with physical maturation and adolescents are occupied with developing intimate relationships with others.

Freud proposed that the personality is governed by three structures or forces: the Id, the Ego, and the Superego. The Id, the "pleasure principle," represents the source of our powerful, instinctual urges, such as sexual and aggressive impulses. It is necessary as it energizes us to act, but cannot go unrestrained. The Ego, the "reality principle," represents our sense of self within reality. It is necessary for telling us what will happen if we act on the Id's impulses and knowing how to control them to protect ourselves. The Superego, the "conscience," represents our sense of morality. It is necessary when Ego protects ourselves but not others, so we also control our social interactions to be ethical and nonharmful to others. For example, when a young child sees a cookie or a toy belonging to someone else, his Id says, "I want that." His Ego says, "If I take that and get caught, I will be in trouble." His Superego says, "Whether I get caught or not, stealing is wrong."

Developing sex/gender identity

Children's development of sexual/gender identification
While different psychological theories/schools of thought agree that sex as a social identity develops through the process of identification, they have different views and explanations for how children develop their social identities as boys or girls. In Freud's view, gender identity develops through processes of differentiation and affiliation. He said once children observe that certain other people have characteristics in common with themselves, they "endeavor to mold the ego after one that had been taken as a model." In other words, they identify with similar other people and try to attain the same attributes. Freud proposed that boys resolve their Oedipal conflicts through identification with the aggressor, i.e. adopting their fathers' characteristics and suppressing sexual impulses toward their mothers. While he focused exclusively on males in this respect, Neo-Freudian psychologists later proposed a female counterpart, the Electra conflict, wherein girls resolve desires for fathers by identifying with mothers and adopting their characteristics. In either case, children differentiate from their opposite-sex parent and identify/affiliate with their same-sex parent.

Processes of developing sex/gender identity
Albert Bandura and other proponents of social learning theory maintain that children learn through a process of observing other people's behavior, observing certain behaviors of others that are rewarded, and then imitating those behaviors to obtain similar rewards. The concept of rewards reinforcing behaviors, i.e. increasing the probability of repeating them, comes from behaviorism or learning theory. Social learning theory is based on behaviorism, but includes additional emphasis on the ideas that learning occurs within a social context and that social interactions are primary influences on learning. According to social learning theory, children observe that males and females engage in different behaviors. They additionally observe that boys and girls receive different rewards for their behaviors. Based on these observations, children then imitate the behaviors appropriate to their own sex that they have seen rewarded in others of their sex to obtain the same rewards. Both behaviorist and social learning theories view gender identity development as being environmentally shaped by consequences; social learning theory focuses on the social environment.

General conclusions of psychologists
Various theories of development, such as psychoanalytic, behaviorist, cognitive, and social learning, have differing views of why and how children develop sexual/gender identities. To address these differences, psychologists have endeavored to produce some general conclusions about young

Copyright © Mometrix Media. You have been licensed one copy of this document for personal use only. Any other reproduction or redistribution is strictly prohibited. All rights reserved.

children's self-concepts of gender. They find that during preschool ages, children gradually develop concepts of what being a girl or a boy in their culture means. These concepts become clearly articulated and shape their behaviors. Between the ages of 2 and 6, children are in the process of putting together the pieces of these gender concepts. Developing sex-appropriate behaviors and developing categories of gender roles both appear to be influenced by a combination and interaction of biological and sociological variables. Psychologists additionally conclude that children perform some mental matching process enabling them to isolate features they share in common with others, and that young children's abilities to observe, imitate, and categorize influence their later concepts of sex-appropriate behaviors. By ages 5–6, most children clearly identify with one sex or the other.

Ego defense mechanisms

Freud identified and described many ego defense mechanisms in his theory. He said these are ways the ego finds to cope with impulses threatening it, and hence the person. Just a few of these that can be apparent in young children's behavior include the following. Regression—for example, if a child has received parental attention exclusively for four years, but then the parents introduce a new baby, not only is parental attention divided between two children, but the baby naturally needs and gets more attention by being a helpless infant. If the child feels displaced/threatened by the younger sibling, s/he may regress from normal four-year-old behaviors to more infantile ones in a bid for similar attention. Projection—if a child feels threatened by experiencing inner aggressive impulses, e.g. hating another person, s/he may project these feelings onto that person, accusing, "You hate me!" Denial—if a child cannot accept feelings triggered by losing a loved one through divorce or death, s/he may deny reality: "S/he will come back."

Erik Erikson's psychosocial theory of human development

In each of Erikson's developmental stages, a central conflict must be resolved; success/failure dictates outcomes. Babies first develop basic trust or mistrust in the world during the first stage. Toddlers are in Erikson's second stage of Autonomy vs. Shame and Self-Doubt. In this stage, children 18 months—3 years are learning muscular control (walking, toilet-training) and developing moral senses of right/wrong. As they gain skills, they want to do more things independently, and they begin to assert their individual wills. Parents are familiar with the associated tantrums, "No!" and other common "Terrible Twos" behaviors. Children receiving appropriate parenting during this stage develop a sense of autonomy through being allowed to attempt tasks realistic for them; to fail and try again; and eventually to master them. Positive outcomes are will/willpower and self-control; negative outcomes are impulsivity and compulsion. Children with parenting at either extreme—being ignored and given no guidance or support; or overly controlled/directed, having everything done for them and never allowed freedom—develop shame, doubting their abilities.

Each of Erikson's nine developmental stages involves a "nuclear crisis" the individual must resolve; success or failure results in positive or negative outcomes. Babies develop basic trust or mistrust; toddlers develop autonomy or shame and self-doubt. Erikson's third stage, Initiative vs. Guilt, involves preschoolers. At this age, young children are exploring the environment further commensurately with their increasing physical/motor, cognitive, emotional, and social skills. They exercise imagination in make-believe/pretend play and pursue adventure. Having gained some control over their bodies in the previous stage, they now attempt to exercise control over their environments. When they succeed in this stage, the positive outcomes are purpose and direction. Children who receive adult disapproval for exerting control over their surroundings—either

Copyright © Mometrix Media. You have been licensed one copy of this document for personal use only. Any other reproduction or redistribution is strictly prohibited. All rights reserved.

because they try to use too much control or because parents are overly controlling—feel guilt. Negative outcomes include excessive inhibition against taking action or ruthless, inconsiderate behavior at the opposite extreme.

Erikson formulated nine stages encompassing the entire human lifespan. The fourth stage corresponds to the end of the early childhood years, when children begin formal schooling. Erikson named this stage, which lasts from around ages 5–6 to puberty, Industry vs. Inferiority. Children in this stage are primarily occupied with learning new academic and social competencies as they attend school, meet more peers and adults, make new friends, and learn to interact in a wider environment. Whereas the focus of Stage 2, Autonomy vs. Shame and Doubt, was self-control and parents were the main relationship; and the focus of Stage 3, Initiative vs. Guilt, was environmental exploration and family was the main relationship; in Stage 4, Industry vs. Inferiority, the focus is on achievements and accomplishments. Friends, neighbors, school, and teachers are the most important relationships. Children's successful resolutions bring positive outcomes of competence and method; negative outcomes are narrowness of abilities and inertia (lack of activity).

Differences between Freud's and Erikson's developmental theories

Erikson's theory was based on Freud's, but whereas Freud's focus was psychosexual, Erikson's was psychosocial. Both emphasized early parent-child relationships. Freud believed the personality was essentially formed in childhood and proposed five stages through puberty and none thereafter; Erikson depicted lifelong development through nine stages. Each stage centers on a "nuclear conflict" to resolve, with positive/negative outcomes of successful/unsuccessful resolutions. Erikson's first, infancy stage (birth—18 months) is Basic Trust vs. Mistrust. When an infant's basic needs—such as being fed, changed, bathed, held/cuddled, having discomfort relieved, and receiving attention, affection, and interaction are met sufficiently and consistently, the baby develops basic trust in the world, gaining a sense of security, confidence, and optimism. The positive outcomes are hope and drive; negative outcomes are withdrawal and sensory distortion. If infant needs are inadequately and/or inconsistently met, the baby develops basic mistrust, with a sense of insecurity, worthlessness, and pessimism.

Lawrence Kohlberg's cognitive-developmental theory

Kohlberg had developed a cognitive theory of moral development, based upon and expanding the concepts of morality Piaget included in his theory of cognitive development. Kohlberg also proposed a cognitive-developmental approach to children's acquisition of sex/gender roles. Piaget and Kohlberg discussed classification or categorization as one of the cognitive abilities that children develop. Just as they learn to categorize various things, e.g. foods, animals, people, etc., they learn that people include female and male categories. They then learn to categorize themselves as either female/girls or male/boys. When children are around 2 years old, they each begin to develop their distinctive sense of self. Once they have differentiated self from the rest of the world, they also begin to be able to develop complex mental concepts. These abilities enable them to develop self-concepts of gender. According to the cognitive-developmental view, once children have developed concepts of their sex/gender, these are maintained despite social contexts and are difficult to change.

Aggression relative to early childhood

Preschoolers typically demonstrate some aggressive behavior, which tends to peak around age 4. Instrumental Aggression is one basic type: younger preschoolers frequently shout, hit, or kick

Copyright © Mometrix Media. You have been licensed one copy of this document for personal use only. Any other reproduction or redistribution is strictly prohibited. All rights reserved.

others to get concrete objects they want. Middle preschoolers are more likely to exhibit Hostile Aggression, i.e. getting even for wrongs or injuries they feel others have done to them. Hostile Aggression occurs in two subtypes: Overt and Relational. Overt Aggression involves physically harming others or threatening to do so, while Relational Aggression involves emotional/social harm, e.g. rejecting/excluding another from a group of friends or spreading malicious rumors about another. Young boys are more likely to engage in Overt Aggression, while young girls are more likely to engage in Relational Aggression. These gender preferences in aggressive behaviors tend to remain the same at all ages if aggression exists. While most young children eventually phase out aggression as they learn other ways of resolving social conflicts, some persist in verbally and/or physically aggressive behavior, causing problems.

Minimizing aggressive behavior in young children

While it is normal for preschoolers to exhibit some physical and verbal aggression until they have learned more mature ways of expressing feelings, getting what they want, and settling disputes, there are things adults can do to influence them such that aggressive behavior does not develop into a predominant method of social interaction. Adults set examples for children, and children learn by observing and imitating those examples. Therefore, parents, caregivers, and teachers should not model verbally and/or physically aggressive behaviors such as calling others names, yelling at others, or punishing others' undesirable behaviors using physical force. Not only should adults avoid disciplining children physically, they should also avoid physically and/or verbally violent interactions with other adults. Social learning theorist Albert Bandura proved that children who viewed violent videos imitated what they observed and engaged in more aggressive behavior, so adults should also prevent young children's exposure to violent TV programming and video games.

Prejudice and discrimination

Prejudice literally means prejudging, i.e. judging someone/something negatively before/without knowing anything about who/what one is judging. Prejudice gives rise to discrimination in that prejudiced ideas motivate unfair, i.e. discriminatory, behaviors toward others. Psychologist Albert Bandura, who developed social learning theory, identified the process whereby children acquire attitudes and behaviors they observe in others, which he named vicarious learning. Children commonly pick up beliefs, attitudes, and behaviors from adults around them, without applying any critical thinking to these. They are often not even aware of the attitudes and beliefs they assume in this way. Thus, they will engage in prejudicial attitudes and discriminatory behaviors without thinking through what they are doing. Though such behavior is not justified, children simply assume it is because of adults' examples. Thus, adults must carefully inspect their own beliefs and attitudes, as well as what they do and say, because these are what children will imitate.

Because many prejudicial attitudes exist in our society on both individualized and institutionalized levels, it is all too easy for children to absorb and emulate them. When children who have been victims of prejudice learn they were attacked not as individuals, but members of a group, this does not eliminate negative effects, but can help them see it in a different perspective. Adults can place prejudice and discrimination in their historical contexts so children realize they are not lone victims but part of a larger group. Correcting false beliefs, as in Albert Ellis's Rational-Emotive Behavior Therapy and other forms of cognitive-behavioral therapy, can be applied by adults' pointing out the irrational, flawed thinking involved and supplying examples contradicting that thinking.

Copyright © Mometrix Media. You have been licensed one copy of this document for personal use only. Any other reproduction or redistribution is strictly prohibited. All rights reserved.

For example, if children have been influenced to think certain groups are less intelligent or lazier than others, adults can show them examples of many members of those groups with outstanding achievements in society. They can do this through book/video biographies, personal anecdotes, and introductions to living people.

Sources of prejudicial thinking
Prejudicial thinking about certain groups of people is uninformed and/or misinformed thinking. It is typically based on fear of the unknown due to lack of knowledge and/or fear due to erroneous beliefs about people. Thus, the best way to dispel prejudice is to provide information where there was none and/or to correct wrong information. When unfamiliar groups become more familiar and when wrong assumptions are corrected, people's misconceptions are replaced by reality and they become less afraid. For example, children having no experience with people from other racial, ethnic, or socioeconomic groups are likely to fear these people (as are many adults). Adults can help young children by furnishing them with many opportunities—not just isolated ones—to interact with people from diverse cultural and socioeconomic milieus. For children to experience true learning, which will supersede negative, uninformed first impressions, they must have multiple such social opportunities. School, outside classes, sports, and camp are activities affording such opportunities.

Combating cultural stereotypes and discrimination
When children experience stereotyping of and discrimination against their cultural group, adults can counter these negative reflections on the group by correcting erroneous opinions they have heard. By giving children plenty of examples of positive accomplishments by members of their group, they convey cultural pride, affording children a sense of empowerment. Adults should consistently model positive, constructive, and no-violent methods of addressing prejudice for children. If prejudice proves ongoing, caregivers and teachers must assertively advocate on behalf of children and their cultures to shut down prejudicial sources. If they hear young children furthering cultural stereotypes they have absorbed, adults should immediately correct their statements and behaviors, explaining why certain words and actions harm others and are unacceptable. Extended discussions with young children are important for putting prejudice into perspective and context to help them understand it. Adults can also apply behavioral methods, such as associating prejudicial behaviors with consequences (e.g. losing a privilege or gaining work) and providing related learning activities to prevent repeated instances.

Bullying

Children who are bullied by others are victims of prejudicial thinking and discriminatory actions. Common negative effects of bullying include rage, feelings of hopelessness, anxiety, and depression. Left untreated, children with these feelings can develop suicidal ideations and actions as they grow older if bullying persists. When young, children have the additional problem of not yet knowing how to manage their negative feelings caused by others' aggression or even how to express them. Adults can give them much-needed help by assisting them in articulating their emotions openly but nonviolently. Adults must realize that young children, especially those who have experienced others' violent treatment, may not recognize that anger can be expressed in any ways other than violent ones. Based on their experience, children may internalize assumptions that they can only act out their anger through self-destructive behaviors. When adults consistently model positive, proactive ways of discussing negative emotions, children observe that more constructive behaviors are possible and learn to adopt these as more effective coping strategies.

Copyright © Mometrix Media. You have been licensed one copy of this document for personal use only. Any other reproduction or redistribution is strictly prohibited. All rights reserved.

Foundations of Early Childhood Education

Psychoanalytic theory

In his development of psychoanalytic theory, Freud (a physician) identified stages of childhood development according to the particular bodily zones where pleasure is focused during each age period. This identification still regularly informs early childhood care and educational practices. For example, infants are in the Oral stage, when nursing provides pleasure as well as nutrition and satisfying hunger. Knowing this, caregivers recognize that babies begin exploring their environments through oral routes. They thus will not punish mouthing of objects; will anticipate and prevent mouthing of unsafe/unsanitary objects; provide suitable objects and activities for oral inspection and orally oriented rewards. Toddlers engaged in toilet-training are in Freud's Anal stage. As they learn to control their bladders and bowels, they also learn to control their impulses and behaviors. Adults knowing this recognize toddlers' willful, stubborn behaviors as normal parts of the process of establishing individual identities and asserting their wishes. Thus, they will not punish these behaviors harshly/inappropriately, but strike a balance between permitting exploration and providing limits, guidance, and support.

According to Freud's theory, preschoolers are in his Phallic stage of psychosexual development. This is the time when they discover their own genitals, so caregivers and educators knowing this will not be distressed at young children's attention to and manipulation of their genitals, and their curiosity and interest in others' genitals as these are not abnormal (unless excessive). Adults who are also aware of Freud's Oedipal conflict in boys and other Neo-Freudian psychologists' corresponding Electra conflict in girls should be neither surprised nor upset when little boys first focus more attention on mothers/female caregivers, and later abandon these attentions to focus on imitating fathers/male caregivers. Freud would say they are demonstrating the Oedipal desire for the mother, which includes fear of castration by the father, and then resolving this conflict through identification with the aggressor/father. Neo-Freudians would say little girls are undergoing a similar process in favoring their fathers and subsequently identifying with their mothers.

Freud theorized that children are in his fourth Latency stage of development at around the same ages when they begin to attend formal schooling. Since Freud's emphasis on development was psychosexual, he identified an erogenous zone where pleasure was focused in each stage of development. The mouth, anus, and genitals are erogenous zones central to Freud's other developmental stages. However, in the stage he termed Latency, there is no erogenous zone of focus. This is because Freud believed that children's sexuality is repressed or submerged during this period. The child's attention is occupied at this time with learning new social and academic skills in the new environment of the school setting. Adults familiar with Freud's basic psychoanalytic concepts realize that children's focus shifts from their relationships with parents to their relationships with friends, classmates, teachers, and other adults during the Latency stage. Children are not rejecting/abandoning parents, but responding to widening social environments. They are more able to learn academic concepts and structures and more complex social interactions and behaviors.

Piaget's stages of cognitive development

According to Piaget's theory, infants are in the Sensorimotor stage of cognitive development. This means they learn through sensory input they get from the environment, motor actions they

Copyright © Mometrix Media. You have been licensed one copy of this document for personal use only. Any other reproduction or redistribution is strictly prohibited. All rights reserved.

perform, and environmental feedback they receive from those actions. They also eventually coordinate their actions and reactions. For example, babies hear and attend to sounds; visually locate sound sources; and learn that some objects make sounds, like rattles. They learn to reach for, grasp, and manipulate objects. They learn when they shake a rattle that it makes a sound, and then repeat this action purposefully to generate the sound. Adults knowing these characteristics will provide infants with many toys they can manipulate, including toys that make noises/music, spin/twirl, or roll/bounce/fly; experiences affording input through all sensory modalities; and positive reinforcement when babies discover new body parts, objects, sights, sounds, textures, smells, and tastes; and demonstrate new behaviors interacting with these. They will not punish repetitious behaviors, like repeatedly throwing items from cribs/high-chair trays, which are part of learning in this stage.

Piaget's second cognitive-developmental stage is Preoperational. Toddlers and preschoolers in this stage typically begin to recognize rudimentary symbolic representation, i.e. that some objects represent other things. This understanding of symbols allows them to begin using words to represent things, people, feelings, and thoughts. Adults can support early childhood language development by frequently conversing with young children, reading books to them, introducing and explaining new vocabulary words, and playing games involving naming and classifying things. Children in this stage also begin pretend/make-believe play through understanding symbols; adults can encourage and support this play, which develops imagination and planning abilities. Preoperational children's thinking is intuitive, not logical; adults understanding this will not expect them to follow/use logical sequences such as doing arithmetic, as they cannot yet perform mental operations. Adults familiar with Piaget's concept of egocentrism realize Preoperational children cannot see others' viewpoints. They thus engage children's attention/interest by beginning from topics related to children's personal selves and activities.

Magical thinking

According to Piaget, magical thinking is the belief that one's thoughts make external events happen. He identified this as a common characteristic of the way children in his Preoperational stage think. Piaget said that preschool children have not yet developed the cognitive ability to perform mental operations. Because they cannot follow or apply logical thought processes, their thinking is irrational and intuitive rather than organized and based on real-world, empirical observations. For example, a Preoperational child may believe that something good happened because s/he wished hard enough for it. Preschoolers also commonly believe their saying/thinking/feeling/wishing something bad toward another caused the other's misfortune. They often blame themselves for divorce or death in the family, thinking these happened because they were "bad." Adults should explain to young children that what they wished, thought, felt, or said did not cause good or bad events, and reassign causes external to the child, e.g. "Mommy and Daddy were not getting along with each other"/"Grandpa was sick"/"It was an accident, not anybody's fault."

Egocentrism and animism as characteristic of Preoperational children

Preoperational children are egocentric, i.e. they view everything as revolving around themselves. Adults aware of this understand that most two-year-olds, for example, neither want to share with others nor understand why they should. Egocentrism also means being unable to see others' perspectives. Adults who take this ability for granted may not realize the simplicity of both some early childhood problems and their solutions. For example, when a preschooler does something physically or emotionally hurtful to another, adults can guide identification of consequences: "Look at her face now. How do you think she feels?" and then guide perspective-taking: "How would you

- 28 -

Copyright © Mometrix Media. You have been licensed one copy of this document for personal use only. Any other reproduction or redistribution is strictly prohibited. All rights reserved.

feel if somebody hit you like you just hit Sally?" This has not occurred to the preschooler, but once s/he is guided to think of it, it can be a revelation. Animism is Preoperational children's attributing human qualities to inanimate objects. Many children's books and TV shows accordingly appeal to young children by animating letters, numbers, or objects (e.g. SpongeBob SquarePants).

Concrete Operations stage vs. Preoperational stage

Piaget said that while preschoolers are in the Preoperational stage and do not think logically because they cannot yet perform mental operations, this ability emerges in the Concrete Operations stage, which tends to coincide with elementary school ages. Concrete Operational children can follow and apply logical sequences to concrete objects they can see and manipulate. This is why they can begin learning mathematical concepts and procedures like addition and subtraction, and grammatical paradigms like verb conjugations. While Preoperational children "centrate" or focus on one attribute of an object, like its appearance, Concrete Operational children "decentrate," accommodating multiple attributes, and can perform and reverse mental operations. For example, a Preoperational child can count pennies, but not understand ten pennies spread into a long row equal ten pennies clustered together. Children in Concrete Operations, instead of focusing on appearance, will use logic and simply count the pennies, showing that each group has the same number regardless of how they look.

Conservation

Piaget identified conservation as a key ability, which Preoperational preschoolers have not yet developed. Piaget found elementary school-age Concrete Operational children develop conservation—the understanding that an object or substance conserves, or retains, its essential properties despite changes in appearance or configuration. For example, adults know a cup of liquid is the same amount regardless of the size or shape of the container holding it. Preoperational children, seeing equal amounts of liquid poured from a tall thin glass to a short wide one or vice versa, will "centrate" (focus exclusively) on either height or width and say one glass holds more. Concrete operational children know logically that the amounts are equal regardless of container shape/appearance. When asked how they know, they use empirical evidence and logic: "Of course it's the same amount; I just saw you pour it from the tall glass to the short one." A universal phenomenon is that after developing conservation, we take it for granted and cannot remember or believe our earlier Preoperational thinking.

Erikson's developmental theory

Erikson's theory is based on Freud's, but focuses on psychosocial rather than psychosexual development. Erikson proposed infants are in his first stage, named for its nuclear conflict of Basic Trust vs. Mistrust. Erikson found if an infant's needs are met adequately and consistently, the baby will form a sense of trust in the world; but if they are not fully and/or regularly met, the baby will form a sense of mistrust in the environment and people. Erikson proposed a positive outcome for resolving the nuclear crisis in each stage; in this stage it is Hope. Caregivers understanding this theory and stage will feed a baby on a regular schedule and not leave the child crying from hunger for long times. They will change the baby's diaper timely when needed rather than letting him/her experience discomfort and cry too long. Moreover, caregivers will meet infant needs for interaction, especially holding and cuddling. Making care/nurturing predictable for babies establishes optimism. The negative outcome of Mistrust is linked to worthless feelings, even suicide.

Copyright © Mometrix Media. You have been licensed one copy of this document for personal use only. Any other reproduction or redistribution is strictly prohibited. All rights reserved.

Erikson's second stage of psychosocial development centers on the nuclear conflict of Autonomy vs. Shame and Doubt. Toddlers in this stage are engaged in learning to walk and toilet-training, involving motor control and self-control. They are also learning to assert themselves. This is one reason for tantrums characteristic of this age group. Toddlers who begin loudly saying "No!" are not merely obstinate or difficult, but are learning to express their wills. Erikson designated Will as the positive outcome of resolving the conflict in this stage, as well as self-control and courage. Children allowed to use their emerging skills to try things on their own become more independent, developing autonomy. Those not allowed to practice and progress in making choices and/or are made to feel ashamed during toilet-training/while learning other new skills, learn to doubt themselves and their abilities instead of developing independence. Adults appreciating this theory and stage let children express preferences and practice new skills, supplying needed encouragement, support, and positive reinforcement without overly restricting, controlling, or punishing them.

In his theory of psychosocial development, Erikson proposed his third stage revolves around the nuclear conflict of Initiative vs. Guilt. Erikson described 3- to 5-year-olds in this stage as being at the "play age." Having developed the ability for make-believe/pretend play, children imitate parents and other adults in their activities. At these ages, children begin taking the initiative to plan and enact scenarios wherein they play roles and use objects to symbolize other things. Through creating situations and stories, they experiment and identify socially with adult roles and behaviors. They are also more actively exploring their environments. Relationships expand from parents to family. The positive outcome/strength of this stage is Purpose. Children thwarted in fulfilling their natural goals and desires develop the negative outcome of Guilt through adults' punishing them for trying to control their environments and/or adults' controlling them too much. Adults understanding this encourage and support pretend play. They encourage and approve children for initiating activities rather than inhibiting or always directing their actions.

Erikson termed the fourth stage of his psychosocial theory of development as centering on the nuclear conflict of Industry vs. Inferiority. Children commonly enter this stage around the years beginning school, also coinciding with the close of the early childhood years. Children at elementary school ages acquire a great many new skills and much new knowledge. This enables them to attempt and accomplish many more things, which they are expected to do in school. Their increased ability and accomplishment engender a positive sense of Industry. Children's most important relationships are no longer only with their parents and family, but with friends, neighbors, classmates, teachers, and other school staff. Hence social interactions are central during this stage. Children feeling unequal to new tasks develop a sense of Inferiority compared to peers. Parents and educators who encourage and reinforce children's desires and attempts to learn and practice new skills and perform tasks help them develop senses of method and competence. Unsupportive/punitive adult responses result in restricted competencies and/or lack of motivation.

Bandura's Social Learning Theory

Psychologist Alfred Bandura developed the primary theory of social learning. While his theory incorporates elements of behaviorism in that environmental rewards and punishments that shape the behaviors and learning of children, Bandura focused more on the social dimension of learning in that he found the context of social interactions the most important medium and influence for learning. Bandura's theory also incorporates elements of cognitive theory by emphasizing the roles played by the cognitive processes of attention, memory, and motivation in learning. Bandura found children learn by observing and imitating the behaviors of models, including adults, older children, and peers. He proposed four conditions required for this learning: Attention, Retention,

Copyright © Mometrix Media. You have been licensed one copy of this document for personal use only. Any other reproduction or redistribution is strictly prohibited. All rights reserved.

Reproduction, and Motivation. Adults understanding Bandura's theory realize children can learn new behaviors by seeing others be rewarded for performing these, and then imitating them; this greatly expands children's learning potential. Bandura also proved that children viewing violent video content engage in more aggressive behaviors, informing adults of the importance of monitoring and controlling children's exposure to media influences.

Hierarchy of needs in Maslow's humanistic theory of self-actualization

Maslow proposed humans are driven by needs, and meeting the most basic needs is prerequisite to meeting more advanced needs. Maslow's needs hierarchy is depicted as a pyramid, with the most fundamental needs at the base. Its five levels are:
1. physiological needs: air, water, sleep, and food necessary for survival
2. security needs: shelter and a safe environment
3. social needs: feeling loved, receiving affection, and belonging to a family and/or group
4. esteem needs: feeling personal value, accomplishment, and social recognition
5. self-actualizing needs: achieving optimal personal growth and realizing one's full potential

For example, babies and young children must have clean air to breathe and be fed and rested to survive before other needs can be addressed. Children must have safe places to live, then their needs for love and belonging can be met. Once a child feels loved and part of a family/group, s/he can develop self-esteem through accomplishments and feeling valued by society. After satisfying these, children can self-actualize.

Carl Rogers' theory

Rogers believed in actualization or realizing one's full potential as did fellow humanist Abraham Maslow. While Maslow applied self-actualization to humans, Rogers applied the "actualization tendency" to all life forms. Rogers gave the name "conditions of worth" to the process he observed whereby others give individuals things based not on need but worthiness. For example, while babies usually receive care based on need, as they grow older, adults establish conditions of worth: children get dessert if they finish dinner/vegetables; they get drinks or snacks after finishing a task/activity/lesson/class; and most significantly, they often get affection on condition of acceptable/desirable behavior. In behaviorism, this is called contingencies of reinforcement: rewards are given contingent on desired behaviors. Rogers would likely disagree with this practice, which he called conditional positive regard. He felt it makes children do what others want, not what they want or need, and teaches them conditional positive self-regard, i.e. self-esteem dependent on external standards. Rogers' remedy was unconditional positive regard—unconditional love and acceptance.

Rogers said all organisms naturally pursue a tendency to actualize or make the best of life. Organismic valuing is the natural tendency to value what is healthy, e.g. avoiding bad-tasting foods, which can be poisonous or rotten. Organismic valuing leads to positive regard/esteem, engendering positive self-regard/self-esteem, reflecting what Rogers called the real self—the person one becomes under optimal conditions. Rogers observed society substitutes conditions of worth for organismic valuing, giving us things based not on our needs but on meeting society's required conditions. Children are taught early they will receive something they want on the condition they do what adults want. This establishes conditional positive regard, meaning children only feel esteemed by others on others' conditions; this develops conditional positive self-regard, or self-esteem dependent on others' esteem. This creates an unattainable ideal self-based on others' standards rather than the real self. For Rogers, incongruence between real and ideal self-causes

Copyright © Mometrix Media. You have been licensed one copy of this document for personal use only. Any other reproduction or redistribution is strictly prohibited. All rights reserved.

neurosis. Rogers' required qualities for effective therapists—congruence/genuineness, empathy, and respect—are equally effective in early childhood education.

Behaviorist or learning theory

Major principles of behaviorism include these: Organisms learn through interacting with the environment. Environmental influences shape behavior. Environmental stimuli elicit responses from organisms. Hypothetical constructs like the mind and/or inner physiological changes are unnecessary for scientifically describing behaviors—everything organisms do, including feeling and thinking. Learning and behavior change are achieved through arranging the learner's environment to elicit certain responses, increasing the probability of repeating those responses by rewarding them (positive reinforcement) and decreasing repetition of unwanted behaviors by punishing (positive punishment) or ignoring them (extinction). Just as Thorndike previously found all animals including humans learn the same way, Skinner also found his principles applied equally to rats, pigeons, and people. His methods have become so popular that early childhood educators routinely give positive reinforcement—verbal praise, treats, and privileges—for performing new skills and demonstrating socially desirable behaviors; teach young children complex tasks in steps (shaping/chaining/task analysis); take away privileges to punish unwanted behaviors (negative punishment); and remove aversive stimuli for complying (negative reinforcement).

Ivan Pavlov's experiments with dogs proved that when a stimulus evoking a reflexive response—drooling at the taste of meat—was repeatedly paired with an unrelated/"neutral" stimulus—a bell ringing—dogs came to associate the unrelated stimulus with the original response and drooled on hearing the bell without tasting meat. This proved generalizable to humans. Edward L. Thorndike's experiments with cats also applied to humans. Thorndike introduced the Law of Effect: we are more likely to repeat behaviors receiving desirable consequences. This set the stage for B. F. Skinner's later work. John B. Watson maintained that because inner states cannot be observed or measured, only observable outer behaviors should be used in psychology and learning. Skinner experimented with operant conditioning, wherein behaviors are trained and shaped through manipulating their antecedents/preceding stimuli and consequences/following stimuli. He expanded behaviorism into a comprehensive theory, including detailed rules for teaching new behaviors and modifying behavior (behavior modification).

Positive and negative reinforcement and positive and negative punishment

Behavioral techniques include positive reinforcement, introducing rewarding stimuli for emitting desired behaviors; negative reinforcement, removing unwanted stimuli for emitting desired behaviors; positive punishment, introducing aversive stimuli for unwanted behaviors; and negative punishment, removing desired stimuli for unwanted behaviors. Research has found positive reinforcement the most powerful of all these. One reason is that people are highly motivated by rewards. Another is that all behaviors meet needs; punishment suppresses certain behaviors, but then other behaviors must emerge to fill the same need. If a child misbehaves to get attention, even scolding/other punishment can constitute attention. But if rewarded for more appropriate behavior to get attention, like asking an available adult or peer for interaction, the child meets the attention need while replacing a maladaptive behavior with an adaptive one. Another reason is punishment's limitations: preschoolers may stop misbehaving after one teacher's punishment, but not with another teacher; punishment not applied consistently loses its effect. Also, punishment can cause resentment, anger, defiance, or fearfulness in young children.

Copyright © Mometrix Media. You have been licensed one copy of this document for personal use only. Any other reproduction or redistribution is strictly prohibited. All rights reserved.

In behaviorism, reinforcement means strengthening the probability a behavior will be repeated. Skinner used the terms positive vs. negative to mean introducing vs. removing, not good vs. bad. Therefore, positive reinforcement is introducing something rewarding immediately after a behavior. When a child's behavior is rewarded, s/he will repeat it to obtain repeated rewards: Johnny gets a treat or praise for putting away his toys; he will do it again. Negative reinforcement is rewarding by removing something unwanted: Johnny dislikes noisy crowds at preschool. One day he wakes up earlier, is taken to preschool earlier, finds it quieter and less crowded; he will want to get up and arrive earlier again. Positive punishment is introducing an aversive consequence for a behavior: Johnny refuses to put toys away; his parents then make him clean up the entire room; he is less likely to repeat the refusal. Negative punishment is removing a desirable stimulus: Johnny refuses to put away toys; his parents prohibit watching TV; he is less likely to keep refusing.

Legislation affecting the education of children with and without disabilities

The 1990 Individuals with Disabilities Education Act (IDEA) was reauthorized in 1997 and numbered Public Law 108-446. It provided more access for children with disabilities to the general education curriculum and extended collaborative opportunities for teachers, other professionals, and families of children with disabilities. No Child Left Behind (NCLB, 2001), the reauthorization of the Elementary and Secondary Education Act (ESEA), stressed accountability for outcomes by identifying schools and districts needing improvement and assuring teacher quality. It required school performance data to include disabled students' standardized test scores. NCLB emphasized giving teachers and administrators better research information and schools more resources, parents more information about their children's progress and the school's performance, and more local flexibility and control in utilizing federal education funds and in improving teacher qualifications, for example, through alternative certifications. And, 2004's IDEA reauthorization, Individuals with Disabilities Education Improvement Act (IDEIA), covers better alignment of NCLB with IDEA, appropriately identifying students needing special education, ensuring reasonable discipline while protecting special needs students defining highly qualified teachers, reducing paperwork, and increasing cooperation to decrease litigation.

IDEA law (the Individuals with Disabilities Education Act)

Public Law 94-142, the Education for All Handicapped Children Act/Education for the Handicapped Act (EHA), passed in 1975; and Public Law 99-457, the EHA Amendments, passed in 1986, provided foundations that were expanded by new 1990 legislation. As a result, EHA was renamed the Individuals with Disabilities Education Act (IDEA). The IDEA's six main principles follow:
1. Publicly funded education cannot exclude any student because of the student's disability.
2. The rights of students with disabilities and of their parents are assured by the protection of due process procedures.
3. The parents of students with disabilities are encouraged to participate in their children's educations.
4. The assessment of all students must be fair and unbiased.
5. All students must be given a free, appropriate public education (FAPE), and it must be provided in the least restrictive environment (LRE) where the student and other students can learn and succeed.
6. Information related to students with disabilities and their families must be kept confidential.

Copyright © Mometrix Media. You have been licensed one copy of this document for personal use only. Any other reproduction or redistribution is strictly prohibited. All rights reserved.

Section 504, Education for the Handicapped Act (EHA), EHA amendments, and ADA

In 1973, Section 504 of the Rehabilitation Act, also called Public Law 93-112, was enacted to ensure individuals with disabilities equal access to federally financed programs and to promote their participation in them. A child must have a physical or mental impairment that substantially limits a major life activity to be eligible for a free, appropriate public education (FAPE) under Section 504. This law stimulated motivation to educate students with disabilities, contributing to the passage of the Education for All Handicapped Children Act, also called Public Law 94-142, in 1975. This law provides that all children with disabilities must receive a FAPE provided in the least restrictive environment possible and individualized. Its procedural safeguards mandate due process. The 1986's EHA amendments, or Public Law 99-457 extended special education to disabled preschoolers aged 3 to 5 years; services to infants and toddlers are at each U.S. state's discretion. And 1990's Americans with Disabilities Act (ADA) requires access for disabled people to public buildings and facilities, transportation, and communication but does not cover educational services.

Recent legal changes to the Americans with Disabilities Act (ADA)

The ADA Amendments Act (ADAAA, 2009) overrules prior Supreme Court decisions narrowly interpreting the ADA. This qualifies many more conditions as disabilities.
1. Physical or mental impairments substantially limiting one or more life activities now include immune system functioning; normal cell growth; brain, and neurological, respiratory, circulatory, endocrine, reproductive, digestive, bowel, and bladder functions, added to the existing activities of eating, sleeping, thinking, communicating, concentrating, lifting, and bending.
2. Impairments include physical (deaf, blind, or wheelchair-bound); conditions (AIDS, diabetes, or epilepsy); mental illnesses and ADHD; record of impairment, for example, cancer in remission and regarded as impaired.
3. Reasonable accommodations mean adaptations or modifications enabling persons with disabilities to have equal opportunities. The ADA describes this regarding equal employment opportunities, but it could also be interpreted relative to equal educational opportunities.
4. Reasonable accommodations that would cause undue hardship, for example, financial, are not required.

Copyright © Mometrix Media. You have been licensed one copy of this document for personal use only. Any other reproduction or redistribution is strictly prohibited. All rights reserved.

Research, Standards, and Trends

Professionalism and professional responsibility

While care and instruction of young children are delivered through a variety of program types, EC educators share common general goals. They appreciate EC as a unique period in life. They work to educate holistically, considering the mind, feelings, and body of the whole child. The educational goals they develop are designed to support each child's fulfilling his/her individual potential within relationship contexts. EC professionals realize children are inseparable from their social milieus of family, society, and culture; they work to relate to and understand children in these contexts, while also appreciating and supporting family ties. They apply their knowledge of child development, teaching according to how children learn and what they need, and apply research in the field to differentiating common assumptions and myths from valid scientific findings. They have appropriate behavioral expectations for children at each developmental stage. EC professionals realize the significance of confidentiality: they never gossip or tell families personal information about other families. Lifelong learners, they set their own professional goals, pursuing ongoing professional development.

Legal responsibilities of EC professionals

Historically, special education was introduced with the purpose of separating special-needs children from their normally developing peers. However, since 1991, the IDEA legislation has established the necessity of inclusion in normal care and educational environments, including EC settings, for children with disabilities. EC professionals know excluding any child is illegal. Another example of legal responsibilities is the "mandated reporter" status of caregivers/teachers/other adults working with children and families. They are legally required to report suspected child abuse and neglect; the law penalizes them for not reporting. For example, an EC teacher sees injuries to a child. S/he knows the mother has a new boyfriend, displays a fearful attitude, and responds evasively to teacher questions. Later, the child tells the teacher the boyfriend hurt him/her. The teacher pities the mother, realizing she needs the boyfriend financially and emotionally, and reporting suspected abuse could make the mother lose her children or their home. Regardless, the teacher must report suspicions by law, which was enacted for stopping violence against children.

Interactions with other adults in the learning environment

Regarding teachers' roles, much of the focus is on observing children and their behaviors, helping children manage peer interactions, and giving children opportunities for developing peer-group social skills. Too often a similar emphasis is not accorded to teachers' reflecting on their interactions and behaviors with other adults; learning to collaborate with other adults; and developing skills for conflict resolution and managing disagreements with other adults. Some experts say teachers should work diligently and deliberately to make adult interactions integral parts of daily classroom activity.

For group ECE settings to attain their goals, adults must make and implement plans collaboratively. However, mandatory staff meetings are commonly occupied with curricular and administrative requirements; beyond these, little or no attention or time is applied to nurturing adult-adult relationships. Adults interact during in-service trainings and professional development experiences, but outside of daily classroom settings. Nevertheless, these experiences can be used as

Copyright © Mometrix Media. You have been licensed one copy of this document for personal use only. Any other reproduction or redistribution is strictly prohibited. All rights reserved.

foundations for better adult-adult communication within ECE contexts. Conscious efforts to develop adult-adult relationships benefiting children's growth, development, and learning are necessary.

Enabling and supporting positive interactions among adults within the ECE setting

Adults engage in positive interactions with each other within ECE programs when they make time to share their anecdotal records and observations of their young students, and collaboratively plan instruction based on their collective contributions. When adults share information and communicate with one another about the children and their families with whom they work, they interact positively together. When EC educators engage in problem-solving activities and dialogues, these help them identify which learning goals and experiences they can make more effective for the children and how they can do this. Adults within ECE settings should engage in reciprocal exchanging of ideas about the EC learning environment and about how to share responsibilities for performing instructional tasks, rearranging classrooms as needed, setting up class projects, taking care of class pets and plants, and other such daily duties.

Adult-adult interactions

Addressing in research and theoretical literature and professional development
ECE research contains little work addressing adults' cooperation and collaborative expertise with each other and the influences of these on children. However, the High/Scope curriculum model, The Creative Curriculum, and similar curriculum models and approaches do address adult-adult interactions by stressing how important teamwork is in planning lessons and sharing responsibilities and information. In addition, some educational experts have written about power struggles and other interactional dynamics in adult-adult relationships that can impede employee performance in a variety of settings. Professional development and training programs rarely include adult conflict-resolution techniques, instruction in working collaboratively, or adult learning principles. Hence educators must consider how their adult-adult interactions can support children's development of competence, capability, and confidence. Sharing instructional goals, planning learning experiences that support goals, and sharing responsibilities as a team for implementing projects establishes climates of safety and trust for children.

Applying the concept of "quality time" to interactions

Educators have noted that attitudes and things we commonly say to children, e.g. "Your actions speak louder than your words" would equally benefit us addressing our own behaviors as adults. Applying the same principles we teach children to interactions among adults in the learning community can positively influence those interactions, which in turn affects adult-child/teacher-student interactions and overall classroom atmospheres. Without such atmospheres conducive to trust and honesty in adult relationships, educators can fall prey to misunderstandings and internalizing negative attitudes, which influence not only coworker interactions but moreover classroom climates. One solution is for adults in ECE to establish occasions affording "quality adult time." Psychotherapist and psychological theorist Virginia Satir, pioneer of family therapy, found interpersonal dynamics influenced by positive adult-adult communication. Trust-building, mutual colleague support, and sharing experiences/feelings—related or unrelated to classrooms— promote adult relationships that benefit teacher-learner relationships and thus enhance young children's development and learning.

Copyright © Mometrix Media. You have been licensed one copy of this document for personal use only. Any other reproduction or redistribution is strictly prohibited. All rights reserved.

Confidentiality of records

In EC settings, records kept about children and their families must be treated with strict confidentiality. EC centers/programs/preschools/agencies should limit access to student records to children's immediate family members; only those employees authorized; and agencies having legal authority to access records. Confidentiality of records and restricted access to them in all centers/programs/preschools/agencies that receive federal funding are mandated by the Family Educational Rights and Privacy Act (FERPA). Moreover, with the ongoing trend toward educational inclusion, many EC settings serve children with disabilities, whose student records are additionally subject to regulations under the federal Individuals with Disabilities Education Act (IDEA), and also to the special education laws of their respective U.S. states. An exception to the laws regarding records confidentiality is mandated reporting by EC personnel of suspected child abuse and neglect. Laws applying to child abuse and neglect supersede FERPA regulations. Legally, EC employees are both required to report suspected abuse and neglect of children, and immune from liability for releasing child records information relevant to their reporting.

> ➤ **Review Video: Confidentiality**
> *Visit* ***mometrix.com/academy*** *and enter* ***Code*: 250384**

Legal issues relative to economic considerations

To furnish and sustain quality care in EC settings is always challenging to care providers. It is even more so during difficult economic times. Many EC centers must face decisions whether to downsize the services they offer or to go out of business. When administrators choose to remain in operation, they encounter equally difficult decisions regarding how to reduce services, but not at the expense of quality. A legal issue related to such economic considerations is that EC personnel are often placed at legal risk when service quality is compromised. While EC employers, employees, young children's parents, and educational researchers are all interested in and pursue a definition of quality care, no single operational definition has been attained. However, EC professionals with ample work experience in EC centers have contributed various definitions. The consensus of their contributions includes the following common elements: a nurturing environment; employees trained in EC development and methods; age-appropriate curricula; sufficient space, equipment, and materials; safety and good maintenance of physical environments; and good parent-teacher communication.

Medical care and treatment

The child care licensing regulations of each U.S. state government mostly govern children's medical care and treatment in EC settings. Overall, state regulations emphasize four areas of medical care and treatment: (1) Health requirements for all employees, such as having no communicable diseases; passing a TB test; having no health conditions preventing active child care; and maintaining accurate employee as well as child health records; (2) Administration by staff of medication to children being served in EC settings; (3) Management by EC staff of emergencies due to illness, injury, and accidents; and (4) Treatment of nonemergency minor illnesses, injuries, and accidents occurring to children in EC settings.

To protect children's health and safety, EC programs/schools/centers must maintain written policies and procedures for emergency and nonemergency care. To protect personnel from litigation, they must adhere scrupulously to written policies and procedures. Litigation for

Copyright © Mometrix Media. You have been licensed one copy of this document for personal use only. Any other reproduction or redistribution is strictly prohibited. All rights reserved.

damages/injury is likely when not following procedures. Not reporting suspected/observed child abuse/neglect and not completing accident reports also invite lawsuits.

Non-emergency medical illnesses

EC programs must keep procedures for, and reports on, non-emergency medical treatment of children on file just as they do for emergency procedures and reporting. Staff must contact and notify a sick child's parents, who decide if the child should leave the center/preschool. If so, parents should transport their child. Parental consent forms should authorize a doctor or nurse to provide routine medical treatment. EC centers/preschools should have sick children wait to be picked up in a location that is separate from other children and activities, but closely supervised by staff. For children with allergies, diabetes, and other chronic medical conditions, EC centers/preschools should not only keep this information on file in records, but also post it accessibly at all times for staff reference. Instructions for any special treatment should be included. For any health impairment(s) a child has that could potentially involve emergency treatment, directions for staff should be visibly posted, including specific employees designated to administer treatment. This protects children from harm and caregivers/educators from legal liability.

Medical emergencies

For a child's non-life-threatening medical emergencies, EC personnel should request transportation by the child's parents. However, if parents cannot transport the child, or in a more severe emergency, EC administrators should call an ambulance. In life-threatening emergencies that preclude waiting for an ambulance, EC administrators must designate the vehicle and responsible employee for transporting the child to the hospital; this information should be posted in the facility's emergency procedures. Administrators should keep the number of staff involved in emergency medical treatment to a minimum. Those employees they designate for involvement should be willing to take on the responsibility and should have current first aid training. The administrators can include a clause in these employees' job descriptions providing for their transporting children in the event of an emergency. The EC facility may also pay for additional or separate liability insurance coverage of the employees they designate as responsible for providing necessary emergency medical treatment.

Administration of medication

The administration of medication to children in EC settings has been subject to much controversy due to obvious issues of dangers and liability. EC centers/programs must write their policies and procedures to include their state government's licensing requirements for medical care and treatment, which they must follow closely. Experts recommend that parent and doctor permission be required for administering any prescription and nonprescription medications to children. EC settings should keep on file written parental consent for each medication, and review these records regularly for changes. They should also post separate charts, easily accessible to staff, with each child's name, medication, dosage, administration time, and teacher initials. These provide documentation of teachers following parent directions and can prevent mistakes. Staff should label all medications with the drug name, child's name, doctor's name and contact information, and administration instructions. EC centers seasonally and frequently contain many children simultaneously recovering from a variety of illnesses; labeling prevents giving children the wrong medication. Empty drug containers should be returned to parents.

Emergency medical treatment and first aid

EC programs and preschools must write specific, detailed procedures regarding emergency treatment and keep these on file. Children's parents, EC administrators, and EC staff need to be informed regarding what will occur in the event of a child's serious illness or injury. EC settings

Copyright © Mometrix Media. You have been licensed one copy of this document for personal use only. Any other reproduction or redistribution is strictly prohibited. All rights reserved.

must also keep written, signed parental consent forms on file, as well as parent contact information, parental physician and hospital preferences, and health insurance information. EC staff should have current, regularly updated first aid training. First aid equipment should be stored in locations accessible to personnel, who should be frequently reminded of these locations. Lists of each staff member's first aid responsibilities and training should be posted, also accessibly. Licensing regulations require EC facilities to notify parents of emergencies; not doing so is subject to legal action. In non-life-threatening emergencies, staff should ask parents to furnish transportation and medical treatment. For grave emergencies, parental consent forms should be filed and updated semi-annually, including physician and hospital names, ambulance service, and other transportation procedures.

Custody issues

EC facilities are affected by two types of issues involving child custody: (1) Parents are pursuing legal and/or physical custody of the child but they are not living together; and (2) State authorities have removed a child from the parents' legal and physical custody. Parents frequently demand the right to visit with and/or take the child home on occasion. Two types of custody are: legal custody, defined as an individual's or agency's right to make decisions on a child's behalf regarding the child's place of residence, medical treatment, and education; and physical custody, defined as an individual's or agency's right and responsibility to provide a child with immediate care, and a household or care facility for the present and immediate future. Physical custody does not include all of the rights of full legal custody. It is serious for a child to be in the middle of a custody battle between divorcing parents or between parents and foster parents; therefore EC facilities need the most concise, clear-cut guidelines possible.

Recommendations to follow pertaining to custody
It is recommended that during a child's enrollment, EC programs procure a signed, dated document clarifying the child's custody status, including names, contact information, and relationships of all individuals authorized to pick up the child. Copies of any separation agreement/court decree should also be filed. Any time EC staff do not recognize an individual coming to pick up a child, they should ask the person to produce photo identification, which they should closely inspect. EC program administrators cannot make decisions regarding who has legal or physical custody of a child they serve. When a parent or other adult enrolls a child in an EC program, that adult is asked to list other persons to be contacted in the event of an emergency. EC administrators are advised to present all parents/guardians with a statement that the EC center will only release their child to someone the enrolling parent/adult listed on the emergency form as authorized to pick up the child.

Non-custodial or non-authorized adults attempting to pick up children
EC centers should always have up-to-date documentation on file of a child's custodial arrangements, signed and dated by the enrolling adult. If an adult not authorized to pick up the child attempts to do so, an EC administrator should inform that adult of the center's policies and procedures regarding custody. They may even show the unauthorized adult their copy of the custodial court order if needed. If the unauthorized adult then departs, the administrator must notify the enrolling adult of the incident; file a written report of it; meet with the custodial adult to clarify custody arrangements anew; document this meeting, including its date and signatures; and file the document in the child's record. If the unauthorized adult refuses to leave and makes a scene or threatens/displays violence, the EC administrator should call the police if needed. The EC center's having a procedure in place for protecting children against emotionally upsetting scenes and/or violent adult behavior is crucial to the children's safety and well-being.

Copyright © Mometrix Media. You have been licensed one copy of this document for personal use only. Any other reproduction or redistribution is strictly prohibited. All rights reserved.

Children not picked up timely by parents/designated others

If a child is not picked up on time from an EC center at the end of its defined day, the EC center has the legal responsibility for the child's welfare as long as the child is on the premises. In the event that a child is left at the EC center for a long time and the parent/authorized adult has not notified the center why and/or when the child will be picked up, EC personnel are advised that keeping the child at the center is less likely to incur legal liability than for the child to stay at an EC staff member's home, for example. If the child has to be removed, it is important for EC staff to inform the police of this and where they are taking the child. If parents are chronically tardy picking up children, EC staff should review the child's information and/or inquire further of parents to ascertain reasons and possible solutions because they are legally responsible for reporting suspected child neglect.

Copyright © Mometrix Media. You have been licensed one copy of this document for personal use only. Any other reproduction or redistribution is strictly prohibited. All rights reserved.

Curricula and Effective Practices

Whole language approach to teaching child literacy

The whole language approach is based on constructivist philosophy and psychology: children construct their own knowledge through their interactions with their environments. In contrast to analytical approaches like phonics and alphabetic learning, constructivism views learning as an individual's unique cognitive experience of acquiring new knowledge, shaped by the individual's existing knowledge and personal perspective. Whole language instruction emphasizes helping children create meaning from their reading and express meaning in their writing. The whole-language philosophy emphasizes cultural diversity, integrating literacy instruction across subject domains, reading high-quality literature, and giving children many opportunities for independent reading, small-group guided reading, and being read to aloud by teachers. Whole language believes children learn to read by writing and vice versa. Realistically purposeful reading and writing are encouraged, as is using texts that motivate children to develop a love for literature. Early grammatical/spelling/technical correctness is not stressed, which can be problematic for children with reading/language processing disorders, who need explicit instruction in decoding skills and strategies.

The whole language approach concentrates on children's seeking, finding, and constructing meaning in language. As such, young children's early technical correctness is not the priority. Whole language teachers do not ignore children's errors. However, they do not make correction more important than overall engagement, understanding, and appreciation of reading, writing, and literature. Instead, teachers make formative assessments taking into account the errors each child makes. Then they design learning experiences for children that give them opportunities and assistance in acquiring mechanically correct linguistic forms and structures. While this holistic approach finds analytical techniques that break language down into components like phonemes and alphabet letters less useful, children with language processing/reading problems need to learn phonemic awareness, phonics, and other decoding skills to develop reading fluency. The National Reading Panel conducted a study (1997–2000) to resolve controversy over phonics vs. whole language as the best teaching method, finding that any effective reading instruction program must teach phonemic awareness, phonics, reading fluency, vocabulary development, and reading comprehension.

Language Experience Approach (LEA)

The LEA teaches beginning reading by connecting students' personal life experiences with written/printed words. A unique benefit is students using their own language and words, enabling them to interact with texts on multiple levels simultaneously. They thus realize they acquire knowledge and understanding through not just instruction, but also their own experiences. Four steps for implementing the LEA with EC groups: (1) Children and teacher choose a topic, like an exciting trip, game, or recent TV show, to discuss with teacher guidance. (2) Each child takes a turn saying a sentence using his/her own words that advances the discussion/story. The teacher writes the children's words verbatim without corrections, visibly and clearly. (3) Every few sentences or several words, the teacher stops and reads the record aloud for children to confirm accuracy. (4) Record review: the teacher points to each word, they read aloud together, or children repeat after the teacher. The teacher gives children copies of the record for independent review and possible compilation into books of LEA stories.

Copyright © Mometrix Media. You have been licensed one copy of this document for personal use only. Any other reproduction or redistribution is strictly prohibited. All rights reserved.

Basal reader approach

The basal reader is America's commonest approach, used in an estimated 75–85 percent of K–8th-grade classrooms. The number of publishers offering basal reading series has decreased to about one-fourth of that in the 20th century, decreasing teacher responsibility for investigating/piloting readers for district approval. Using basal readers is a skills-based/bottom-up approach. Teaching smaller-to-larger reading subskills in systematic, rigid sequence assists students' transition from part to whole. Texts graded by reading level contain narration and exposition organized thematically by unit, including children's literature and diverse other genres. Phonics and other specific instructional strands with practice assignments develop skills, which are assessed with end-of-unit tests. For young children, text decoding is enabled through exact control of vocabulary items and word analysis skills, "big [enlarged] books," and word and picture cards. 20th-century and older series sacrificed comprehension and enjoyment for vocabulary control and skill acquisition, but 21st-century series vary methods more (like multiple story versions or book excerpts enabling selection sharing), affording children more motivation to read.

Directed reading activity

Using basal readers, the DRA comprises:
1. The teacher prepares children for reading by stimulating their motivation and introducing new concepts and/or vocabulary.
2. Students read silently, guided by teacher questions and statements.
3. The teacher develops student comprehension and students discuss characters, plots, or concepts to further comprehension.
4. After silent reading, students read aloud and read answers to teacher questions, known as "purposeful rereading."
5. Students' follow-up workbook activities/practice review comprehension and vocabulary.

Some selections may include enrichment activities relating them to writing, art, drama, or music. The DR-TA approach is designed to develop critical readers through instruction in group comprehension. It requires children's active engagement in reading by processing information, asking questions, and receiving feedback as they read. The first phase of DR-TA is the teacher's direction of student thought processes throughout reading. The second phase involves developing student skills according to their needs as identified in phase 1, and additional extension or follow-up activities.

Directed reading activity (DRA) vs. directed reading-thinking activity (DR-TA)

(1) One main difference is that the DR-TA approach gives teachers all the responsibility and greater flexibility for developing lessons. As such it contains fewer directions than the DRA approach, which contains specific materials and questions to use, specific guidelines, and is more teacher-manual-oriented and materials-oriented. Therefore DR-TA can be used for not only basal readers, but also planning lessons in other curriculum areas involving reading; the DRA approach applies more directly to basal reader programs. (2) DRA manuals use mostly literal, factual questions, requiring only convergent thinking for student responses. However, in DR-TA, questions also demand divergent (creative) thinking of students, stimulating higher-level reading comprehension and interpretation. (3) New vocabulary is pretaught in the DRA approach before children read. The DR-TA approach excludes preteaching, realistically requiring student decoding of new vocabulary words during reading. (4) DRA manuals specify when to teach which skills for reading

Copyright © Mometrix Media. You have been licensed one copy of this document for personal use only. Any other reproduction or redistribution is strictly prohibited. All rights reserved.

comprehension. DR-TA approaches do not, requiring more questioning expertise and acceptance of some alternative student responses by teachers.

Manipulatives used for preschool math learning

Young children learn primarily through visually inspecting, touching, holding, and manipulating concrete objects. While they are less likely to understand abstract concepts presented abstractly, such concepts are likelier accessible to preschoolers through the medium of real things they can see, feel, and manipulate. Manipulatives are proven as effective learning devices; some early math curricula (e.g. Horizons) even require them. They are also particularly useful for children with tactile or visual learning styles. Many math manipulatives are available for sale, e.g. linking cubes; 3-dimensional geometric shapes and "geoboards"; large magnetized numbers for whiteboards; weights, scales, and balances for measurements; math blocks; math games; number boards and color tiles; flash cards; play money, toy cash registers, and activities; objects for sorting and patterning; or tangrams for recognizing shapes, reproducing and designing patterns, and spatial problem-solving. Teachers can create homemade math manipulatives using bottle caps/lids; seashells, pebbles/stones; buttons; keys; variously sized, shaped, and colored balls; coffee stirrers; or cardboard tubes from paper products.

Process skills that preschool science programs help develop

Experts find three process skills that good EC science programs help develop are observation, classification, and communication. Young children are inherently curious about the world and hence enjoy many activities involving inquiry and discovery. Teachers can uncover science in many existing preschool activities. For example, since young children relate to activities focusing on themselves, teachers can have them construct skeletons of dry pasta, using their pictures as heads. Cooking activities involve science, as do art activities. Teachers can have children explore various substances' solubility in water, which colors are produced by mixing which other colors, etc. They can have them compare/contrast similarities/differences among objects. They can create inexpensive science centers using animal puppets; models; thematically-related games, puzzles, books, and writing materials; mirrors, prisms, magnifiers; scales, magnets; and various observable, measurable objects. Teachers should regularly vary materials to sustain children's interest.

Using inquiry and discovery in science

EC teachers are advised to "teach what they know," i.e. use materials with which they are familiar. For example, teachers who like plants can have young children plant beans, water and watch them grow, moreover incorporating this activity with the story "Jack and the Beanstalk." Teachers can bring in plants, leaves, and flowers for children to observe and measure their sizes, shapes, or textures. Experts recommend teachers utilize their everyday environments to procure learning materials, such as pine needles and cones; loose feathers and leaves found outdoors; animal fur from pets or groomers; and/or snakeskins or turtle shells from local pet stores. Experts advise teachers to use their observational skills during inquiry and discovery activities: if children apply nonstandard and/or unusual uses of some materials, teachers should observe what could be a new discovery, wherein students teach adults new learning, too. Teachers should let children play with and explore new materials to understand their purposes, uses, and care before using them in structured activities.

Copyright © Mometrix Media. You have been licensed one copy of this document for personal use only. Any other reproduction or redistribution is strictly prohibited. All rights reserved.

Developing physical coordination, fine motor skills, and large muscle skills

Preschoolers are more likely to fall because their lower bodies are not yet developed equally to their upper bodies, giving them higher centers of gravity. Therefore, seeing how long they can balance on one foot and hopping exercises help improve balance and coordination. Hopping races let preschoolers participate in groups and observe peer outcomes, which can also enhance self-confidence and supporting others. "Freeze dancing" (like Musical Chairs without the chair-sitting), without eliminations, provides physical activity and improves coordination. Using writing implements, tying shoes, and playing with small items develop fine motor skills. With preschoolers, it is more effective and developmentally appropriate to incorporate fine motor activities into playtime than to separate quiet activity from play. For example, on nature walks, teachers can have children collect pebbles and twigs and throw them into a stream, developing coordination and various muscles. Running, skipping, and playing tag develop large muscle skills. Kicking, throwing, and catching balls give good unstructured exercise without game rules preschoolers cannot understand. Preschoolers' short attention spans preclude long activity durations.

Aesthetic experiences

Aesthetic experiences focusing on color

To help children learn color names and develop sensory discrimination and classification abilities, some art museums offer preschool lessons, which teachers can also use as models. For example, a teacher can read a children's story or sing a song about color, then present a painting/artwork for children to examine, and then a separate display with circles/squares/ovals of colors used by the artist, asking children to name these and any other colors they know, and identify any other colors the artist used not represented in the second display. The teacher then demonstrates how mixing produces other colors. After this demonstration with children's discussion, the teacher gives each child a piece of heavy-duty paper and a brush. The teacher pours about an inch-sized puddle of each of the three primary colors—red, blue, and yellow—in the middle of each child's paper. The teacher then tells the children to use their brushes to explore mixing colors and see the variety of other colors they can create.

Aesthetic experiences involving shape

Giving young children learning activities that focus on shape used in art helps them develop their abilities to form concepts and identify discrepancies. Manipulating basic geometric shapes also stimulates their creative thinking skills and imaginations, as well as developing early geometric math skills. For example, an EC teacher can first read aloud a children's book about shapes, of which many are available. After reading it through, the teacher can go back through the story asking children to point to and name shapes they recognize. Then the teacher can show children an artwork. Using line drawings and/or solid geometric shapes, they discuss what shapes the artist used. The teacher can help children arrange solid shapes to form different images (people, flowers, houses). The teacher can then give children paper pulp trays/heavy paper/board, assorted wooden/cardboard/plastic shapes, and instructions to think and arrange shapes they can make with them, and then give them glue to affix the shapes to their trays/paper/board. They can paint their creations after the glue dries.

Element of line in visual art

Activities focusing on line in art help young children expand their symbol recognition, develop their comparison-making ability, and facilitate shape recognition. Teachers can begin by singing a song or reading a children's story about lines. Then they can present one painting/drawing/artwork and

Copyright © Mometrix Media. You have been licensed one copy of this document for personal use only. Any other reproduction or redistribution is strictly prohibited. All rights reserved.

help children point at various kinds of lines that the artist used. The teacher can draw various line types on a separate piece of paper, e.g. wavy, pointy, spiral, and ask children to find similar lines in the artwork. Then the teacher can ask children to try drawing these different lines themselves. Teachers should also inform children of various tools for drawing lines and let them experiment with these, e.g. crayons, pencils, markers, chalk, paint. An EC teacher can also supply butcher paper or other roll paper for each child to lie down on in whatever creative body positions they can make. The teacher outlines their body shapes with a marker. Then the teacher has the children explore drawing different kinds of lines, using various kinds of drawing tools, to enhance and personalize their individual body outlines.

Element of texture in art

Preschoolers learn much through looking at and touching concrete materials. Activities involving visual and tactile examination and manipulation plus verbal discussion enhance young children's representational/symbolic thinking abilities. Such activities also enable children to explore various ways of representing different textures visually. Teachers can provide "feely bags/boxes"— bags/boxes with variously textured items inside, e.g. sandpaper, fleece, clay, wool, or tree bark—for children to feel and describe textures before seeing them, and identify objects based on feel. A teacher can then show children a selected artwork; they discuss together which textures are included, e.g. smooth, rough, jagged, bumpy, sharp, prickly, soft, or slippery. The teacher can then demonstrate using plaster/thickened paste/clay how to create various textures using assorted tools (e.g. tongue depressors, plastic tableware, chopsticks, small toys, or child-safe pottery tools) and have children experiment with discovering and producing as many different textures as they can. After children's products dry, they can paint them the next day.

Social skills

Experts find it crucial for young children's later success in school and life to have experiences that develop understanding of their own and others' emotions; constructive management of their strong feelings; and skills in forming and maintaining relationships. Young children use earlier developed motor skills like pushing/shoving, biting, hitting, or kicking, to get what they want rather than later developing verbal skills. Since physical aggression is antisocial, social development includes learning more acceptable, verbal emotional expressions. "Punch and Judy"–type puppet-shows depicting aggression's failures entertain preschoolers; discussing puppet behavior develops social skills. Teachers have children say which puppets they liked/disliked and considered good/bad; what happened; what might happen next; and how puppets could act differently. Teachers can reinforce children's discussion of meeting needs using words, not violence. Many read-aloud stories explain why people behave certain ways in social contexts; discussion/question-and-answer groups promote empathy, understanding, and listening skills. Assigning collaborative projects, like scrapbooking in small groups, helps young children learn cooperation, turn taking, listening, and verbally expressing what they want.

Affective learning experiences

Providing affective experiences supports young children's emotional development, including understanding and expressing their emotions. These enable development of emotional self-regulation/self-control. Emotional development is also prerequisite to and supportive of social interactions and development. Affective activities also help teachers understand how children feel, which activities they find most fascinating, and/or why they are not participating. "Feelings and

Copyright © Mometrix Media. You have been licensed one copy of this document for personal use only. Any other reproduction or redistribution is strictly prohibited. All rights reserved.

Faces" activities are useful. For example, a teacher can have each child draw four different "feeling" faces on paper plates—e.g. happy, sad, angry, confused, excited—and discuss each.

A teacher can offer various scenarios, like learning a new song, painting a picture, getting a new pet, or feeling sick, and ask children how they feel about each. Then the teacher can give them new paper plates, having them draw faces showing feelings they often have. Gluing Popsicle sticks to the plates turns them into "masks." The teacher can prompt the children on later days to hold up their masks to illustrate how they feel on a given day and about specific activities/experiences.

<u>Promoting emotional development, physical activity, and creativity</u>
Early childhood teachers can help children understand their feelings and others' feelings, express their emotions, engage in physical exercise, use creative thinking, and have fun by using emotional movement activities. For example, the teacher can begin with prompting the children to demonstrate various types of body movements and postures, like crawling, walking, tiptoeing, skipping, hopping, crouching, slouching, limping, or dancing. Then the teacher can ask the children which feelings they associate with each type of movement and body position. The teacher can play some music for children to move to, and give them instructions such as "Move like you are happy....like you are sad....like you are scared....like you are surprised....like you are angry...." Teachers can also use "freeze"/"statue" dances or games, wherein children move to music and must freeze in position like statues when the music stops; for affective practice, teachers instruct children to depict a certain emotion each time they freeze in place.

Indoor and outdoor space

Indoor and outdoor EC learning environments should be safe, clean, and attractive. They should include at least 35' square indoors and 75' square outdoors of usable play space per child. Staff must have access to prepare spaces before children's arrival. Gyms/other larger indoor spaces can substitute if outdoor spaces are smaller. The youngest children should be given separate outdoor times/places. Outdoor scheduling should ensure enough room, plus prevent altercations/competition among different age groups. Teachers can assess if enough space exists by observing children's interactions and engagement in activities. Children's products and other visuals should be displayed at child's-eye level. Spaces should be arranged to allow individual, small-group, and large-group activity. Space organization should create clear pathways enabling children to move easily among activities without overly disturbing others, should promote positive social interactions and behaviors; and activities in each area should not distract children in other areas.

Learning environments

<u>Arranging indoor learning environments according to curricular activities</u>
EC experts indicate that rooms should be organized to enable various activities, but not necessarily to limit activities to certain areas. For example, mathematical and scientific preschool activities may occur in multiple parts of a classroom, though the room should still be laid out to facilitate their occurrence. Sufficient space for infants to crawl and toddlers to toddle are necessary, as are both hard and carpeted floors. Bolted-down/heavy, sturdy furniture is needed for infants and toddlers to use for pulling up, balancing, and cruising. Art and cooking activities should be positioned near sinks/water sources for cleanup. Designating separate areas for activities like block-building, book-reading, musical activities, and dramatic play facilitates engaging in each of these. To allow ongoing project work and other age-appropriate activities, school-aged children should have separate areas. Materials should be appropriate for each age group and varied. Equipment/materials for sensory

Copyright © Mometrix Media. You have been licensed one copy of this document for personal use only. Any other reproduction or redistribution is strictly prohibited. All rights reserved.

stimulation, manipulation, construction, active play, dramatic play, and books, recordings, and art supplies, all arranged for easy, independent child access and rotated for variety, are needed.

<u>Arranging learning environments related to children's personal, privacy, and sensory needs</u>
In any EC learning environment, the indoor space should include easily identifiable places where children and adults can store their personal belongings. Since EC involves children in groups for long time periods, they should be given indoor and outdoor areas allowing solitude and privacy while still easily permitting adult supervision. Playhouses and tunnels can be used outdoors, small interior rooms and partitions indoors. Environments should include softness in various forms like grass outdoors; carpet, pillows, and soft chairs indoors; adult laps to sit in and be cuddled; and soft play materials like clay, Play-Doh, finger paints, water, and sand. While noise is predictable, even desirable in EC environments, undue noise causing fatigue and stress should be controlled by noise-absorbing elements like rugs/carpets, drapes, acoustical ceilings and other building materials. Outdoor play areas supplied/arranged by school/community playgrounds should be separated from roadways and other hazards by fencing and/or natural barriers. Awnings can substitute for hills, and inclines/ramps for shade, when these are not naturally available. Surfaces and equipment should be varied.

Early childhood behavior management

Repetition and consistency are two major elements for managing young children's behavior. Adults must always follow and enforce whichever rules they designate. They must also remember that they will need to repeat their rules over and over to make them effective. Behaviorism has shown it is more powerful to reward good behaviors than punish bad behaviors. Consistently rewarding desired behaviors enables young children to make the association between behavior and reward. Functional behavior analysis can inform adults: knowing the function of a behavior is necessary to changing it. For example, if a toddler throws a tantrum out of frustration, providing support/scaffolding for a difficult task, breaking it down to more manageable increments via task analysis, and giving encouragement would be appropriate strategies; but if the tantrum was a bid for attention, adults would only reinforce/strengthen tantrum recurrence by paying attention. Feeling valued and loved within a positive relationship greatly supports young children's compliance with rules. The "10:1 Rule" prescribes at least 10 positive comments per 1 negative comment/correction.

Managing the normal behavior of young children

Before reacting to young children's behaviors, adults should make sure children understand the situation. They should state rules simply and clearly; repeat them frequently for a long time for young children to remember and follow them; and state and enforce rules very consistently to avoid confusion. Adults should tell children clearly what they expect of them. They should never assume they need do nothing when children follow rules; they should consistently give rewards for compliance. Adults should also explain to young children why they are/are not receiving rewards by citing the rule they did/did not follow. Adults can arrange the environment to promote success. For example, if a child throws things that break windows, adults can remove such objects and substitute softer/more lightweight items. Organization is also important. Adults should begin with a simple, easy-to-implement plan and adhere to it. They should record children's progress; analyzing the records shows what does/does not work and why, enabling new/revised plans.

Copyright © Mometrix Media. You have been licensed one copy of this document for personal use only. Any other reproduction or redistribution is strictly prohibited. All rights reserved.

Including families in children's education

First, ECE personnel can make sure that communication between the school/program and family is reciprocal and regular. EC educators should promote and support the enhancement and application of parenting skills. They should also acknowledge that parents have an integral part in supporting children's learning. All school personnel should make parents feel welcome in school, and moreover should seek parents' help and support. When school administrators, teachers, and other staff make educational decisions that affect the children and their families, they should always be sure that the children's parents are involved in these decisions. In addition, educational personnel should not just work on children's educational goals, learning objectives, and curricular and instructional planning and design on their own, keeping the school or program isolated; they should make use of all available community resources. Instead of trying to educate young children within a school bubble, educators who collaborate with their communities realize benefits of stronger families, schools, and child learning.

Flexibility and variety are key elements for involving diverse families, with changing situations and needs, in ECE. Adaptable approaches include these: Educators include families in designing children's Individual Family Service Plans (IFSPs) for preschoolers. They ask families to develop their own goals for educational participation. They create volunteer calendars, encouraging parents to collaborate when able. They communicate with families regularly, using speech if written/printed language presents barriers. They establish media libraries for parents/families to browse and check out resources. They facilitate parental meeting attendance and school visits by providing transportation and child care. They adapt to parental work schedules by convening meetings at alternative times of day. They often send families communications about both their children and class content, including information regarding important developmental milestones and methods for nurturing growth and development. They offer families individualized, specific strategies for home use. They recruit interested family members to help in preschool. They also function as clearinghouses to facilitate family access to community supports like local health care agencies, businesses, and universities.

Copyright © Mometrix Media. You have been licensed one copy of this document for personal use only. Any other reproduction or redistribution is strictly prohibited. All rights reserved.

Children and Families

Genetic and environmental influences

Young children are subject to both genetic and environmental influences upon their relative risk of displaying antisocial behaviors. Research into factors influencing early childhood behavior identifies both genetic variables and environmental ones, like corporal punishment, affecting young children's propensities toward antisocial behavior. Children experiencing more corporal punishment display greater behavior problems; children at greater genetic risk also do. However, boys at higher genetic risk for behavior problems who also experience more corporal punishment exhibit the most antisocial behavior. Therefore, both genetic risk factors and corporal punishment significantly predict preschoolers' antisocial behavior. Additionally, the nature-nurture interaction of genetic risk factors and environmental punishment is statistically significant for young boys but not young girls. Such evidence shows that environmental learning is not wholly responsible for antisocial behavior: genetic variables predispose some young children to antisocial behaviors more than others.

Research-supported observations about genetic and biological influences

Adopted children with one or both biological parents having histories of alcohol abuse, criminal records, and/or major psychiatric illness are at double the risk for drug abuse as those having biological parents without such histories. While this risk is genetic, differential environmental influences can exacerbate or mitigate children's biological risk for engaging in addictive behaviors. For example, adopted children who experience difficulties in their adopted families, such as deaths or divorce, are at higher risk of developing drug abuse problems. Conversely, children whose biological parents' histories put them at higher genetic risk for abusing drugs—but who were adopted into loving, stable families—are less at risk for developing addictions. Researchers conclude that children with higher genetic risks for addiction are more vulnerable to adverse environmental influences in their adopted families than children with lower genetic risks. Also, genetic risks become less powerful in adoptive families having lower environmental risk factors.

Maturational factors

Many physiological factors affect the development of babies and young children. These dictate which kinds of learning activities are appropriate or ineffective for certain ages. For example, providing a newborn with visual stimuli from several feet away is wasted, as newborns cannot yet focus on distant objects. Adults cannot expect infants younger than about 5 months to sit up unsupported, as they have not yet developed the strength for it. Adults cannot expect toddlers who have not yet attained stable walking gaits to hop or balance upon one foot successfully. It is not coincidental that first grade begins at around 6 years: younger children cannot physically sit still for long periods and have not developed long enough attention spans to prevent distraction. This is also why kindergarten classes feature varieties of shorter term activities and more physical movement. Younger children also have not yet developed the self-regulation to keep from shouting out on impulse, getting up and running around, etc.—behaviors disruptive to formal schooling but developmentally normal.

Copyright © Mometrix Media. You have been licensed one copy of this document for personal use only. Any other reproduction or redistribution is strictly prohibited. All rights reserved.

Birth order

Neo-Freudian psychologist Alfred Adler proposed that a child's birth order relative to other children in a family is associated with corresponding influences on the child's personality and behaviors. For example, Adler found that the only child is regarded as a miracle of birth by parents with no prior experience of having a baby. This child receives the undivided attention of both parents, who may be overprotective of the child and/or spoil him/her. Some general characteristics of only children include preferring adults' company, using adult language, enjoying being the center of attention from adults, and finding it difficult to share with other children. Adler said the oldest/older child has been "dethroned"/displaced by a younger sibling and must learn to share. Parents often have very high expectations of the oldest/older child, give him/her much responsibility, and expect him/her to set an example for younger siblings. Older/oldest children may turn to fathers once a sibling is born. They may feel entitled to power, developing strict/authoritarian attitudes/behaviors. Given encouragement, they can develop helpful attitudes/behaviors.

In his psychoanalytic theory, Alfred Adler included birth order as one family influence on child personality development. For example, he found that the youngest child in a family, like an only child, is never "dethroned" or displaced by a new sibling. However, unlike an only child, the youngest sibling has many "parents" in the form of older siblings who help to raise, instruct, and influence him/her. Youngest siblings are often spoiled by the attentions of parents plus older siblings. Some youngest children continue to feel and behave like the "baby" of the family indefinitely. Many youngest children, always being littlest, wish to be bigger than siblings. As they grow, youngest siblings may make grandiose plans that never succeed. Adler found with twins, one is usually more active or stronger, and is often perceived by the parents as older—s/he may have been born a minute earlier and/or they perceive him/her as more mature. The stronger twin may develop as the leader; the other may develop problems with identity.

Psychoanalyst and theorist Adler included birth order as one factor in his study of influences on personality development. He identified general tendencies associated with each family birth position. For example, the second-born child was described by Adler as having a "pacemaker" in that there is always an older sibling ahead of this child. Adler found that the results of this position include the child's becoming more competitive out of attempts to overtake the elder sibling. He noted that competition could devolve into sibling rivalry. A second child might develop into a rebellious sort or might develop a habit of always trying to "top" or exceed everybody else's accomplishments. Adler described the middle child in a family as being "sandwiched" between older and younger siblings, so that s/he can feel "squeezed out" of any privileged or significant position. Some middle children may grow up to fight against injustice or unfairness; others may encounter difficulty establishing places for themselves. Some middle children develop even-tempered dispositions, with no extreme opinions and "take-it-or-leave-it" attitudes.

Adlerian psychoanalytic theory includes family birth order as an influence on personality development and behavior. For example, Adler described a child who is born after an older child has died as having a "ghost" ahead of him/her. Such a child, called a "ghost child," is likely to be subject to overprotection by the mother, who fears losing him/her after losing a child previously. The child may respond to parental overprotectiveness by taking advantage of the parent to get what s/he wants. Alternatively, some "ghost" children resent feeling parental comparisons to the deceased child, whose memory parents have idealized; in this case, the child may rebel. Adler said adoptive parents can be so grateful to have a child and so anxious to make up for the child's loss of biological parents, that they may spoil him/her; thus, the adopted child is more liable to develop

Copyright © Mometrix Media. You have been licensed one copy of this document for personal use only. Any other reproduction or redistribution is strictly prohibited. All rights reserved.

very demanding, spoiled behaviors. The adopted child may ultimately either resent his/her biological parents for rejecting/leaving him/her or idealize them, negatively comparing the adoptive parents.

Adler found that the ways children are perceived and treated by parents and siblings relative to their birth order contribute to their personality formation and behavior. For example, Adler stated the only boy with girl siblings, surrounded by females when the father is not there, can develop either of opposite extremes: he may engage excessively in behaviors to prove he is the "man of the family" or develop effeminate behaviors through identifying with surrounding females. Adler found when a child is the only girl among male siblings, her older brothers can behave protectively toward her. An only girl among boys may make efforts to please the father and develop either of two opposing extremes: becoming a tomboy to compete with brothers or developing very feminine behaviors to differentiate from them. In families with all-male or all-female children, Adler noted parents who wanted a child of the other sex might dress one child as the opposite sex. The child may either exploit this role reassignment or strongly object to it.

Murray Bowen's Family Systems Theory

Dr. Bowen identified four basic family relationship patterns within what he called the Nuclear Family Emotional System. These patterns dictate where problems develop when the family system is under tension. Bowen labeled these patterns Marital Conflict; Dysfunction in One Spouse; Impairment of One or More Children; and Emotional Distance, which latter is associated with the first three. In Impairment of One or More Children, the parents focus their anxieties on one or more of their children. Their perception of the child(ren) is either negative or idealized. The more the parents focus on one child, the more that child reciprocally focuses on them, becoming more reactive to parental expectations, needs, and attitudes than siblings are. This process undermines the child's differentiation of self, a key factor in healthy individual development according to Bowen. The child becomes more susceptible to internalizing or externalizing family tensions, affecting his/her social relationships, school performance, and physical and mental health.

Family Projection Process

In the Family Projection Process, Dr. Murray Bowen found that parents can project their anxieties onto their children. When parents worry overly that something is wrong with one child, they may see everything the child does as proof of that worry. Their excessive efforts to remedy the child's "problem" can actually cause the child to develop the problem in reality, as the child's self-image becomes aligned with parental perceptions. While parents with such worries usually feel guilty of not giving the "problem" child enough attention, they have in fact directed more attention to this child than his/her siblings. Bowen found that children less engaged in this process have more realistic, mature relationships with parents and develop into more goal-oriented, less reactive, and less emotionally needy individuals. Both parents participate equally in the process in different ways; both are insecure relative to the child, but Bowen said typically one parent pretends to feel secure with the other's complicity.

In his theory, Bowen referred to the way parents transmit their emotional issues to children as the Family Projection Process, which involves three steps: (1) A parent focuses on a child, fearing something is wrong with that child. (2) The parent perceives the child's behavior as confirmation of this fear. (3) The parent then treats the child as though something really is wrong. When parents try to "fix" what they perceive is a problem in the child, their perception can become a self-fulfilling prophecy as the child eventually embodies that perception. For example, if parents perceive a child

Copyright © Mometrix Media. You have been licensed one copy of this document for personal use only. Any other reproduction or redistribution is strictly prohibited. All rights reserved.

as helpless and are always helping her excessively, the child's self-image comes to mirror the parents' perception; the child becomes de facto helpless and dependent even though she may not have been so initially. The more intense this process is, the greater relationship sensitivities children develop, beyond those of their parents.

Nutrition

Raw or lightly steamed vegetables are best because excess heat destroys nutrients and frying adds fat calories. Fresh, in-season and flash-frozen fruits are more nutritious/less processed than canned. Adults should monitor young children's diets to limit highly processed produce, which can have excessive sugar, salt, or preservatives. Good protein sources include legumes, nuts, lean poultry, and fish. Adults should take care with young children to avoid choking hazards by cutting foods into bite-sized pieces. Serving nut butters instead of whole nuts is safer, but spread thinly on whole-grain breads/crackers or vegetable pieces, because young children can choke on large globs of nut butter as well. Omega-3 fatty acids from salmon, mackerel, herring, flaxseeds, and walnuts control inflammation, prevent heart arrhythmias, and lower blood pressure. Monounsaturated fats from avocados, olives, peanuts, their oils, and canola oil prevent heart disease, lower bad cholesterol, and raise good cholesterol. Polyunsaturated fats from nuts, seeds, and corn, soy, sesame, sunflower, and safflower oils lower cholesterol. These fats/oils should be served in moderation, avoiding saturated fats.

Babies are typically nourished via mother's milk or infant formula, and then with baby food; however, young children mostly eat the same foods as adults by the age of 2 years. Though they eat smaller quantities, young children have similar nutritional needs to those of adults. Calcium can be more important in early childhood to support the rapid bone growth occurring during this period; young children should receive 2–3 servings of dairy products and/or other calcium-rich foods. For all ages, whole-grain foods are nutritionally superior for their fiber and nutrients than refined flours, which have had these removed. Refined flours provide "empty calories" causing wider blood-sugar fluctuations and insulin resistance—Type 2 diabetes risks—than whole grains, which stabilize blood sugar and offer more naturally occurring vitamins and minerals. Darkly and brightly colored produce are most nutritious. Adults should cut foods into small, bite-sized pieces to prevent choking in young children, who have not yet perfected their biting, chewing, and swallowing skills.

Young children have smaller stomachs than adults and cannot eat as much at one time as teens or adults. However, it is common practice for today's restaurants to provide oversized portions. The historical tradition of encouraging young children to "clean their plates" is ill-advised considering these excessive portions and the abundance of food in America today. Adults can help young children by teaching them instead to respond to their own bodies' signals and eat only until they are satisfied. Adults can also place smaller portions of food on young children's plates and request to-go containers at restaurants to take leftovers home. Because young children cannot eat a lot at once, they must maintain their blood sugar and energy throughout the day by snacking between meals. However, "snack foods" need not be high in sugar, salt, and unhealthy fats. Cut pieces of fresh fruits and vegetables, whole-grain crackers and low-fat cheeses, and portable yogurt tubes make good snacks for young children.

Unhealthy fats, hydration, sugar drinks, fruit juices, and portion sizes
Saturated fats from meats and full-fat dairy should be limited; they can cause health problems like high cholesterol, cardiovascular disease, obesity, and diabetes. Trans fats are produced chemically by hydrogenating normally liquid unsaturated fats and converting them to solid, saturated fats as in margarine and shortening used in many baked goods. These are considered even unhealthier than

Copyright © Mometrix Media. You have been licensed one copy of this document for personal use only. Any other reproduction or redistribution is strictly prohibited. All rights reserved.

regular saturated fats and should be avoided. (The words "partially hydrogenated" in the ingredients signal trans fats.) Infants derive enough water from mother's milk/formula, but young children should be given plenty of water and/or milk in "sippy cups" to stay hydrated. The common practice of giving young children fruit juice should be avoided. Even without added sugars, fruit juices crowd out room in small stomachs for food nutrients and cause dental cavities and weaken permanent teeth before they erupt. Children can also gain weight, as juice calories do not replace food calories the way actual fruit does with its fiber and solids. Young children should eat two-thirds of adult-sized portions.

Feeding strategies

Early childhood is an age range often associated with "finicky" eaters. Adults can experiment by substituting different foods that are similar sources of protein or other nutrients to foods young children dislike. Preparing meals to look like happy faces, animals, or have appealing designs can entice young children to eat varied foods. Engaging children age-appropriately in selecting and preparing meals with supervision can also motivate them to consume foods when they have participated in their preparation. Adults should model healthy eating habits for young children, who imitate admired adults' behaviors. Early childhood is when children form basic food-related attitudes and habits and so is an important time for influencing these. Children are exposed to unhealthy foods in advertising, at school, in restaurants, and with friends, so adult modeling and guidance regarding healthy choices are important to counteract these influences. However, adults should also impart the message early that no foods are "bad"/forbidden, allowing some occasional indulgences in small amounts, to prevent the development of eating disorders.

Sleep

Sleep allows the body to become repaired and recharged for the day and is vital for young children's growth and development. Children aged 2–5 years generally need 10–12 hours of sleep daily. Children 5–7 years old typically need 9–11 hours of sleep. Their sleep schedules should be fairly regular. While occasionally staying up later or missing naps for special events is not serious, overall inconsistent/disorganized schedules cause lost sleep and lethargic and/or cranky children. Some young children sleep fewer hours at night but need long daytime naps, while others need longer, uninterrupted nighttime sleep but seldom nap. Young children are busy exploring and discovering new things; they have a lot of energy and are often excited even when tired. Because they have not developed much self-regulation, they need adult guidance to calm down enough to go to sleep and will often resist bedtimes. Adults should plan bedtime routines. These can vary, but their most important aspect is consistency. Children then expect routines' familiar steps, and anticipating these comfort them.

The majority of early childhood experts think young children should not have adults in their rooms every night while they fall asleep. They believe this can interfere with young children's capacity for "self-soothing" and falling asleep on their own, making them dependent on an adult presence to fall asleep. Parents/caregivers are advised to help children relax until sleepy, and then leave, saying "Good night" and "I love you." Young children frequently feel more comfortable going to bed with a favorite blanket or stuffed animal and/or a night light. Regardless, fears and nightmares are still fairly common in early childhood. "Family beds," i.e. children sleeping in the same bed or adjacent beds with parents, are subject to controversy. However, this is traditional in many developing countries and was historically so in America. Whatever the individual family choice, it should be consistent as young children will be frustrated by inconsistent practices and less likely to develop good sleeping habits.

Copyright © Mometrix Media. You have been licensed one copy of this document for personal use only. Any other reproduction or redistribution is strictly prohibited. All rights reserved.

Relationship of sleep quality to blood sugar control in children with Type 1 (juvenile) diabetes

Researchers find blood sugar stability problematic for many children with Type 1 (juvenile) diabetes, despite all efforts by parents and children to follow diabetic health care rules, because of sleep differences. Diabetic children spend more time in lighter than deeper stages of sleep compared to nondiabetic children. This results in higher levels of blood sugar and poorer school performance. Lighter sleep and resulting daytime sleepiness tend to increase blood sugar levels. Sleep apnea is a sleep disorder that causes a person's breathing to be interrupted often during sleeping. These breathing interruptions result in poorer sleep quality, fatigue, and daytime sleepiness. Sleep apnea has previously been associated with Type 2 diabetes—historically adult-onset, though now children are developing it, too. It is now known that apnea is also associated with Type 1 diabetes in children: roughly one-third of diabetic children studied have sleep apnea, regardless of their weight (being overweight can contribute to apnea). Sleep apnea is additionally associated with much higher blood sugars in diabetic children.

Bedtime routines

Bedtime routines serve as transitions from young children's exciting, adventurous daytime activities to the tranquility needed for healthful rest. Adults should begin routines by establishing and enforcing a rule that daytime activities like rough-and-tumble physical play or TV watching stop at a specific time. While preschoolers may be less interested in computer/video games than older children, establishing limits early will help parents enforce stopping these activities at bedtime when they are older, too. Bath time is one good way to begin bedtime routines. Toys and games make baths fun, and bath washes with lavender and other soothing ingredients are now available to relax young children. Also, since young children eat smaller meals, healthy bedtime snacks are important. Too much/too little food will disrupt sleep, and too much liquid can cause bedwetting. Adults should plan nighttime snacks appropriately for the individual child. Bedtime reading promotes interest in books and learning, adult-child/family bonding, and calms children. Singing lullabies, hugging, and cuddling also support bonding, relax children, and make them feel safe and secure.

Transitioning from sleeping in cribs to regular beds

One of young children's significant transitions from infancy is moving from a crib to a "big bed." Some become very motivated to escape cribs. For example, some bright, adventurous toddlers and even babies have untied padded crib bumpers, stacked them, and climbed out of the crib. For such children, injury is a greater danger from a crib than a bed. Others, whose cognitive and verbal skills are more developed than motor skills, may stand/jump up and down, repeatedly calling, "Hey, I'm up!" until a parent comes. These children should be moved to regular beds, with guardrails and/or body pillows to prevent rolling/falling-out accidents. If a child is moved to a bed to free the crib for a new baby, this should be done weeks ahead of the infant's arrival if possible, to separate these two significant life events. Most young children are excited about "grown-up" beds. Some, if hesitant, can sleep in the crib and nap in the bed for a gradual transition until ready for the bed full-time.

Hygiene

Dental hygiene

Even while young children still have their deciduous/"baby" teeth, dental hygiene practices can affect their permanent/adult teeth before they erupt. For example, excessive sugar can weaken adult teeth before they even appear above the gumline. Adults should not only teach young children how important it is to brush their teeth twice and floss once daily at a minimum; moreover, they

- 54 -

Copyright © Mometrix Media. You have been licensed one copy of this document for personal use only. Any other reproduction or redistribution is strictly prohibited. All rights reserved.

should model these behaviors. Children are far more likely to imitate parents' dental hygiene practices than do what parents only tell them but do not do themselves. Integrating tooth brushing into morning and bedtime routines promotes the habit. Adults can help motivate resistant children with entertaining toothbrushes that play music, spin, light up, and/or have cartoon illustrations. Young children have not developed the fine motor skills sufficient for flossing independently and will need adult supervision until they are older. Individual flossers are easier for them to use with help than traditional string dental floss.

Hand-washing
A major change during early childhood is that hygiene transforms from something adults do for children to something children learn to do themselves. Toddlers are typically learning toilet-training, getting many germs on their hands. Preschoolers today are also often exposed to germs in daycare or school settings. Adults must explain to young children using concrete, easily understood terms how germs spread; how hand-washing removes germs; and when and how to wash their hands. Adults also need to remind children frequently to wash their hands until it becomes a habit. Remind them hand-washing is required before eating, after toileting, after being outdoors, after sneezing/coughing, and after playing with pets. Because young children have short attention spans and can be impatient, they are unlikely to wash long or thoroughly enough. Adults can encourage this by teaching children to sing "Happy Birthday" or other 15- to 20-second songs/verses while washing, both assuring optimal hand-washing duration and making the process more fun.

Bathing
While infants are bathed by adults, by the time they are toddlers or preschoolers, they generally have learned to sit in a bathtub and wash themselves. However, regardless of their ability to bathe, young children should never be left unsupervised by adults in the bath. Young children can drown very quickly, even in an inch of water; an adult should always be in the bathroom. Also, adults should not let young children run bathwater: they are likely to make it too cold or hot. Adults can prevent scalding accidents by turning down the water heater temperature. The adult should adjust water temperature and test it on his/her own inner arm (an area with more sensitive skin). Parents/caregivers should choose baby shampoos, soaps, and washes that do not irritate young eyes or skin, and keep adult bath products out of children's reach and sight. Very active children may need to bathe daily; others suffering dry, itchy skin should bathe every other day and/or have parents/caregivers apply mild moisturizing lotion.

Exercise

Young children need daily physical exercise to strengthen their bones, lungs, hearts, and other muscles. Throwing, catching, running, jumping, kicking, and swinging actions develop young children's gross motor skills. Children sleep better with regular physical activity and are at less risk for obesity. Playing actively with other children also develops social skills, including empathy, sharing, cooperation, and communication. Family playtimes strengthen bonding and let parents model positive exercise habits. Outdoor play is fun for youngsters; running and laughing lift children's moods. Pride at physical attainments moreover boosts children's self-images and self-esteem. At least 60 minutes of physical activity most days is recommended for children. This includes jungle gyms, slides, swings, and other playground equipment; family walks, bike-riding, playing backyard catch, baseball, football, or basketball; adult-supervised races or obstacle courses; and age-appropriate community sports activities/leagues. Adults should plan and supervise activities to prevent injuries. They should also provide repeated sunscreen applications for outdoor activities to prevent sunburn and long-term skin damage.

Copyright © Mometrix Media. You have been licensed one copy of this document for personal use only. Any other reproduction or redistribution is strictly prohibited. All rights reserved.

<u>Physical activities for winter months and/or inclement weather</u>
While summer is typically the season of the most physical activity as it allows outdoor activities and the greatest choice of activities, adults can also provide many opportunities for young children to enjoy and benefit from exercise in winter and bad weather. Many young children like participating (at their own levels) in their parents' workouts to exercise videos. Adults can arrange "dance parties" in the living room for young children on cold/rainy days. Current video games, like Dance Dance Revolution, promote physical movement to music, making it fun while developing attention, cognitive processing, coordination, timing, and footwork. Parents can enroll their young children in indoor dance, gymnastics, karate, swimming, or ice-skating lessons and/or help them join indoor basketball, soccer, ice hockey, volleyball, or other sports teams. Families can attend local ice-skating rinks or bowling alleys for recreation. Many community facilities offer discounted fees, scholarships, or even free programs for families with financial considerations. Some companies also offer employees' families access to recreational centers/activities.

Exposure to TV and other media

Preschool-aged children are not yet cognitively able to distinguish between reality and fantasy. Therefore, overly violent or intense content in TV or other media can frighten them. Additionally, exposure to video violence has been proven to increase aggressive behaviors in young children. Moreover, using TV as a babysitter for long times excludes more cognitively stimulating and interactive pursuits. Parents/caregivers can provide young children with paints, crayons, and modeling clay. They can play board games and simple card games, do puzzles, sing songs, and read stories with young children. Pretend/make-believe play develops during early childhood, so adults can encourage their playing "house," "dress-up," or "auto shop." Park/playground trips afford outdoor play and physical activity/exercise. Visiting local museums, zoos, or planetariums combine education and entertainment with outings. In multiple-child families, it is important for each child to get some one on one time with parents regularly, even in unstructured activities like going to the hardware store with Daddy or keeping Mommy company while she washes dishes.

Cultures and cultural values

The culture in a society influences, even determines, our individual values, as do both historical and current social and political occurrences. Our values then influence the ways in which children are valued and raised. As American educators, we can understand the "American" perspective on early childhood better through understanding cultural diversity. We tend to fixate on our own culture's beliefs of truth as the only existing reality, but depending on our personal histories and values and current conditions, there can actually be multiple right ways of doing things. For example, Western cultures value children's early attainment of independence and individuality, but Eastern cultures value interdependence and group harmony more than individualism. In affluent societies, letting children explore the environment early and freely is valued, but in poor and/or developing societies, parents protect children, keeping them close and even carrying them while working, and thus do not value early freedom and exploration.

Individualistic vs. collectivistic cultures

Anthropologists have classified various world cultures along a continuum of how individualistic or interdependent their structures and values are. Investigating these differences is found to afford much insight and application for early childhood education. The predominant culture in America is considered very individualistic. Children are encouraged to assert themselves and make their own choices to realize their highest potentials, with the ultimate goal of individual self-fulfillment.

- 56 -

Copyright © Mometrix Media. You have been licensed one copy of this document for personal use only. Any other reproduction or redistribution is strictly prohibited. All rights reserved.

Collectivistic/sociocentric cultures, however, place the highest importance on group well-being; if collective harmony is disrupted by individual assertiveness, such self-assertion is devalued. Some educators characterize this contrast as the difference between standing out (individualist) and fitting in (collectivist). Researchers note that when asked to finish "I am..." statements, members of interdependent cultures tend to supply a family role, religion, or organization (e.g. "a father/a Buddhist"); whereas members of individualistic cultures cite personal qualities (e.g. "intelligent/hardworking"). Research finds American culture most individualistic, Latin American and Asian cultures most interdependent, and European cultures in the middle.

Age, ethnicity, and income

Research traces many variations in well-being and health to early childhood. These differences come from inequities in service access and treatment, congenital health problems, and early exposure to greater familial and community risk factors. Child groups at risk that are overrepresented in our population include young children, low-income children, and minority children. More young children than older children are likely to live in economically disadvantaged families. As of 2005, more than 10 million children aged 0–5 years lived in the U.S. 20 percent of these were in families classified as poor, i.e. with income below the federal poverty level (FPL), and 42 percent were in families designated low-income, i.e. with income below double the FPL. Of more than 2 million American children aged 0–5 living in families identified as extremely poor, i.e. with income less than half the FPL, minority groups were also overrepresented. The younger the children are, the greater the adverse effects of poverty are on their developmental outcomes.

Racial and ethnic origin

Children are at higher risk for inadequate development when they are born prematurely or with low birth weights. Recent research found racial and ethnic disparities in these birth conditions. For example, rates of low birth weights in 2004 were almost double for African-Americans as for whites (13.4 percent versus 7.1 percent). Latinos had similar but slightly lower risk than whites for low birth weight (6.9 percent versus 7.1 percent). Native American/Alaska Natives had slightly higher risk than white (7.5 percent versus 7.1 percent), as did Asian/Pacific Islanders (7.9 percent versus 7.1 percent). In oral health, 28 percent of preschoolers have had tooth decay. Moreover, data show that in children aged 2–5 years, oral disease increased 15.2 percent from 1994–2002, equaling 600,000 more children. It was found 13.9 percent of children aged 2–5 years were overweight or obese. Risk for overweight/obesity is higher for low-income and minority children. These groups are also at higher risk for poorer quality and continuity in asthma treatment. Asthma's prevalence as well as asthma-related morbidity and deaths are higher in African-American children than white children.

Proportionately more mothers in minority and low-income groups—up to 40 percent—suffer maternal depression than in other parts of the population. Maternal depression is associated with poor mother-child bonding; lower child scores in language and reading; and higher prevalence of depression and other mental health problems later in children. Low-income and minority families are at higher risk for developmental difficulties and mental health issues. According to U.S. surveys, about one-third or over 3 million of young children have two or more health and developmental risk factors. These risk factors include maternal mental health, maternal education, family poverty, and race/ethnicity. Each added risk factor increases the probability of either greater developmental risk or worse health status. Risk increases exponentially with multiple factors. One risk factor doubles risk; two factors more than triple it; three causes almost five times the risk; and four risk factors represent 14 times the risk of developmental delay or poor health.

Copyright © Mometrix Media. You have been licensed one copy of this document for personal use only. Any other reproduction or redistribution is strictly prohibited. All rights reserved.

Relationship of environment, social and emotional support, self-image, and success

Researchers have recently found that a child's sense of self is significant in predicting success in life. Even when a child's family environment involves multiple stressors, having a good relationship with one parent mitigates a child's psychosocial risks. As a child grows older, a close, supportive, lasting relationship with an adult outside the family can confer similar protection. Such relationships promote self-esteem in a child. Children with positive self-esteem are more able to develop feelings of control, mastery, and self-efficacy to achieve tasks, and they are more able to manage stressful life experiences. Such children demonstrate more initiative in forming relationships and accomplishing tasks. They reciprocally derive more positive experiences from their environments. Children with positive self-concepts pursue, develop, and sustain experiences and relationships that support success. Their positive self-images are further enhanced by these successes, generating additional supportive relationships and experiences. While we often hear about negative cycles of poverty, abuse, or failure, positive cycles of success can be equally as self-perpetuating.

Economically deprived and culturally diverse environments

Historically, disadvantages of poverty have been the focus of research; e.g. lack of toys, inadequate verbal interactions limiting visual discrimination and linguistic development or risk factors like less education, poorer nutrition, family stressors, medical illness, inadequate social stimulation, and insufficient social-service support leading to school dropouts, delinquency, unemployment, and perpetuated poverty. However, more recent research also identifies poverty's advantages, including opportunities for young children to play with peers and older children with little adult intervention, promoting empathy, cooperation, self-control, self-reliance, and sense of belonging; experience with multiple teaching styles, especially modeling, observation, and imitation; and language acquisition within a culturally-specific context through rich cultural traditions of stories, songs, games, and toys. These findings illuminate the resiliency or stress resistance of some children. Recent research also identifies protective factors against risk factors. These protections contribute to child resiliency, including the child's personality traits; having stable, supportive, cohesive family units; and having external support systems promoting positive values and coping skills.

Effects of racial, ethnic, and economic disparities

Parenting, home safety, and school readiness

According to the National Survey on Early Childhood Health, significant differences are reported in Latino and African-Americans' parenting practices, home routines, and home safety measures. These differences are associated with differing degrees of positive early childhood development. Research studies have also revealed that American children in minority groups, on the average, demonstrate lower school readiness levels when they begin formal education than white American children do. The research furthermore shows that most of these differences in school readiness levels are associated with differences in family income. Researchers also comment that disparities among racial and ethnic groups in their school readiness and subsequent academic achievement in school may be additional contributors to discrimination against minority racial and ethnic groups by teachers and other educational personnel.

Copyright © Mometrix Media. You have been licensed one copy of this document for personal use only. Any other reproduction or redistribution is strictly prohibited. All rights reserved.

<u>Health care aspects of immunizations, regular providers, and satisfaction</u>
Although the disparity in childhood immunizations between white and minority infants and toddlers has decreased, still, fewer minority children are receiving standard immunizations than white children in America. For example, the preschool rates for receiving each major vaccination from 2003–2004 in America were the lowest among non-Latino black, Native American, and Alaskan Native children. One sign of health service quality and continuity is having a regular health care provider. Recent national surveys have found that while more than 80 percent of children under the age of 5 in economically affluent families are seen at physicians' offices or HMOs for care when sick, not much more than 54 percent of children under age 5 in economically poor families are seen for sick care. The National Survey of Early Childhood Health has found African-American and Latino parents report more dissatisfaction with pediatricians and more unmet needs for early childhood development services than white parents. Twice as many Latino as white parents felt providers never or only occasionally understood their individual child's needs.

Differing socioeconomic and racial effects on mental, emotional, and social health

According to the National Survey of Child and Adolescent Well-Being, in recent years over 40 percent of toddlers and over 68 percent of preschoolers who were in contact with the child welfare system had high levels of need, developmentally and behaviorally. But overall, fewer than 23 percent of these children were getting services to address these needs. Thus, young children of socioeconomically disadvantaged families were found to have more developmental and behavioral problems than children in other socioeconomic groups, yet were also less likely to receive help with such problems. Another social and emotional difference related to racial group membership has been reflected by levels of violence in the family. 2003 data found that over 15 percent of African-American families experienced violent conflicts, compared to below 9 percent of white families and over 11 percent of Latino families. Racial groups classified as "other" constituted over 12 percent. Experts concede that styles of disagreeing can be influenced by cultural and demographic variables. However, they find the strongest influence on conflicts becoming violent to be parental stress.

Inequity in health insurance coverage for children of minority groups

Research has demonstrated that after taking health insurance status into account, there are no significant socioeconomic differences in how family organization and doctor/health care practitioner visits are related. Furthermore, research has shown that having health insurance coverage decreases differences in developmental and health outcomes for young children. However, despite these findings, children of minority groups are less likely than their nonminority peers to have either private or public health care coverage. Regarding access to health care services, it has been found that parents whose first language was not English were only half as likely to get preventive health care for their infants as native English-speaking families. This inequity in service delivery was found to be constant across white, African-American, and Latino families that had infants, but not in Asian-American families having infants.

Unequal health care treatment of young minority children in America

According to data collected by the National Survey of Early Childhood Health, minority families have less communication and guidance from pediatric health care providers than white families. For example, African-American parents were found to make significantly fewer phone calls than white parents to pediatric health care practices. Latino parents made fewer than half the calls that white parents did; African-American parents made fewer than three-fourths of the calls white parents did. This survey also found that pediatricians and other pediatric health care service

Copyright © Mometrix Media. You have been licensed one copy of this document for personal use only. Any other reproduction or redistribution is strictly prohibited. All rights reserved.

providers were more likely to emphasize topics of household alcohol and drug use and community violence when they talked with minority patient families than they did in discussions with white patient families. African-American children are found far more likely to have special health care needs than white children; yet researchers find that even after controlling for health status, insurance, and other pertinent variables, health care providers are still nearly twice as likely not to refer minority children to specialists and consultants.

Leveling inequalities in early childhood care, health, and education

Eliminating unequal treatment in early childhood has significant benefits, including lowering overall national rates of poverty; improving overall health and education measures; saving long-term health care costs; decreasing disabilities; and lengthening lives by decreasing mortality rates. The effects of low income and racism on young children and their families are complex, and these influences interact with one another. Therefore it is impossible or extremely difficult to solve problems generated by one of these social factors without including the other associated influencing factors. Because of the interrelationships of variables, strategies on a system level have the most potential for effectiveness. For example, job training and placement programs that could help parents economically are limited in effectiveness if quality child care is not also available to those parents. Enhancing educational programs could improve academic performance, but not if young students are too hungry to benefit from instruction. And the measurement and monitoring of developmental, health, and educational outcomes will not change their disparity unless treatment inequities are resolved.

Early Childhood Comprehensive Systems (ECCS)

According to the National Center for Children in Poverty, Early Childhood Comprehensive Systems (ECCS) initiatives in each U.S. state have the ability to further methods that can decrease socioeconomically related health care inequities in early childhood, which generates positive impacts for the rest of children's lives. To raise and shape consciousness of health care issues affected by income and race, experts recommend that ECCS establish connections between projects/programs designed to eradicate poverty and racism and efforts in developing early childhood systems. Another consciousness-raising strategy recommended for ECCS is to work at increasing the general public's awareness of racial, ethnic, and economic disparities in early childhood health care and to work at increasing such awareness in health professionals, educators, early care providers, and other significant stakeholders who regularly provide services to young children. ECCS can also include racial/ethnic data in performance monitoring; encourage state SCHIP and Medicaid agencies to do the same; analyze state data for disparities in risk, access, and outcomes, including small-area analyses, geocoding, etc.; and identify and measure unequal treatment through data analysis.

Experts in early childhood development find that state ECCS should target their support toward communities with larger populations of minority and low-income families. Inasmuch as local systems have limited resources, some state ECCS might need to allocate more of these resources to communities having higher risks of adverse outcomes for children. ECCS can also provide assistance to communities by helping them assess their local assets, strengths, needs, and risk factors. Early childhood development experts emphasize that state ECCS should focus their efforts on improving the quality of health care services that are available within communities where all or the majority of residents are members of minority groups and/or have low socioeconomic status.

Copyright © Mometrix Media. You have been licensed one copy of this document for personal use only. Any other reproduction or redistribution is strictly prohibited. All rights reserved.

Another way in which state ECCS can strengthen the supports available in communities for citizens who are subject to unequal health care treatment according to their demographic groups is to offer and provide incentives for community development projects that are designed to decrease health care treatment disparities based on racial/ethnic and economic differences.

Early childhood experts advise that each U.S. state's ECCS should implement strategies designed to monitor health care providers and services for cultural and linguistic competency, and to improve these competencies. One example of such improvement is ensuring that specific training in cultural and linguistic competency and cross-cultural competency is integrated into the training of both health care providers and early childhood educators. ECCS can also be responsible for seeing that parent education materials and resources in health care are translated into the native languages of local families who are not native English speakers, and supporting interpreter and translator services for communities having families needing these. Experts find that ECCS can additionally improve child and family health services by supporting various early childhood service settings in employing nonprofessional/community health workers. Moreover, ECCS can help further equality and consistency of health care across varied demographic groups by applying research evidence-based guidelines regarding health care, family support, early learning, and related services and programs.

Zone of Proximal Development (ZPD)

Vygotsky identified an area or range of skills wherein a learner can complete a task s/he could not yet complete independently, given some help. He termed this area the Zone of Proximal Development. Vygotsky found if a child is given assistance, guidance, or support from someone who knows more—especially another child just slightly more advanced in knowledge and/or skills—the first child can not only succeed at a task s/he is still unable to do alone; but that child also learns best through accomplishing something just slightly beyond his/her limits of expertise to do alone. Jerome Bruner coined the term "scaffolding" to describe temporary support that others give learners for achieving tasks. Scaffolding is closely related to the ZPD in that only the amount of support needed is given, and it allows the learner to accomplish things s/he could not complete autonomously. Scaffolding is gradually withdrawn as the child's skills develop, until the child reaches the level of expertise needed to complete the task on his/her own.

Montessori Method

Maria Montessori's method emphasizes children's engagement in self-directed activities, with teachers using clinical observations to act as children's guides. In introducing and teaching concepts, the Montessori Method also employs self-correcting ("autodidactic") equipment. This method focuses on the significance and interrelatedness of all life forms, and the need for every individual to find his/her place in the world and to find meaningful work. Children in Montessori schools learn complex math skills and gain knowledge about diverse cultures and languages. Montessori philosophy puts emphasis on adapting learning environments to individual children's developmental levels. The Montessori Method also believes in teaching both practical skills and abstract concepts through the medium of physical activities. Montessori teachers observe and identify children's movements into sensitive periods when they are best prepared to receive individual lessons in subjects of interest to them that they can grasp readily. Children's senses of autonomy and self-esteem are encouraged in Montessori programs. Montessori instructors also strive to engage parents in their children's education.

Copyright © Mometrix Media. You have been licensed one copy of this document for personal use only. Any other reproduction or redistribution is strictly prohibited. All rights reserved.

What Montessori calls "work" refers to developmentally appropriate learning materials. These are set out so each student can see the choices available. Children can select items from each of Montessori's five sections: Practical Life, Sensorial, Language Arts, Mathematics and Geometry, and Cultural Subjects. When a child is done with a work, s/he replaces it for another child to use and selects another work. Teachers work one on one with children and in groups; however, the majority of interactions are among children, as Montessori stresses self-directed activity. Not only teachers but also older children help younger ones in learning new skills, so Montessori classes usually incorporate 2- or 3-year age ranges. Depending on students' ages and the individual school, Montessori schooldays are generally half-days, e.g. 9 a.m.–noon or 12:30 p.m. Most Montessori schools also offer afternoon and/or early evening options. Children wanting to "do it myself" benefit from Montessori, as do special-needs children. Individualized attention, independence, and hands-on learning are emphasized. Montessori schools prefer culturally diverse students and teach about diverse cultures.

The Practical Life area of Montessori classes helps children develop care for self, others, and the environment. Children learn many daily skills, including buttoning, pouring liquids, preparing meals, and cleaning up after meals and activities. The Sensorial area gives young children experience with learning through all five senses. They participate in activities like ordering colors from lightest to darkest; sorting objects from roughest to smoothest texture; and sorting items from biggest to smallest/longest to shortest. They learn to match similar tastes, textures, and sounds. The Language Arts area encourages young children to express themselves in words, and they learn to identify letters, match them with corresponding phonemes (speech sounds), and manually trace their shapes as preparation for learning reading, spelling, grammar, and writing. In the Mathematics and Geometry area, children learn to recognize numbers, count, add, subtract, multiply, divide, and use the decimal system via hands-on learning with concrete materials. In the Cultural Subjects area, children learn science, art, music, movement, time, history, geography, and zoology.

Schedules of reinforcement in behaviorism

Continuous schedules of presenting rewards or punishments are fixed. Fixed ratio schedules involve introducing reinforcement after a set number of instances of the targeted behavior. For example, when asking a preschooler to put away materials, a teacher might present punishment for noncompliance only after making three consecutive requests. The disadvantage is, even young children know they can get away with ignoring the first two requests, only complying just before the third. Fixed interval schedules introduce reinforcement after set time periods. Again, the disadvantages are, even multiply disabled infants quickly learn when to expect reinforcement, rather than associating it with how long they have engaged in a desired behavior; young children only change their behavior immediately before the teacher will observe and reward it. Variable ratio and variable interval schedules apply reinforcement following irregular numbers of responses or irregular time periods, respectively. The advantage of variable schedules is, since children cannot predict when they will receive reinforcements, they are more likely to repeat/continue desired behaviors more and for longer times.

Bank Street Curriculum

Lucy Sprague Mitchell founded the Bank Street Curriculum, applying theoretical concepts from Jean Piaget, Erik Erikson, John Dewey, and others. Bank Street is called a Developmental Interaction Approach. It emphasizes children's rich, direct interactions with wide varieties of ideas, materials, and people in their environments. The Bank Street method gives young children opportunities for

Copyright © Mometrix Media. You have been licensed one copy of this document for personal use only. Any other reproduction or redistribution is strictly prohibited. All rights reserved.

physical, cognitive, emotional, and social development through engagement in various types of child care programs. Typically, multiple subjects are included and taught to groups. Children can learn through a variety of methods and at different developmental levels. By interacting directly with their geographical, social, and political environments, children are prepared for lifelong learning through this curriculum. Using blocks, solving puzzles, going on field trips, and doing practical lab work are among the numerous learning experiences Bank Street offers. Its philosophy is that school can simultaneously be stimulating, satisfying, and sensible. School is a significant part of children's lives, where they inquire about and experiment with the environment and share ideas with other children as they mature.

The Bank Street Developmental Interaction Approach to teaching recommends that children at the oldest early childhood ages of 5–6 years should have classrooms that are efficient, organized, conducive to working, and designed to afford them sensory and motor learning experiences. Classrooms should include rich varieties of appealing colors, which tend to energize children's imaginations and activity and encourage them to interact with the surroundings and participate in the environment. "Interest corners" in classrooms are advocated by the Bank Street approach. These are places where children can display their art works, use language, and depict social life experiences. This approach also recommends having multipurpose tables in the classroom that children can use for writing, drawing, and other classroom activities. The Bank Street Developmental Interaction Approach also points out the importance of libraries in schools, not just for supporting classroom content, but for providing materials for children's extracurricular reading.

The Bank Street Developmental Interaction Approach requires educators to create well-designed classrooms: this curriculum approach finds children are enabled to develop discipline by growing up in such controlled environments. Teachers are considered to be extremely significant figures in their young students' lives. The Bank Street Approach requires that teachers always treat children with respect, to enable children to develop strong senses of self-respect. Teachers' having faith in their students and believing in their ability to succeed are found to have great impacts on young children's performance and their motivation to excel in school and in life. The Bank Street Curriculum emphasizes the importance of providing transitions from one type of activity to another. It also stresses changing the learning subjects at regular time intervals. This facilitates children's gaining a sense of direction and taking responsibility for what they do. Bank Street views these practices as helping children develop internal self-control, affording them discipline for dealing with the external world.

Froebel's educational theory

Friedrich Froebel (1782–1852) invented the original concept and practice of Kindergarten. His theory of education had widespread influences, including using play-based instruction with young children. Froebel's educational theory emphasized the unity of humanity, nature, and God. Froebel believed the success of the individual dictates the success of the race, and that school's role is to direct students' will. He believed nature is the heart of all learning. He felt unity, individuality, and diversity were important values achieved through education. Froebel said education's goals include developing self-control and spirituality. He recommended curricula include math, language, design, art, health, hygiene, and physical education. He noted school's role in social development. According to Froebel, schools should impart meaning to life experiences; show students relationships among external, previously unrelated knowledge; and associate facts with principles. Froebel felt human potential is defined through individual accomplishments. He believed humans generally are productive and creative, attaining completeness and harmony via maturation.

Copyright © Mometrix Media. You have been licensed one copy of this document for personal use only. Any other reproduction or redistribution is strictly prohibited. All rights reserved.

Froebel, 19th-century inventor of Kindergarten, developed an influential educational theory. He found that observation, discovery, play, and free, self-directed activity facilitated children's learning. He observed that drawing/art activities develop higher level cognitive skills and that virtues are taught through children's games. He also found nature, songs, fables, stories, poems, and crafts effective learning media. He attributed reading and writing development to children's self-expression needs. Froebel recommended activities to develop children's motor skills and stimulate their imaginations. He believed in equal rather than authoritarian teacher-student relationships, and advocated family involvement/collaboration. He pointed out the critical nature of sensory experiences, and the value of life experiences for self-expression. He believed teachers should support students' discovery learning rather than prescribing what to learn. Like Piaget, Dewey, and Montessori, Froebel embraced constructivist learning, i.e. children construct meaning and reality through their interactions with the environment. He stressed the role of parents, particularly mothers, in children's educational processes.

Friedrich Froebel originated the concept and practice of Kindergarten (German for "child's garden") in 1837. His educational theory had great influence on early childhood education. Froebel's theory addressed society's role in education. He saw education as defined by the "law of divine unity," which stated that everything is connected and humanity, nature, and God are unified. Froebel believed all developments are by God's plan; he found the social institution of religion an important part of children's education. He emphasized parental and sibling involvement in child education. He theorized that culture is changed not by acquiring ideas, but by the productivity, work, and actions of the individual. Froebel believed all children deserve respect and individual attention; should develop their individual potentials; and can learn, irrespective of social class or religion, providing they are developmentally ready for given specific content. Regarding consensus, Froebel's view was religious: he believed God's supreme plan determined social and moral order. He felt people should share common experiences and learn unity, while also respecting diversity and individuality.

Siegfried Engelmann

Engelmann (b. 1931) cofounded the Bereiter-Engelmann Program with Carl Bereiter with funding from the U.S. Office of Education. This project demonstrated the ability of intensive instruction to enhance cognitive skills in disadvantaged preschool-aged children, establishing the Bereiter-Engelmann Preschool Program. Bereiter and Engelmann also conducted experiments reexamining Piaget's theory of cognitive development, specifically concerning the ability to conserve liquid volume. They showed, contrary to Piaget's contention that this ability depended solely on a child's cognitive-developmental stage, it could be taught. Engelmann researched curriculum and instruction, including preschoolers with Down syndrome and children from impoverished backgrounds, establishing the philosophy and methodology of Direct Instruction. He designed numerous reading, math, spelling, language, and writing instruction programs, and also achievement tests, videos, and games. Engelmann worked with Project Head Start and Project Follow Through. The former included his and Wesley Becker's comparison of their Engelmann-Becker model of early childhood instruction with other models in teaching disadvantaged children. The latter is often considered the biggest controlled study ever comparing teaching models and methods.

In the 1960s, Siegfried Engelmann noted a lack of research into how young children learn. Wanting to find out what kinds of teaching effected retention, and what the extent was of individual differences among young learners, Engelmann conducted research, as Piaget had done, using his own children and those of colleagues and neighbors. With a previous advertising background, Engelmann formed focus groups of preschool children to test-market teaching methods. Main

Copyright © Mometrix Media. You have been licensed one copy of this document for personal use only. Any other reproduction or redistribution is strictly prohibited. All rights reserved.

features of the curricula Engelmann developed included emphasizing phonics and computation early in young children's instruction; using a precise logical sequence to teach new skills; teaching new skills in small, separate, "child-sized" pieces; correcting learners' errors immediately; adhering strictly to designated teaching schedules; constantly reviewing to integrate new learning with previously attained knowledge; and scrupulous measurement techniques for assessing skills mastery. To demonstrate the results of his methods for teaching math, Engelmann sent movies he made of these to educational institutions. They showed that with his methods, toddlers could master upper-elementary-grade-level computations, and even simple linear equations.

Direct Instruction method

Direct Instruction (DI) is a behavioral method of teaching. Therefore, learner errors receive immediate corrective feedback, and correct responses receive immediate, obvious positive reinforcement. DI has a fast pace—10–14 learner responses per minute overall—affording more attention and less boredom; reciprocal teacher-student feedback; immediate indications of learner problems to teachers; and natural reinforcement of teacher activities. DI thus promotes more mutual student and teacher learning than traditional "one-way" methods. Children are instructed in small groups according to ability levels. Their attention is teacher-focused. Teacher presentations follow scripts designed to give instruction the proper sequence, including prewritten prompts and questions developed through field-testing with real students. These optimized prepared lessons allow teachers to attend to extra instructional and motivational aspects of learning. Cued by teachers, who control the pace and give all learners with varying response rates chances for practice, children respond actively in groups and individually. Small groups are typically seated in semicircles close to teachers, who use visual aids like blackboards and overhead projectors.

Project Follow Through

In 1967, President Lyndon B. Johnson declared his War on Poverty. This initiative included Project Follow Through, funded by the U.S. Office of Education and Office of Economic Opportunity. Research had previously found that Project Head Start, which offered early educational interventions to disadvantaged preschoolers, had definite positive impacts; but these were often short-lived. Project Follow Through was intended to discover how to maintain Head Start's benefits. Siegfried Engelmann and Wesley Becker, who had developed the Engelmann-Becker instructional model, invited others to propose various other teaching models in communities selected to participate in Project Follow Through. The researchers asked parents in each community to choose from among the models provided. The proponents of each model were given funds to train teachers and furnish curriculum. Models found to enhance disadvantaged children's school achievement were to be promoted nationally. Engelmann's Direct Instruction model showed positive results surpassing all other models. However, the U.S. Office of Education did not adopt this or other models found best.

A huge comparative study of curriculum and instruction methods, Project Follow Through incorporated three main approaches: Affective, Basic Skills, and Cognitive. Affective approaches used in Project Follow Through included the Bank Street, Responsive Education, and Open Education models. These teaching models aim to enhance school achievement by emphasizing experiences that raise children's self-esteem, which is believed to facilitate their acquisition of basic skills and higher-order problem-solving skills. Basic Skills approaches included the Southwest Labs, Behavior Analysis, and Direct Instruction models. These models find that mastering basic skills facilitates higher-order cognitive and problem-solving skills, and higher self-esteem. Cognitive approaches included the Parent Education, TEEM, and Cognitively Oriented Curriculum models.

Copyright © Mometrix Media. You have been licensed one copy of this document for personal use only. Any other reproduction or redistribution is strictly prohibited. All rights reserved.

These models focus on teaching higher-order problem-solving and thinking skills as the optimal avenue to enhancing school achievement, and to improving lower-order basic skills and self-esteem. Affective and Cognitive models have become popular in most schools of education. Basic Skills approaches are less popular, but are congruent with other, very effective methods of specialized instruction.

Constance Kamii

Professor of early childhood education Constance Kamii, of Japanese ancestry, was born in Geneva, Switzerland. She attended elementary school in both Switzerland and Japan, completing secondary school and higher education degrees in the United States. She studied extensively with Jean Piaget, also of Geneva. She worked with the Perry Preschool Project in the 1960s, fueling her subsequent interest in theoretically grounded instruction. Kamii believes in basing early childhood educational goals and objectives upon scientific theory of children's cognitive, social, and moral development; and moreover that Piaget's theory of cognitive development is the sole explanation for child development from birth to adolescence. She has done much curriculum research in the U.S., and published a number of books, on how to apply Piaget's theory practically in early childhood classrooms. Kamii agrees with Piaget that education's overall, long-term goal is developing children's intellectual, social, and moral autonomy. Kamii has said, "A classroom cannot foster the development of autonomy in the intellectual realm while suppressing it in the social and moral realms."

Kamii and DeVries

Constance Kamii and Rhetta DeVries formulated the Kamii-DeVries Constructivist Perspective model of preschool education. It is closely based upon Piaget's theory of child cognitive development and on the Constructivist theory to which Piaget and others subscribed, which dictates that children construct their own realities through their interactions with the environment. Piaget's particular constructivism included the principle that through their interacting with the world within a logical-mathematical structure, children's intelligence, knowledge, personalities, and morality develop. The Kamii-DeVries approach finds that children learn via performing mental actions, which Piaget called operations, through the vehicle of physical activities. This model favors using teachers experienced in traditional preschool education, who employ a child-centered approach, and establish active learning settings, are in touch with children's thoughts, respond to children from children's perspectives, and facilitate children's extension of their ideas. The Kamii-DeVries model has recently been applied to learning assessments using technology (2003) and to using constructivism in teaching physics to preschoolers (2011).

High/Scope Curriculum

The High/Scope Curriculum, developed by David P. Weikart and colleagues, takes a constructivist approach influenced by Piaget's theory, advocating active learning. The High/Scope curriculum model identified a total of 58 "key experiences" it finds critical for preschool child development and learning. These key experiences are subdivided into ten main categories:
  1. Creative representation, which includes recognizing symbolic use, imitating, and playing roles
  2. Language and literacy, which include speaking, describing, scribbling, and narrating/dictating stories
  3. Initiative and social relations, including solving problems, making decisions and choices, and building relationships

Copyright © Mometrix Media. You have been licensed one copy of this document for personal use only. Any other reproduction or redistribution is strictly prohibited. All rights reserved.

4. Movement, including activities like running, bending, stretching, and dancing
5. Music, which includes singing, listening to music, and playing musical instruments
6. Classification, which includes sorting objects, matching objects or pictures, and describing object shapes
7. Seriation, or arranging things in prescribed orders (e.g. by size or number)
8. Numbers, which for preschoolers focuses on counting
9. Space, which involves activities like filling and emptying containers
10. Time, including concepts of starting, sequencing, and stopping actions.

David Weikart and colleagues developed the High/Scope Curriculum in the 1960s and 1970s, testing it in the Perry Preschool and Head Start Projects, among others. The High/Scope philosophy is based on Piaget's Constructivist principles that active learning is optimal for young children; that they need to become involved actively with materials, ideas, people, and events; and that children and teachers learn together in the instructional environment. Weikart and colleagues' early research focused on economically disadvantaged children, but the High/Scope approach has since been extended to all young children and all kinds of preschool settings. This model recommends dividing classrooms into well-furnished, separate "interest areas," and regular daily class routines affording children time to plan, implement, and reflect upon what they learn, and to participate in large and small group activities. Teachers establish socially supportive atmospheres; plan group learning activities; organize settings and set daily routines; encourage purposeful child activities, problem-solving, and verbal reflection; and interpret child behaviors according to High/Scope's key child development experiences.

The High/Scope Curriculum frequently incorporates computers as regular program components, including developmentally appropriate software, for children to access when they choose. School days may be full-day or part-day, determined by each individual program. Flexible hours accommodate individual family needs and situations. High/Scope programs work in both child care and preschool settings. High/Scope was originally designed to enhance educational outcomes for young children considered at-risk due to socioeconomically disadvantaged, urban backgrounds, and was compatible with Project Head Start. This model of early childhood curriculum and instruction advocates individualizing teaching to each child's developmental level and pace of learning. As such, the High/Scope approach is found to be effective for children who have learning disabilities, and also for children with developmental delays. It works well with all children needing individual attention. High/Scope is less amenable to highly structured settings that use more adult-directed instruction.

Head Start Program

Head Start was begun in 1964, extended by the Head Start Act of 1981, and revised in its 2007 reauthorization. It is a program of the U.S. Department of Health and Human Services designed to give low-income families and their young children comprehensive services of health, nutrition, education, and parental involvement. While Head Start was initially intended to "catch up" low-income children over the summer to reach kindergarten readiness, it soon became obvious that a six-week preschool program was inadequate to compensate for having lived in poverty for one's first five years. Hence the Head Start Program was expanded and modified over the years with the aim of remediating the effects of system-wide poverty upon child educational outcomes. Currently, Head Start gives local public, private, nonprofit, and for-profit agencies grants for delivering comprehensive child development services to promote disadvantaged children's school readiness by improving their cognitive and social development. It particularly emphasizes developing early reading and math abilities preschoolers will need for school success.

Copyright © Mometrix Media. You have been licensed one copy of this document for personal use only. Any other reproduction or redistribution is strictly prohibited. All rights reserved.

The Early Head Start program developed as an outgrowth of the original Head Start Program. Head Start initially aimed to remediate the deprivation of poor preschool-aged children by providing educational services over the summer to help them attain school readiness by kindergarten. Because educators and researchers soon discovered the summer program was insufficient to make up for poor children's lack of preparation, Head Start was expanded to become more comprehensive. Head Start was established in 1964 and expanded by the Head Start Act in 1981. After research had accumulated considerable evidence of how important children's earliest years are to their ensuing growth and development, the U.S. Department of Health and Human Services Administration for Children and Families' Office of Head Start established the Early Head Start Program in 1995. Early Head Start works to improve prenatal health; improve infant and toddler development; and enhance healthy family functioning. It serves children from 0–3 years. Like the original program, Early Head Start stresses parental engagement in children's growth, development, and learning.

Emergent literacy theory

According to the theory of emergent literacy, even infants encounter written language. Two- and three-year-olds commonly can identify logos, labels, and signs in their homes and communities. Also, young children's scribbles show features/appearances of their language's specific writing system even before they can write. For example, Egyptian children's scribbles look more like Egyptian writing; American children's scribbles look more like English writing. Young children learn to read and write concurrently, not sequentially; the two abilities are closely interrelated. Moreover, though with speech, receptive language comprehension seems easier/sooner to develop than expressive language production, this does not apply to reading and writing: first learning activities involving writing are found easier for preschoolers than those involving reading. Research finds that form follows function, not the opposite: young children's literacy learning is mostly through meaningful, functional, purposeful/goal-directed real-life activities. Literacy comprises not isolated, abstract skills learned for their own sake, but rather authentic skills applied to accomplish real-life purposes, the way children observe adults using literacy.

Through extensive research, emergent literacy theorists have found that: (1) Young children develop literacy through being actively involved in reading and rereading their favorite storybooks. When preschoolers "reread" storybooks, they have not memorized them; rather, theorists find this activity to exemplify young children's reconstruction of a book's meaning. Similarly, young children's invented spellings are examples of their efforts to reconstruct what they know of written language; they can inform us about a child's familiarity with specific phonetic components. (2) Adults' reading to children, no matter how young, is crucial to literacy development. It helps children gain a "feel" for the character, flow, and patterns of written/printed language, and an overall sense of what reading feels like and entails. It fosters positive attitudes toward reading in children, strongly motivating them to read when they begin school. Being read to also helps children develop print awareness and formulate concepts of books and reading. (3) Influenced by Piaget and Vygotsky, emergent literacy theory views reading and writing as developmental processes having successive stages.

Emergent literacy vs. reading readiness

Historically, early childhood educators viewed "reading readiness" as a time during young children's literacy development when they were ready to start learning to read and write, and taught literacy accordingly. However, in the late 19th and early 20th centuries, research has found

Copyright © Mometrix Media. You have been licensed one copy of this document for personal use only. Any other reproduction or redistribution is strictly prohibited. All rights reserved.

that children have innate learning capacities and that skills emerge under the proper conditions. Educational researchers came to view language as developing gradually within a child rather than a child's being ready to read at a certain time. Thus, the term "emergent" came to replace "readiness," while "literacy" replaced "reading" as referring to all of language's interrelated aspects of listening, speaking, writing, and viewing, as well as reading. Traditional views of literacy were based only on children's reading and writing in ways similar to those of adults. However, more recently, the theory of emergent literacy has evolved through the findings of research into the early preschool reading of young children and their and their families' associated characteristics.

The emergent literacy theoretical perspective yields an instructional model for the learning and teaching of reading and writing in young children that is founded on building instruction from the child's knowledge. Emergent literacy theory's assumption is that young children already know a lot about language and literacy by the time they enter school. This theory furthermore regards even 2- and 3-year-olds as having information about how the reading and writing processes function, and as having already formed particular ideas about what written/printed language is. From this perspective, emergent literacy theory then dictates that teaching should build upon what a child already knows and should support the child's further literacy development. Researchers conclude that teachers should furnish open-ended activities allowing children to show what they already know about literacy; to apply that knowledge; and to build upon it. From the emergent literacy perspective, teachers take the role of creating a learning environment with conditions that are conducive to children's learning in ways that are ideally self-motivated, self-generated, and self-regulated.

Literacy practices that are not developmentally appropriate

Research finds some preschools are like play centers, but not optimal for literacy because their curricula exclude natural reading and writing activities. Researchers have also identified a trend in many kindergartens to ensure children's "reading readiness" by providing highly academic programs, influencing preschool curricula to get children "ready" for such kindergartens. Influenced and even pressured by kindergarten programs' academic expectations, parents have also come to expect preschools to prepare their children for kindergarten. However, experts find applying elementary-school programs to kindergartens and preschools developmentally inappropriate. Formal instruction in reading and writing and worksheets are not suitable for younger children. Instead, research finds print-rich preschool environments both developmentally appropriate and more effective. For example, when researchers changed classrooms from having a "book corner" to having a centrally located table with books plus paper, pencils, envelopes, and stamps, children spent 3 to 10 times more time on direct reading and writing activities. Children are found to take naturally to these activities without prior formal reading and writing lessons.

Planning a play-based curriculum

To plan a curriculum based on children's natural play with building blocks (Hoisington, 2008), a teacher can first arrange the environment to stimulate further such play. Then s/he can furnish materials for children to make plans/blueprints for and records and models of buildings they construct. The teacher can make time during the day for children to reflect upon and discuss their individual and group building efforts. Teachers can also utilize teaching strategies that encourage children to reflect on and consider in more depth the scientific principles related to their results. A teacher can provide building materials of varied sizes, shapes, textures, and weights, and props to add realism, triggering more complex structures and creative, dramatic, emotional, and social development. Teachers can take photos of children's structures as documents for discussions,

Copyright © Mometrix Media. You have been licensed one copy of this document for personal use only. Any other reproduction or redistribution is strictly prohibited. All rights reserved.

stimulating language and vocabulary development. Supplying additional materials to support and stick together blocks extends play-based learning. Active teacher participation by offering observations and asking open-ended questions promotes children's standards-based learning of scientific, mathematical, and linguistic concepts, processes, and patterns.

When children play at building with blocks, for example, they investigate material properties such as various block shapes, sizes, and weights and the stability of carpet vs. hard floor as bases. They explore cause-and-effect relationships; make conclusions regarding the results of their trial-and-error experiments; draw generalizations about observed patterns; and form theories about what does and does not work to build high towers. Ultimately, they construct their knowledge of how reality functions. Teachers support this by introducing relevant learning standards in the play context meaningful to children. For example, math standards including spatial awareness, geometry, number, operations, patterns, and measurement can be supported through planning play. By encouraging and guiding children's discussion and documentation of their play constructions, and supplying nonfictional and fictional books about building, a teacher also integrates learning goals and objectives for language and literacy development. Teachers can plan activities specifically to extend learning in these domains, like counting blocks; comparison/contrast; matching; sorting; sequencing; phonological awareness; alphabetic awareness; print awareness; book appreciation; listening, comprehension, speech, and communication.

Thematic teaching units

To develop a thematic teaching unit, a teacher designs a collection of related activities around certain themes or topics that crosses several curriculum areas or domains. Thematic units create learning environments for young children that promote all children's active engagement, as well as their process learning. By studying topics children find relevant to their own lives, thematic units build upon children's preexisting knowledge and current interests, and also help them relate information to their own life experiences. Varied curriculum content can be more easily integrated through thematic units, in ways that young children can understand and apply meaningfully. Children's diverse individual learning styles are also accommodated through thematic units. Such units involve children physically in learning; teach them factual information in greater depth; teach them learning process-related skills, i.e. "learning how to learn"; holistically integrate learning; encourage cohesion in groups; meet children's individual needs; and provide motivation to both children and their teachers.

Project Approach

The Project Approach (Katz and Chard, 1989) entails having young children choose a topic interesting to them, studying this topic, researching it, and solving problems and questions as they emerge. This gives children greater practice with creative thinking and problem-solving skills, which supports greater success in all academic and social areas. For example, if a class of preschoolers shows interest in the field of medicine, their teacher can plan a field trip to a local hospital to introduce a project studying medicine in depth. During the trip, the teacher can write down/record children's considerations and questions, and then use these as guidelines to plan and conduct relevant activities that will further stimulate the children's curiosity and imagination. Throughout this or any other in-depth project, the teacher can integrate specific skills for reading, writing, math, science, social studies, and creative thinking. This affords dual benefits: enabling both children's skills advancement, and their gaining knowledge they recognize is required and applies in their own lives. Children become life-long learners with this recognition.

Copyright © Mometrix Media. You have been licensed one copy of this document for personal use only. Any other reproduction or redistribution is strictly prohibited. All rights reserved.

Integrated curriculum

An integrated curriculum organizes early childhood education to transcend the boundaries between the various domains and subject content areas. It unites different curriculum elements through meaningful connections to allow study of wider areas of knowledge. It treats learning holistically and mirrors the interactive nature of reality. The principle that learning consists of series of interconnections is the foundation for teaching through use of an integrated curriculum. Benefits of integrated curricula include an organized planning mechanism; greater flexibility; and the ability to teach many skills and concepts effectively, include more varied content, and enable children to learn most naturally. By identifying themes children find most interesting, teachers can construct webs of assorted themes, which can provide the majority of their curriculum. Research has proven the effectiveness of integrated teaching units for both children and their teachers. Teachers can also integrate new content into existing teaching units they have identified as effective. Integrated units enable teachers to ensure children are learning pertinent knowledge and applying it to real-life situations.

EC teachers can incorporate many skills into units organized by theme. This includes state governments' educational standards/benchmarks for various skills. Teachers can base units on topics of interest to young children, e.g. building construction, space travel, movie-making, dinosaurs, vacations, nursery rhymes, fairy tales, pets, wildlife, camping, the ocean, and studies of particular authors and book themes. Beginning with a topic that motivates the children is best; related activities and skills will naturally follow. In planning units, teachers should establish connections among content areas like literacy, physical activity, dramatic play, art, music, math, science, and social studies. Making these connections permits children's learning through their strongest/favored modalities and supports learning through meaningful experiences, which is how they learn best. Theme-based approaches effectively address individual differences and modality-related strengths, as represented in Gardner's theory of Multiple Intelligences. Thematic approaches facilitate creating motivational learning centers and hands-on learning activities, and are also compatible with creating portfolio assessments and performance-based assessments. Teachers can encompass skill and conceptual benchmarks for specific age/developmental levels within engaging themes.

Integrating subject/domain content across the curriculum has been used for years at every educational level, from higher education to early childhood education. However, recent demands for accountability, as exemplified and escalated by No Child Left Behind, can distract educators from holistic and overall learning toward preoccupation with developing isolated skills and using test scores to measure achievement. But rather than discarding teaching methods proven effective, early childhood educators need to integrate newer, mandate-related practices into existing plans and methods. Teaching integrated curricula in early childhood classrooms has proven effective for both children and teachers. Integrating learning domains and subject content in turn integrates the child's developing skills with the whole child. When teachers use topics children find interesting and exciting, in-depth projects focusing on particular themes, and good children's literature, they give children motivation to learn the important concepts and skills they need for school and life success. Children should bring home from preschool not only further developed skills, but also knowledge useful and meaningful in life.

Copyright © Mometrix Media. You have been licensed one copy of this document for personal use only. Any other reproduction or redistribution is strictly prohibited. All rights reserved.

Diverse Needs of All Children

Characteristics of infants and young children with intellectual disabilities

Newborns with intellectual disabilities, especially of greater severity, may not demonstrate normal reflexes, such as rooting and sucking reflexes, necessary for nursing. They may not show other temporary infant reflexes such as the Moro, Babinski, swimming, stepping, or labyrinthine reflexes, or they may demonstrate weaker versions of some of these. In some babies, these reflexes will exist but persist past the age when they normally disappear. Babies with intellectual disabilities are likely to display developmental milestones at later-than-typical ages. The ages when they do display milestones vary according to the severity of the disability and by individual. Young children with intellectual disabilities are likely to walk, self-feed, and speak later than normally developing children. Those who learn to read and write do so at later ages. Children with mild intellectual disabilities may lack curiosity and have quiet demeanors; those with profound intellectual disabilities are likely to remain infantile in abilities and behaviors throughout life. Intellectually disabled children will score below normal on standardized IQ tests and adaptive behavior rating scales.

Infections that can cause intellectual disabilities
Congenital cytomegalovirus (CMV) is passed to fetuses from mothers, who may be asymptomatic. About 90% of newborns are also asymptomatic; 5% to 10% of these have later problems. Of the 10% born with symptoms, 90% will have later neurological abnormalities, including intellectual disabilities. Congenital rubella, or German measles, is also passed to fetuses from unvaccinated and exposed mothers, causing neurological damage including blindness or other eye disorders, deafness, heart defects, and intellectual disabilities. Congenital toxoplasmosis is passed to fetuses by infected mothers, who can be asymptomatic, with a parasite from raw or undercooked meat that causes intellectual disabilities, vision or hearing loss, and other conditions. Encephalitis is brain inflammation caused by infection, most often viral. Meningitis is inflammation of the meninges, or membranes, covering the brain and is caused by viral or bacterial infection; the bacterial form is more serious. Both encephalitis and meningitis can cause intellectual disabilities. Maternal human immunodeficiency virus (HIV) and acquired immunodeficiency syndrome (AIDS) can be passed to fetuses, destroying immunity to infections, which can cause intellectual disabilities. Maternal listeriosis, a bacterial infection from contaminated food, animals, soil, or water, can cause meningitis and intellectual disabilities in surviving fetuses and infants.

Environmental, nutritional, and metabolic influences
Environmental deprivation syndrome results when developing children are deprived of necessary environmental elements—physical, including adequate nourishment (malnutrition); climate or temperature control (extremes of heat or cold); hygiene, like changing and bathing; and so on. It also includes lack of adequate cognitive stimulation, which can stunt a child's intellectual development, and neglect in general. Malnutrition results from starvation; vitamin, mineral, or nutrient deficiency; deficiencies in digesting or absorbing foods; and some other medical conditions. Environmental radiation, depending on dosage and time of exposure, can cause intellectual disabilities. Congenital hypothyroidism (underactive thyroid) can cause intellectual disabilities, as can hypoglycemia (low blood sugar) from inadequately controlled diabetes or occurring independently and infant hyperbilirubinemia. Bilirubin, a waste product of old red blood cells, is found in bile made by the liver and is normally removed by the liver; excessive bilirubin buildup in babies can cause intellectual disabilities. Reye syndrome, caused by aspirin given

Copyright © Mometrix Media. You have been licensed one copy of this document for personal use only. Any other reproduction or redistribution is strictly prohibited. All rights reserved.

children with flu or chicken pox, or following these viruses or other upper respiratory infections, or from unknown causes, produces sudden liver and brain damage and can result in intellectual disabilities.

Genetic abnormalities affecting the nervous system

Rett syndrome is a nervous system disorder causing developmental regression, particularly severe in expressive language and hand function. It is associated with a defective protein gene on an X chromosome. Having two X chromosomes, females with the defect on one of them can survive; with only one X chromosome, males are either miscarried, stillborn, or die early in infancy. Rett syndrome produces many symptoms, including intellectual disabilities. Tay-Sachs disease, an autosomal recessive disorder, is a nervous system disease caused by a defective gene on chromosome 15 resulting in a missing protein for breaking down gangliosides, chemicals in nerve tissues that build up in cells, particularly brain neurons, causing damage. Tay-Sachs is more prevalent in Ashkenazi Jews. The adult form is rare; the infantile form is commonest, with nerve damage starting *in utero*. Many symptoms, including intellectual disabilities, appear at 3 to 6 months and death occurs by 4 to 5 years. Tuberous sclerosis, caused by genetic mutations, produces tumors damaging the kidneys, heart, skin, brain, and central nervous system. Symptoms include intellectual disabiltiies, seizures, and developmental delays.

Genetic or inherited metabolic disorders

Adrenoleukodystrophy is an X-linked genetic trait. Some female carriers have mild forms, but it affects more males more seriously. It impairs metabolism of very long-chain fatty acids, which build up in the nervous system (as well as adrenal glands and male testes). The childhood cerebral form, manifesting at ages 4 to 8, causes seizures, visual and hearing impairments, receptive aphasia, dysgraphia, dysphagia, intellectual disabilities, and other effects. Galactosemia is an inability to process galactose, a simple sugar in lactose, or milk sugar. By-product buildup damages the liver, kidneys, eyes, and brain. Hunter syndrome, Hurler syndrome, and Sanfilippo syndrome each cause the lack of different enzymes; all cause an inability to process mucopolysaccharides or glycosaminoglycans (long sugar-molecule chains). Hurler and Sanfilippo (but not Hunter) syndromes are autosomal recessive traits, meaning both parents must pass on the defect. All cause progressive intellectual disabilities. Lesch-Nyhan syndrome, affecting males, is a metabolic deficiency in processing purines. It causes hemiplegia, varying degrees of intellectual disabilities, and self-injurious behaviors. Phenylketonuria (PKU), an autosomal recessive trait, causes lack of the enzyme to process dietary phenylalanine, resulting in intellectual disabilities.

Prescription drugs, substances of abuse, and diseases in pregnant mothers

Warfarin, a prescription anticoagulant drug to thin the blood and prevent excessive clotting, can cause microcephaly (undersized head) and intellectual disabilities in an infant when the mother has taken it during pregnancy. The prescription antiseizure drug Trimethadione can cause developmental delays in babies when it has been taken by pregnant mothers. Maternal abuse of solvent chemicals during pregnancy can also cause microcephaly and intellectual disabilities. Maternal crack cocaine abuse during pregnancy can cause severe and profound intellectual disabilities and many other developmental defects in fetuses, which become evident when they are newborns. Maternal alcohol abuse can cause fetal alcohol syndrome, which often includes intellectual disabilities, among many other symptoms. Maternal rubella (German measles) virus can cause intellectual disabilities as well as visual and hearing impairments and heart defects. Maternal herpes simplex virus can cause microcephaly, intellectual disabilities, and microophthalmia (small or no eyes). The varicella (chicken pox) virus in pregnant mothers can also cause intellectual disabilities as well as muscle atrophy in babies.

Copyright © Mometrix Media. You have been licensed one copy of this document for personal use only. Any other reproduction or redistribution is strictly prohibited. All rights reserved.

Attachment styles identified by Mary Ainsworth

Mary Ainsworth worked with John Bowlby, discovering the first empirical evidence supporting his attachment theory. From her Strange Situation experiments, she identified secure, insecure and avoidant, insecure and resistant, and insecure and disorganized attachment styles. Securely attached children show normal separation anxiety when mother leaves and happiness when she returns, avoid strangers when alone but are friendly with mother present, and use mother as a safe base for environmental exploring. Insecure and resistant children show exaggerated separation anxiety, ambivalence and resistance to mother upon reuniting, fear strangers, cry more, and explore less than secure or avoidant babies. Insecure and avoidant children show no separation anxiety or stranger anxiety and little interest on reunions with mother and are comforted equally by mother or strangers. Insecure and disorganized types seem dazed and confused, respond inconsistently, and may mix resistant and ambivalent and avoidant behaviors. Secure styles are associated with sensitive, responsive caregiving and children's positive self-images and other images, resistant and ambivalent styles with inconsistent caregiving, and avoidant with unresponsive caregivers. Avoidant, resistant, and disorganized styles, associated with negative self-images and low self-esteem, are most predictive of emotional disturbances.

Learning disabilities (LDs) and their respective characteristics

Dyslexia, the most common LD, means deficiency or inability in reading. It primarily affects reading but can also interfere with writing and speaking. Characteristics include reversing letters and words, for example, confusing b and d in reading and writing; reading won as now, confusing similar speech sounds like /p/ and /b/, and perceiving spaces between words in the wrong places when reading. Dyscalculia is difficulty doing mathematical calculations; it can also affect using money and telling time. Dysgraphia means difficulties specifically with writing, including omitting words in writing sentences or leaving sentences unfinished, difficulty putting one's thoughts into writing, and poor handwriting. Central auditory processing disorder causes difficulty perceiving small differences in words despite normal hearing acuity; for example, couch and chair may be perceived as cow and hair. Background noise and information overloads exacerbate the effects. Visual processing disorders affect visual perception despite normal visual acuity, causing difficulty finding information in printed text or from maps, charts, pictures, graphs, and so on; synthesizing information from various sources into one place; and remembering directions to locations.

Variables having the potential to cause learning disabilities

LDs are basically neurological disorders. Though they are more specific to particular areas of learning than global disorders like intellectual disabilities, scientific research has found correlations between LDs and many of the same factors that cause intellectual disabilities, including prenatal influences like excessive alcohol or other drug consumption, diseases, and so on. Once babies are born, glandular disorders, brain injuries, exposure to secondhand smoke or other toxins, infections of the central nervous system, physical trauma, or malnutrition can cause neurological damage resulting in LDs. Hypoxia and anoxia (oxygen loss) before, during, or after birth is a cause, as are radiation and chemotherapy. These same influences often cause behavioral disorders as well as LDs. Another factor is genetic: Both LDs and behavior disorders have been observed to run in families. While research has not yet identified specific genetic factors, heritability does appear to be a component in influencing learning and behavioral disorders.

Neurological damage found in LD and ADHD children

Copyright © Mometrix Media. You have been licensed one copy of this document for personal use only. Any other reproduction or redistribution is strictly prohibited. All rights reserved.

Various neurological research studies have revealed that children diagnosed with LDs and ADHD have at least one of several kinds of structural damage to their brains. Scientists have found smaller numbers of cells in certain important regions of the brains of some children with learning and behavioral disorders. Some of these children are found to have brain cells of smaller than normal size. In some cases, dysplasia is discovered; that is, some brain cells migrate into the wrong area of the brain. In some children with learning and behavioral disorders, blood flow is found to be lower than normal to certain regions in the brain. Also, the brain cells of some children with learning and behavioral disabilities show lower levels of glucose metabolism; glucose (blood sugar) is the brain's main source of fuel, so inadequate utilization of glucose can affect the brain's ability to perform some functions related to cognitive processing, as in LDs, and to attention and impulse control, as in ADHD.

Anxiety disorders

Anxiety disorders include generalized anxiety disorder (GAD), obsessive-compulsive disorder (OCD), posttraumatic stress disorder (PTSD), panic disorder, social phobia, and specific phobias. All share a common characteristic of overwhelming, irrational, and unrealistic fears. GAD involves excessive worrying about anything or everything and free-floating anxiety. Anxiety may be about real issues but is nonetheless exaggerated and spreads, overtaking the child's life. OCD involves obsessive and preoccupied thoughts and compulsive or irresistible actions, including often bizarre rituals. Germ phobia, constant hand washing, repeatedly checking whether tasks are done or undone, and collecting things excessively are common. PTSD follows traumatic experiences/events. Children have frequent, extreme nightmares, crying, flashbacks wherein they vividly perceive or believe they are experiencing the traumatic event again, insomnia, depression, anxiety, and social withdrawal. Symptoms of panic disorder are panic attacks involving extreme fear and physical symptoms like a racing heart, cold hands and feet, pallor, hyperventilation, and feeling unable to move. Children with social phobia develop fear and avoidance of day care, preschool, or other social settings. Specific phobias are associated with specific objects, animals, or persons and are often triggered by traumatic experiences involving these.

> ➤ **Review Video:** <u>**Anxiety Disorders**</u>
> *Visit **mometrix.com/academy** and enter **Code:** 366760*

Emotional disturbances

Researchers have investigated emotional disturbances but have not yet established known causes for any. Some disturbances, for example the major mental illness schizophrenia, seem to run in families and hence include a genetic component; childhood schizophrenia exists as a specific diagnosis. Factors contributing to emotional disturbances can be biological or environmental but more often are likely a combination of both. Dysfunctional family dynamics can often contribute to child emotional disorders. Physical and psychological stressors on children can also contribute to the development of emotional problems. Some people have attributed emotional disturbances to diet, and scientists have also researched this but have not discovered proof of cause and effect. Bipolar disorder is often successfully treated with the chemical lithium, which affects sodium flow through nerve cells, so chemical imbalance may be implicated as an etiology. Pediatric bipolar disorder, which has different symptoms than adult bipolar disorder, correlates highly with histories of bipolar and other mood disorders or alcoholism in both parents.

Pediatric bipolar disorder

Copyright © Mometrix Media. You have been licensed one copy of this document for personal use only. Any other reproduction or redistribution is strictly prohibited. All rights reserved.

Bipolar, formerly called manic-depressive disorder, has similar depressive symptoms in children as adults. However, children's mood swings often occur much faster, and children show more symptoms of anger and irritability than other adult manic symptoms. Bipolar children's most common symptoms include frequent mood swings; extreme irritability; protracted (up to several hours) tantrums or rages; separation anxiety; oppositional behavior; hyperactivity, impulsivity, and distractibility; restlessness and fidgetiness; silly, giddy, or goofy behavior; aggression; racing thoughts; grandiose beliefs or behaviors; risk-taking; depressed moods; lethargy; low self-esteem; social anxiety; hypersensitivity to environmental or emotional triggers; carbohydrate (sugar or starch) cravings; and trouble getting up in the morning. Other common symptoms include bed-wetting (especially in boys), night terrors, pressured or fast speech, obsessive or compulsive behaviors, motor and vocal tics, excessive daydreaming, poor short-term memory, poor organization, learning disabilities, morbid fascinations, hypersexuality, bossiness and manipulative behavior, lying, property destruction, paranoia, hallucinations, delusions, and suicidal ideations. Less common symptoms include migraines, bingeing, self-injurious behaviors, and animal cruelty.

Conduct disorder

Factors contributing to conduct disorders in children include genetic predispositions, neurological damage, child abuse, and other traumatic experiences. Children with conduct disorders display characteristic emotional and behavioral patterns. These include aggression: They bully or intimidate others, often start physical fights, will use dangerous objects as weapons, exhibit physical cruelty to animals or humans, and assault and steal from others. Deliberate property destruction is another characteristic—breaking things or setting fires. Young children are limited in some of these activities by their smaller size, lesser strength, and lack of access; however, they show the same types of behaviors against smaller, younger, weaker, or more vulnerable children and animals, along with oppositional and defiant behaviors against adults. Also, while truancy is impossible or unlikely in preschoolers, and running away from home is less likely, young children with conduct disorders are likely to demonstrate some forms of seriously violating rules, another symptom of this disorder.

Childhood-onset schizophrenia

The incidence of childhood-onset schizophrenia is rare, but it does exist. One example of differential diagnosis involves distinguishing qualitatively between true auditory hallucinations and young children's "hearing voices" otherwise: In the latter case, a child hears his or her own or a familiar adult's voice in his or her head and does not seem upset by it, while in the former, a child may hear other voices, seemingly in his or her ears, and is frightened and confused by them. Tantrums, defiance, aggression, and other acting-out, externalized behaviors are less frequent in childhood-onset schizophrenia than internalized developmental differences, for example, isolation, shyness, awkwardness, fickleness, strange facial expressions, mistrust, paranoia, anxiety, and depression. Children demonstrate nonpsychotic symptoms earlier than psychotic ones. However, it is difficult to use prepsychotic symptoms as predictors due to variance among developmental peculiarities. While psychiatrists find the course of childhood-onset schizophrenia somewhat more variable than in adults, child symptoms resemble adult symptoms. Childhood-onset schizophrenia is typically chronic and severe, responds less to medication, and has a more guarded prognosis than adolescent- or adult-onset schizophrenia.

Psychotic disorders

Copyright © Mometrix Media. You have been licensed one copy of this document for personal use only. Any other reproduction or redistribution is strictly prohibited. All rights reserved.

Psychosis is a general psychiatric category referring to thought disturbances or disorders. The most common symptoms are delusions that is, believing things that are not true, and hallucinations, that is, seeing, hearing, feeling, tasting, or smelling things that are not there. While early childhood psychosis is rarer than at later ages, psychiatrists confirm it does occur. Moreover, prognosis is poorer for psychosis with onset in early childhood than in adolescence or adulthood. Causes can be from known metabolic or brain disorders or unknown. Younger children are more vulnerable to environmental stressors. Also, in young children, thoughts distorted by fantasy can be from normal cognitive immaturity, due to lack of experience and a larger range of normal functioning, or pathology; where they lie on this continuum must be determined by clinicians. Believing one is a superhero who can fly can be vivid imagination or delusional; having imaginary friends can be pretend play or hallucinatory. Other developmental disorders can also cloud differential diagnosis.

Visual impairments

Historically, it was thought that VI children developed more slowly than normal; however, it is now known that ages for reaching developmental milestones are equally variable in VI babies as in others and that they acquire milestones within equal age ranges. One developmental difference is in sequence: VI children tend to utter their first words or subject-verb 2-word sentences earlier than other children. Some VI children also demonstrate higher levels of language development at younger-than-typical ages. For example, they may sing songs from memory or recall events from the past at earlier ages than other children. This is a logical development in children who must rely more on input to their hearing and other senses than to their vision when the latter is impaired. Totally blind babies reach for objects later, hence explore the environment later; hand use, eye-hand coordination, and gross and fine motor skills are delayed. Blind infants' posture control develops normally (rolling, sitting, all-fours, and standing), but mobility (raising on arms, pulling up, and walking) are delayed.

Visual impairments in babies and young children

Syndrome-related and other malformations like cleft iris or lens dislocation causing VI can have prenatal origins. Cataracts clouding the eye's lens can be congenital, traumatic, or due to maternal rubella. Eyes can be normal, but impairment in the brain's visual cortex can cause VI. Infantile glaucoma, like adult glaucoma, causes intraocular fluid buildup pressure and VI. Conjunctivitis and other infections cause VI. Strabismus and nystagmus are ocular-muscle conditions, respectively causing eye misalignments and involuntary eye movements. Trauma damaging the eyeball(s) is another VI cause. The optic nerve can suffer from atrophy (dysfunction) or hypoplasia, that is, developmental regression, usually prenatally due to neurological trauma; acuity cannot be corrected. Refractive errors like nearsightedness, farsightedness, and astigmatism are correctable. Retinoblastoma, or behind-the-eye tumors, can cause blindness and fatality; surgical or chemotherapeutic treatment is usually required before age 2. Premature infants can have retinopathy of prematurity or retrolental fibroplasia. Cryotherapeutic treatment seems to stop disease progression. Its effects range from none to severe VI (approximately 25% of children) to complete blindness.

Blindness

Blind babies and children are more dependent than others on adults, affecting development. With control of their inner realities but not of their outer environments, blind children may withdraw, seeking and responding less to social interaction. They may not readily develop concepts of the external world or self-concepts as beings separate from the world and the understanding that they can be both agents and recipients of actions relative to the environment. Mother-infant smiling

Copyright © Mometrix Media. You have been licensed one copy of this document for personal use only. Any other reproduction or redistribution is strictly prohibited. All rights reserved.

initiates recognition, attachment, and communication in sighted babies; blind infants smile on hearing mother's voice at 2 months. Only tactile stimuli like tickling and nuzzling evoke regular smiling in blind babies. Missing facial expressions and other visual cues, blind children have more complicated social interactions. They often do not understand the basics of playing with others and seem emotionally ambivalent or uninterested and uncommunicative. Peers may reject or avoid them; adults often overprotect them. Self-help skills like chewing, scooping, self-feeding, teeth brushing, grooming, and toilet training are delayed in blind children.

<u>Impacts of blindness upon cognitive development</u>
Blind children have more difficulty determining and confirming characteristics of things, hence defining concepts and organizing them into more abstract levels; their problem-solving is active but harder, and they construct different realities than sighted children. Blind babies typically acquire object permanence (the understanding that unseen objects still exists) a year later than normal; they learn to reach for objects only by hearing. Understanding cause-and-effect relationships is difficult without visual evidence. Blind babies and toddlers take longer to understand and object's constancy regardless of their orientation in space, affecting their ability to orient toys and their own hands. Blind children can identify object size differences and similarities, but classifying object differences and similarities in other attributes requires longer times and more exposures to various similar objects. Blind children's development of the abilities to conserve object properties like material or substance, weight, amount and volume, length, and liquid volume is later than normal.

Speech and language impairments

In speech, most phonological disorders are articulatory; that is, children fail to pronounce specific speech sounds or phonemes correctly beyond the normal developmental age for achieving accuracy. Stuttering, disfluency, and rate and rhythm disorders cause children to repeat phonemes, especially initial word sounds; to repeat words; to prolong vowels or consonants; or to block, that is, straining so hard to produce a sound that, pressure builds, but no sound issues. Their speech rates may also speed and slow irregularly. Children with voice disorders can have voices that sound hoarse, raspy, overly nasal, higher- or lower-pitched than normal, overly weak or strident, and whispery or harsh. Hoarseness is common with vocal nodules and polyps. Cleft palate commonly causes hypernasality. In language, one of the most common impairments is delayed language development due to environmental deprivation, intellectual disabilities, neurological damage or defects, hearing loss, visual impairment, and so on. Children with neurological damage or disorders may exhibit aphasias, language disorders characterized by receptive difficulty with understanding spoken or written language, or expressive difficulty constructing spoken or written language.

<u>Factors that can contribute to speech and language impairments</u>
Some speech and language disorders in children have unknown causes. Others have known causes such as hearing loss: Speech and language are normally acquired primarily through the auditory sense, so children with impaired hearing have delayed and impaired development of speech and language. Brain injuries, neurological disorders, viral diseases, and some medications can also cause problems with developing language or speech. Children with intellectual disabilities are more likely to have delayed language development, and their speech is also more likely to develop more slowly and to be distorted. Cerebral palsy causes neuromuscular weakness and incoordination of speech. When severe, it can cause inability to produce recognizable speech sounds; some children without speech can still vocalize, and some cannot. A cleft palate or lip and other physical impairments affect speech. Inadequate speech-language modeling at home inhibits speech-language development. Vocal abuse in children (screaming, coughing, throat clearing, or excessive

- 78 -

Copyright © Mometrix Media. You have been licensed one copy of this document for personal use only. Any other reproduction or redistribution is strictly prohibited. All rights reserved.

talking) can cause vocal nodules or polyps, causing voice disorders. Stuttering can be related to maturation, anxiety or stress, auditory feedback defects, or unknown causes.

Hearing impairments

Half or more (50% to 60%) of infant hearing losses have genetic origins—Down and other genetically based syndromes or the existence of parental hearing loss. About 25% or more of infant hearing losses are caused by maternal infections during pregnancy, such as cytomegalovirus (CMV), postnatal complications like blood transfusions or infection with meningitis, or traumatic head injuries. Included in this 25% or more are babies having nongenetic neurological disorders or conditions that affect their hearing. Malformations of the ears, head, or face can cause hearing loss in babies. Babies spending 5 days or longer in neonatal intensive care units (NICUs) or having complications while in the NICU are also more likely to suffer hearing loss. Around 25% of babies are diagnosed with hearing loss whose etiology is unknown.

Signs of hearing impairments

If an infant does not display a startle response at loud noises, this is a potential sign of hearing loss. This can also indicate other developmental disabilities, but because hearing loss is the most prevalent disability among newborns, hearing screening is a priority. Between birth and 3 or 4 months old, babies should turn toward the source of a sound; if they do not, it could indicate hearing loss. A child who does not utter first words like mama or dada by age 1 could have hearing impairment. When babies or young children do not turn their heads when their names are called, adults may mistake this for inattention or ignoring; however, children turning upon seeing adults, but not upon hearing their names, can indicate hearing loss. Babies and children who seem to hear certain sounds but not others may have partial hearing losses. Delayed speech-language development or unclear speech, not following directions, saying "Huh?" often, and wanting higher TV or music volumes can indicate hearing loss in children.

Physical and health impairments

In the special education field of early childhood education, other health impairment is a term referring to health and physical conditions that rob a child of strength, vitality, or alertness or that cause excessive alertness to environmental stimuli, all having the end result of impeding the child's ability to attend or respond to the educational environment. Health problems can be acute, that is short-term or temporary but serious, or chronic, that is, long-term, persistent, or recurrent. Some examples of such health and physical impairments include: cerebral palsy, spina bifida, amputations or missing limbs, muscular dystrophy, cystic fibrosis, asthma, rheumatic fever, sickle-cell anemia, nephritis or kidney disease, leukemia, Tourette syndrome, hemophilia, diabetes, heart disease, AIDS, and lead poisoning. All these conditions and others can interfere with a child's development and ability to attend and learn. In addition to seizure disorders, which often cause neurological damage, seizure-controlling medications also frequently cause drowsiness, interfering with attention and cognition. Attention deficit and attention deficit hyperactivity disorders (ADD and ADHD) limit attention span, focus, and concentration and thus are sometimes classified as health impairments requiring special education services.

Characteristics of babies and children with physical and health impairments

The characteristics of children having various physical or health impairments can range from having no limitations to severe limitations in their activities. Children with cerebral palsy, for example, usually have deficiencies in gross and fine motor development and deficits in speech-language development. Physical and health conditions causing severe debilitation in some children

Copyright © Mometrix Media. You have been licensed one copy of this document for personal use only. Any other reproduction or redistribution is strictly prohibited. All rights reserved.

not only seriously limit their daily activities but also cause multiple primary disabilities and impair their intellectual functioning. Other children with physical or health impairments function at average, above-average, or gifted intellectual and academic levels.

An important consideration when working with babies and young children having physical or health impairments is handling and positioning them physically. Correctly picking up, holding, carrying, giving assistance, and physically supporting younger children and arranging play materials for them based on their impairment is not only important for preventing injury, pain, and discomfort; it also enables them to receive instruction better and to manipulate materials and perform most efficiently. Preschoolers with physical impairments also tend to have difficulty with communication skills, so educators should give particular attention to facilitating and developing these.

Developmental delays

Developmental delays can come from genetic or environmental causes or both. Infants and young children with intellectual disabilities are most likely to exhibit developmental delays. Their development generally proceeds similarly to that of normal children but at slower rates; milestones are manifested at later-than-typical ages. Sensory impairments such as with hearing and vision can also delay many aspects of children's development. Children with physical and health impairments are likely to exhibit delays in their motor development and performance of physical activities. Another factor is environmental: Children deprived of adequate environmental stimulation commonly show delays in cognitive, speech-language, and emotional and social development. Children with autism spectrum disorders often have markedly delayed language and speech development; many are nonverbal. Autistic children also typically have impaired social development, caused by and inability or difficulty with understanding others' emotional and social nonverbal communications. When they cannot interpret these, they do not know how to respond and also cannot imitate them; however, they can often learn these skills with special instruction.

<u>Characteristics in infants and young children that can indicate developmental delays</u>
Developmental delays mean that a child does not reach developmental milestones at the expected ages. For example, if most babies normally learn to walk between 12 and 15 months of age, a 20-month-old who is not beginning to walk is considered as having a developmental delay. Delays can occur in cognitive, speech-language, social-emotional, gross motor skill, or fine motor skill development. Signs of delayed motor development include stiff or rigid limbs, floppy or limp body posture for the child's age, using one side of the body more than the other, and clumsiness unusual for the child's age. Behavioral signs of children's developmental delays include inattention, or shorter than normal attention span for the age; avoiding or infrequent eye contact; focusing on unusual objects for long times or preferring objects over social interaction; excessive frustration when attempting tasks normally simple for children their age; unusual stubbornness; aggressive and acting-out behaviors; daily violent behaviors; rocking; excessive talking to oneself; and not soliciting love or approval from parents.

IDEA's legal definition of traumatic brain injury

TBI is defined by the IDEA law (the Individuals with Disabilities Education Act) as "an acquired injury to the brain from external physical force, resulting in total or partial functional disability or psychosocial impairment, or both, that adversely affect a child's educational performance." This definition excludes injuries from birth trauma, congenital injuries, and degenerative conditions. TBI is the foremost cause of death and disability in children (and teens) in the USA.

Copyright © Mometrix Media. You have been licensed one copy of this document for personal use only. Any other reproduction or redistribution is strictly prohibited. All rights reserved.

The most common causes of TBI in children include falls, motor vehicle accidents, and physical abuse. In spite of the IDEA's definition, aneurysms and strokes are examples of internal traumas that can also cause TBI in babies and young children. External head injuries that can result in TBI include both open and closed head injuries. Shaken baby syndrome is caused by forcibly shaking an infant. This causes the brain literally to bounce against the insides of the skull, causing rebound injuries, resulting in TBI and even death.

Characteristics traumatic brain injuries
TBI can impair a child's cognitive development and processing. It can impede the language development of children, which is dependent upon cognitive development. Children who have sustained TBI often have difficulties with attention, retention and memory; reasoning, judgment, understanding abstract concepts and thinking abstractly, and problem-solving abilities. TBIs can also impair a child's motor functions and physical abilities. The sensory and perceptual functions of children with TBI can be abnormal. Their ability to process information is often compromised. Their speech can also be affected. In addition, TBIs can impair a child's psychosocial behaviors. Memory deficits are commonest, tend to be more long lasting, and are often area specific; for example, a child may recall personal experiences but not factual information. Other common characteristics of TBI include cognitive inflexibility or rigidity, damaged conceptualization and reasoning, language loss or poor verbal fluency, problems with paying attention and concentrating, inadequate problem solving, and problems with reading and writing.

Multiple disabilities

The term multiple disabilities refers to any combination of more than one disabling condition. For example, a child may be both blind and deaf due to causes such as having rheumatic fever in infancy or early childhood. Anything causing neurological damage before, during, or shortly after birth can result in multiple disabilities, particularly if it is widespread rather than localized. For example, infants deprived of oxygen or suffering traumatic brain injuries *in utero*, during labor or delivery, or postnatally can sustain severe brain damage. So can babies having encephalitis or meningitis and those whose mothers abused drugs prenatally. Infants with this type of extensive damage can often present with multiple disabilities, including intellectual disabilities, cerebral palsy, physical paralysis, mobility impairment, visual impairment, hearing impairment, and speech-language disorders. They may have any combination of or all of these disabilities as well as others. In addition to a difficulty or inability with normal physical performance, multiply disabled children often have difficulty acquiring and retaining cognitive skills and transferring or generalizing skills among settings and situations.

Prematurity or preterm birth

Babies born before 37 weeks' gestation are classified as premature or preterm. Premature infants can have difficulty with breathing, as their lungs are not fully developed, and with regulating their body temperatures. Premature infants may be born with pneumonia, respiratory distress, extra air or bleeding in the lungs, jaundice, sepsis or infection, hypoglycemia (low blood sugar), severe intestinal inflammation, bleeding into the brain or white-matter brain damage, or anemia. They have lower-than-normal birth weights, body fat, muscle tone, and activity. Additional typical characteristics of premature infants include apnea (interrupted breathing); lanugo (a coating of body hair that full-term infants no longer have); thin, smooth, shiny, translucent skin through which veins are visible; soft, flexible ear cartilage; cryptorchidism (undescended testicles) and small, non-

Copyright © Mometrix Media. You have been licensed one copy of this document for personal use only. Any other reproduction or redistribution is strictly prohibited. All rights reserved.

ridged scrotums in males; enlarged clitorises in females; and feeding difficulties caused by weak or defective sucking reflexes or incoordination of swallowing with breathing.

<u>Disabling conditions that can result from premature births</u>
Physicians find it impossible to predict the long-term results of prematurity for any individual baby based on an infant's gestational age and birth weight. However, some related immediate and long-term effects can be identified. Generally, the lower the birth weight and the more prematurely a child is born, the greater the risk is for complications. Infants born at less than 34 weeks of gestation typically cannot coordinate their sucking and swallowing and may temporarily need feeding or breathing tubes or oxygen. They also need special nursery care until able to maintain their body temperatures and weights. Long-term complications of prematurity can include bronchopulmonary dysplasia, a chronic lung condition; delayed physical growth and development; delayed cognitive development; mental or physical delays or disabilities; and blindness, vision loss, or retinopathy of prematurity (formerly called retrolental fibroplasia). While some premature infants sustain long-term disabilities, some severe, other babies born prematurely grow up to show no effects at all; and any results within this range can also occur.

Copyright © Mometrix Media. You have been licensed one copy of this document for personal use only. Any other reproduction or redistribution is strictly prohibited. All rights reserved.

Diagnosis, Assessment, and Evaluation

Informal assessment instruments

EC teachers assess pre-K children's performance in individual, small-group, and whole-class activities throughout the day using informal tools that are teacher-made, school/program/district-furnished, or procured by school systems from commercial educational resources. For classroom observations, teachers might complete a form based on their observations during class story or circle time, organized using three themes per day, each targeting different skills—social-emotional, math, alphabet knowledge, oral language, or emergent writing. They note the names of children demonstrating the specified skill and those who might need follow-up, and provide needed one-on-one interventions daily. For individual observations, teachers might fill out a chart divided into domains like physical development; oral language development; math; emergent reading; emergent writing; science and health; fine arts; technology and media; social studies; social-emotional development; and approaches to learning, noting one child's strengths and needs in each area per chart. In addition to guided observation records, teachers complete checklists; keep anecdotal and running records; and assemble portfolio assessments of children's work. Tracking children's progress informs responsive instructional planning.

Formal assessment instruments

Formal assessment instruments are typically standardized tests, administered to groups. They give norms for age groups/developmental levels for comparison. They are designed to avoid administrator bias and capture children's responses only. Their data can be scaled and be reported in aggregate to school/program administrators and policymakers. The Scholastic Early Childhood Inventory (SECI) is a formal one on one instrument to assess children's progress in four domains found to predict kindergarten readiness: phonological awareness, oral language development, alphabet knowledge, and mathematics. Other instruments measuring multiple developmental domains include the Assessment, Evaluation and Programming System (0–6 years) for planning intervention; the Bayley Scale for Infant Development (1–42 months) for assessing developmental delays; the Brigance Diagnostic Inventory of Early Development (0–7 years) for planning instruction; the Developmental Profile II (0–6 years) to assess special needs and support IEP development; the Early Coping Inventory (4–36 months) and Early Learning Accomplishment Profile (0–36 months), both for planning interventions; and the Infant-Toddler Developmental Assessment (0–42 months) to screen for developmental delays.

Screening and assessment instruments

Differences among screening and assessment instruments

A variety of screening and assessment instruments exist for EC measurement. Some key areas where they differ include which developmental domains are measured by an instrument; for which applications an instrument is meant to be used; to which age ranges an instrument applies; the methods by which a test or tool is administered; the requirements for scoring and interpreting a test, scale, or checklist; whether an instrument is appropriate for use with ethnically diverse populations; and whether a tool is statistically found to have good validity and reliability.

EC program administrators should choose instruments that can measure the developmental areas pertinent to their program; support their program's established goals; and include all EC ages

Copyright © Mometrix Media. You have been licensed one copy of this document for personal use only. Any other reproduction or redistribution is strictly prohibited. All rights reserved.

served in their program. Instruments' administration, scoring, and interpretation methods should be congruent with program personnel's skills. Test/measure administration should involve realistic time durations. Instruments/tools should be appropriate to use with ethnically diverse and non-English-speaking children and families. Tests should also be proven psychometrically accurate and dependable enough.

Typical applications of screening and assessment instruments

The ways in which screening and assessment instruments applicable to ECE are used include a wide range of variations. For example, ECE programs typically need to identify children who might have developmental disorders or delays. Screening instruments are used to identify those children showing signs of possible problems who need assessments, not to diagnose problems. Assessment instruments are used to develop and/or confirm diagnoses of developmental disorders or delays. Assessment tools are also used to help educators and therapists plan curricular and treatment programs. Another important function of assessment instruments is to determine a child's eligibility for a given program. In addition, once children are placed in ECE programs, assessment tools can be used to monitor their progress and other changes occurring through time. Moreover, program administrators can use assessment instruments to evaluate children's achievement of the learning outcomes that define their program goals—and by extension, the teachers' effectiveness in furthering children's achievement of those outcomes.

Measuring development by different screening and assessment instruments

The available screening and assessment instruments for EC development cover a wide range in scope and areas of focus. Some measures are comprehensive, assessing young children's progress in many developmental domains including sensory, motor, physical, cognitive, linguistic, emotional, and social. Some other instruments focus exclusively on only one domain, such as language development or emotional-social development. Some instruments even focus within a domain upon only one of its facets, e.g. upon attachment or temperament within the domain of emotional-social development. In addition, some tools measure risk and resiliency factors influencing developmental delays and disorders. Programs like Head Start that promote general EC development should select comprehensive assessment instruments. Outreach programs targeting better identification of children having untreated and/or undetected mental health problems should choose instruments assessing social-emotional development. Clinics treating children with regulatory disorders might select an instrument measuring temperament. Prevention programs helping multiple-needs families access supports and services could use a measure for risk and resiliency factors. Multifaceted EC programs often benefit most from using several instruments in combination.

Age ranges included in various screening and assessment instruments

An important consideration for screening and assessment in early childhood is that EC development is very dynamic and occurs rapidly. Hence screening and assessment instruments must be sensitive to such frequent and pronounced developmental changes. Some instruments target specific age ranges like 0–36 months. Others cover wider ranges, e.g. children aged 2–16 years. The latter may have internal means of application to smaller age ranges; for example, sections respectively for 3–6-month-old babies, 7–12-month-olds, and 12–18-month-olds. Or they indicate different scoring and interpretation criteria by age; for example, some screening tools specify different numbers of test items depending on the child's age to indicate a need for assessment.

Copyright © Mometrix Media. You have been licensed one copy of this document for personal use only. Any other reproduction or redistribution is strictly prohibited. All rights reserved.

Choosing screening and assessment instruments covering the entire age range served in an ECE program is advantageous—not only because they can be used with all child ages in the program, but also because they can be administered and readministered at the beginning and end of programs and/or in between, to compare and monitor changes, which is difficult with separate, age-specific tests.

Scoring and interpretation of various screening and assessment instruments

Some instruments are fairly simple to score and interpret, needing little training of EC personnel. For example, paper-and-pencil questionnaires/surveys often only need the numbers/points for each item response added up for a total score; or a group of scores is obtained by summing values within sections. Interpreting some screening scores can be as simple as noting whether a child's score surpasses a designated cut-off value that signals assessment is needed. Such screenings can be scored and interpreted right after administration, and readily shared with parents and other stakeholders. Assessment instruments using more complicated scoring and interpretation include such procedures as weighting item values; reversing point values for certain items; converting raw scores into standardized scores or percentages; and referring to tables giving national norms for comparison. Standardized tests, including preschool IQ scales, commonly involve such methods. Assessors often need considerable training; advanced psychometric education and experience; thorough knowledge of EC development; and additional time to score and interpret these tests. Results may be discussed in separately scheduled meetings.

Screening and assessment tools that use structured tasks

Screening and assessment instruments that use structured tasks involve a list of behaviors and/or skills that a child is expected to attain by a certain age range or developmental level. The administrators must present various activities or tasks to a child, and then record the details of the child's performance of each activity or task. Instruments using structured tasks require EC staff training for administration. They take over 20 minutes to complete. EC programs/schools/agencies must buy testing equipment/materials and single-use recording forms. Because paper-and-pencil questionnaires/surveys are easy to administer; apply across various settings, e.g. preschools, pediatricians' waiting rooms, homes, etc.; cost comparatively little; require minimal administrator training; and are frequently short, they are appropriate for screening use. While formal/informal observational tools, structured/semi-structured interview tools, and structured-task tools take more training, time, and expense, they also provide more detailed information, making them useful for determining diagnoses and/or developing individualized care/instruction plans. Instruments using multiple methods, e.g. collecting data from various settings and respondents, yield the most comprehensive information.

Formal and informal observations

Some instruments require EC staff to watch a child's behavior and/or interactions with parents/caregivers and/or peers. Formal observations involve watching activities structured for the screening/assessment instrument. Informal observations involve watching a child's activities in natural settings like at home or in preschool during play times. Formal observation tools typically require staff to be trained to administer them. The trained observers' findings can include records of which developmentally normal behaviors a child has attained, incidences of problem behaviors noted, descriptions and evaluations of the quality of a child's social interactions with other people, and other observations of the child's behaviors that can inform screening and assessment. Observational screening and assessment instruments usually take more than 20 minutes for administration. Publishers of observational tests typically charge EC programs to order single-use recording forms; some allow them to purchase templates and then reproduce the forms.

Copyright © Mometrix Media. You have been licensed one copy of this document for personal use only. Any other reproduction or redistribution is strictly prohibited. All rights reserved.

Paper-and-pencil reports

The most common form of paper-and-pencil report about infants and young children are questionnaires. Parents, caregivers, and teachers read printed questions or statements and respond by selecting Yes or No to a question or a number/level on a Likert-type scale showing the degree to which they agree with a statement. For self-administration, instruments must contain questions/statements written on reading levels accessible to the respondents and in their native languages. Alternatively, some questionnaires or surveys can be read to the respondent by an interviewer trained in or familiar with administration of the chosen instrument. Such self-reporting instruments usually take fewer than 20 minutes to finish, and ECE program personnel need comparatively little training to administer them. However, employees may need further training to score and/or interpret responses, or already-trained specialists may score and interpret them in some cases. ECE schools/programs/agencies can obtain some self-reporting instruments free of charge; other tools' publishers charge for response forms; and others charge only for initially obtaining their materials, allowing purchasers to reproduce them thereafter.

Interviews

In EC programs conducting assessments, personnel usually conduct interviews with a child's parents, teachers, and/or caregivers. Interviews can be made in structured formats, i.e. the administrator reads prescribed questions as written to the interviewee, or semi-structured formats, wherein the administrator uses his/her judgment to add more questions to the written ones until s/he determines that the information provided is complete enough. Interview questions vary, covering subjects of parental concern, the child's identified areas of strengths and accomplishments, the child's identified areas of deficits or needs, the interactions between parents and child, and the child's behavior. Interviews can be brief, but usually they are longer than paper-and-pencil self-reporting questionnaires, surveys, or checklists. EC personnel frequently need to be trained to administer published interview-based instruments. Publishers typically charge schools/programs/agencies for ordering multiple, single-use response forms, or they may require a one-time order and allow them to reproduce the forms from their initial purchase to use for multiple administrations.

Test-retest reliability

Test-retest reliability is how consistent/stable an instrument's results are across administrations. An instrument with good test-retest reliability yields the same results when administered twice or more to the same child within a short time. For example, the same assessor gives a child the same test twice within a few days or weeks, comparing the results. The more similar the results between/among administrations, the higher the test-retest reliability. This implies the instrument measures an attribute/construct that is stable over a short time. Due to the inherent rapidity and dynamism of EC development, we expect significant developmental changes over years and months; but over only weeks or days, we expect little or no substantial change. Therefore, instruments whose results are not stable over a short time are less utile for EC screening/assessment. For example, a child's scoring with "typical development" on one administration but "possible delay/disorder" a week later means the instrument does not define the child's developmental needs, and thus is not reliable.

Copyright © Mometrix Media. You have been licensed one copy of this document for personal use only. Any other reproduction or redistribution is strictly prohibited. All rights reserved.

Inter-rater reliability

Inter-rater reliability is how consistent/stable an instrument's results are across different individual administrators/raters. Good inter-rater reliability means the instrument will give the same/similar results for the same child, at the same time, in the same setting, when administered by different people. This shows that the instrument measures a quality/construct that remains stable regardless of who administers the test. Significant differences among different raters' results present problems, especially with instruments using unstructured interviews, observations, or structured tasks. For example, if one rater scores a child as possibly having a developmental delay or disorder while another rater using the same test scores the same child as within the range of normal development, the instrument does not identify the child's true developmental needs and is unreliable. When different assessors (like parent vs. teacher) observe a child in different settings, though, like home vs. preschool, and/or at different times, varying results are expected and not necessarily indicative of inter-rater unreliability because children's behaviors can vary by setting.

Internal consistency

A testing instrument is said to have internal consistency when its individual items correlate strongly with each other and with the total test score. This means that all of the individual items (questions, stimuli, tasks, etc.) measure parts of the same construct that the test is intended to measure. A test with low internal consistency could be measuring additional attributes that the authors did not define or mean for the test to measure. Children with disparate developmental needs could thus receive similar scores, based on different test items. With comprehensive screening and assessment instruments that cover multiple domains of development, EC educators should look for internal consistency within each subscale of the test or within each domain tested. However, they should not necessarily expect internal consistency among the different domains or at the level of the test's full-scale/overall score. For example, they should not expect high correlation between a test's subscale measuring a child's language skills development and its subscale measuring a child's gross motor skills development.

Concurrent validity

When a screening or assessment instrument yields results comparable to those of another instrument whose validity has been previously established, it has good concurrent validity. Since the test used for comparison was already found valid, users have confidence in its results. Therefore, their confidence is warranted in another test showing high concurrent validity with the established test. For example, the Stanford-Binet Intelligence Scales and the Wechsler Preschool and Primary Scales of Intelligence (WPPSI) are both well-established IQ tests with demonstrated statistical validity and reliability. So if EC educators have found or been given a new instrument for measuring intelligence, they are likely to find that its authors have compared the test's results to the results obtained by the Stanford-Binet and/or WPPSI. Educators who have confidence in the Stanford-Binet and/or the WPPSI are then justified in having comparable confidence in the new test if its results were found similar to those of the established tests, indicating its high concurrent validity.

Content validity

Whether a test instrument measures the entire content area it purports to measure is known as content validity. It determines whether a test can yield accurate and fair measures of the totality of the construct that the assessor wants to test. For example, if a screening instrument is intended to

Copyright © Mometrix Media. You have been licensed one copy of this document for personal use only. Any other reproduction or redistribution is strictly prohibited. All rights reserved.

measure social-emotional development in a young child, it should include individual test items covering the range of this domain's important components. A screening test that covers a child's interactions with caregivers but not with peers; screens attention but not initiation of play; or screens for social skills but not communication skills would not address all elements of social-emotional development and thus not have good content validity. EC educators can use instruments with high content validity to generalize with more confidence about how a child's test performance predicts his/her levels of functioning in real life. By contrast, if a test has low content validity, generalizations about the tested child's development can exceed the test's scope and be inaccurate and/or unrealistic.

Predictive validity

A screening/assessment instrument's prediction of a child's behavior in real life is predictive validity. For example, an instrument screening for social-emotional disorders in preschool children might predict tantrum and/or oppositional behaviors in kindergarten. In another example, you would expect a screening instrument for social-emotional disorders to differentiate between children with normal/typical social-emotional development and those with mental health disorders. If a screening tool identifies a child with a potential mental health disorder and has high predictive validity, a complete clinical diagnostic evaluation of the screened child would diagnose a mental health disorder. Sensitivity is the instrument's accuracy—here, in identifying developmental disorders/delays, if it correctly identifies 9 of 10 children really having disorders/delays, it has 90 percent sensitivity. Specificity conversely would be accuracy in identifying children without disorders/delays. Despite high sensitivity and specificity, screeners yield some errors. False-positives over-identify delays/disorders where none exist; false-negatives under-identify existing delays/disorders. Unnecessary concern is a consequence of false-positives; lack of prevention/early intervention/treatment is a more serious consequence of false-negatives.

> ➤ **Review Video:** <u>Testing Validity</u>
> *Visit* ***mometrix.com/academy*** *and enter* ***Code: 315457***

Internal consistency

Whether a test's individual items contribute to measuring the construct the test is supposed to measure is internal consistency. It is determined by how much the test's individual items correlate with one another and with the overall score. A test with high internal consistency more accurately measures the specific content area/developmental domain/construct it means to measure. A test with low internal consistency poses problems when children who might have very different needs get the same score. For example, if a test meant to measure aggression has low internal consistency, its individual items are not correlated with one another or the overall score, implying it tests more than one construct. Two children given this test could score beyond the cutoff level indicating diagnosis or assessment need, but their scores could be due to completely different individual test items. Since individual test items do not correlate, the two children might have markedly different needs. Furthermore, those needs may not be related to aggression, since the test probably unintentionally measures additional constructs.

Norm-referenced versus criterion-referenced tests

Norm-referenced tests compare a child's test results to those of a comparison group of other children in the same age group, grade, or developmental level. This comparison group is called a normative or standardization sample. Norm-referenced tests show how an individual child's

Copyright © Mometrix Media. You have been licensed one copy of this document for personal use only. Any other reproduction or redistribution is strictly prohibited. All rights reserved.

performance compares to that of the general population of children. Criterion-referenced tests compare a child's test results to a predetermined standard of performance for the child's age group/grade/level. They show how an individual child's performance compares to standards established by educational experts. Norm-referenced tests are useful for determining whether a child is similar to the "average" child and identifying children performing significantly above or below average. Criterion-referenced tests are good for measuring the extent to which an individual child has mastered areas or domains of development and for monitoring changes over time in the child's levels of mastery.

Elements of applying assessment results to planning instruction

ECE settings should provide organized outlines of developmentally appropriate guidelines for their children, including when and how to introduce and reinforce guidelines at each learning stage. These outlines are foundations for anecdotal observations and authentic assessments tracking developmental progress. ECE programs supply opportunities and activities to develop each discrete skill, including copious review and practice young children require for retention. Teachers should plan learning experiences meaningfully promoting developing identified guidelines and addressing children's interests. ECE settings should have organized progress-tracking systems following developmental sequences. These help teachers determine whether a child can move to the next level or prior skills that need additional reinforcement. Tracking systems should be easy to maintain and immediately give teachers basic information regarding each child's level of functioning for planning activities and discussions. Teachers should then create "ready reference" charts/graphs of assessment and monitoring results, giving an idea of the class/group's general functioning level, to inform activity/lesson planning and additional support needed for individual children—one on one for those below class/group level, enriched for those above it.

Good communication with children's parents

When teachers send home a letter to parents explaining classroom practices and giving contact information at the beginning of the school year, parents perceive them as approachable and available. When a teacher calls each parent/guardian during school's first two weeks, parents appreciate and enjoy conversations. Calls also make it easier for teachers to contact parents later in the year regarding child issues if needed. Experts find it effective to mail postcards home, addressed to children or parents. Establishing simple class websites including teacher contact information facilitates parental access. Teachers' printing business cards and attaching them to their first parent letters conveys professionalism. Teachers using Internet/e-mail/print to publish weekly/monthly class newsletters informally keep parents apprised of children's instruction and teach parents to expect communication. Teachers can send parents invitations to visit prior to school/program Open Houses: teachers are perceived as more approachable when more parents are comfortable in classrooms. Having children write appreciation letters to parents for Open Houses encourages children to invite parents; parents also perceive teacher appreciation by association.

Screening young children for developmental disorders

If a child's development is suspected of being delayed—for example, the child is not reaching developmental milestones during expected age ranges—a developmental screening may be administered. Screening tests are quickly performed and yield more general results. The hospital or doctor's office may give a questionnaire to the parent or caregiver to complete for a screening. Alternatively, a health or education professional may administer a screening test to the child. Screening tests are not intended to diagnose specific conditions or give details; they are meant to

Copyright © Mometrix Media. You have been licensed one copy of this document for personal use only. Any other reproduction or redistribution is strictly prohibited. All rights reserved.

identify children who may have some problem. Screenings can over-identify or under-identify developmental delays in children. Hence, if the screening identifies a child as having developmental delay(s), the child is then referred for a developmental evaluation—a much longer, more thorough, comprehensive, in-depth assessment using multiple tests, administered by a psychologist or other highly-trained professional. Evaluation provides a profile of a child's strengths and weaknesses in all developmental domains. Determination of needs for early intervention services or treatment plans is based on evaluation results.

If a young child has been screened for developmental disorders or delays within the past 6 months and no changes have been observed or reported, repeat screening may be waived. Initial screenings are required. Hearing and vision screenings are mandatory in screening young children. Formal developmental measures are also required, which may include screening tests of motor skills development, cognitive development, social-emotional development, and self-help skills development. Formal screening tests of speech-language development are also required. Additional tests recommended during screening include informal measures. For example, checklists, rating scales, and inventories may be used to screen a child's behavior, mood, and performance of motor skills, cognitive skills, self-help skills, and social and emotional skills. On checklists, parents or caregivers check whether the child does or does not demonstrate listed behaviors, or assessors may complete them via parent or caregiver interviews or interviewing and observing the child. Rating scales ask parents, caregivers, and assessors to rate a child's behaviors, affect, mood, and so on, within a range of numbered and labeled descriptions. Inventories list demonstrated skills and needs. Behavioral observations and existing records and information are also used.

Collaborative approaches
Historically, the tradition was to conduct kindergarten screenings of children entering schools around age 5. However, in recent years, school districts have developed community referral networks to assist in the processes of Child Find, screening, evaluation, and referral for early intervention and early childhood special education and related services. Current models are more informal, proactive, and collaborative. Cooperative educational interagency service efforts give parents information about normal early childhood development and available community resources and offer opportunities for developmental screenings of their young children. Specific procedures are governed by individual U.S. state laws. Generally, district networks implementing current models send developmental review forms to parents to complete in advance, and then they attend a developmental screening at a community site. Parents discuss normal early childhood growth and development with program staff, while in the same room, trained professionals observe their children as they play. Children's vision and hearing are also screened. Parents can discuss their children's current development with psychologists, early childhood educators, or counselors. Thereafter, they can learn about community resources.

Data that a developmental evaluation of a young child needs to incorporate

The child's social history should be obtained. This is typically done by a social worker. Details of the child's developmental progress heretofore; the family's composition, socioeconomic status, and situation; and the child's and family's health and medical histories and status should be emphasized. A physician's or nurse's medical assessment is required, including a physical examination, and if indicated, a specialist's examination. A psychologist typically assesses intellectual and cognitive development; at least one such test is generally required. At least one test of adaptive behavior is also required to assess emotional-social development. Self-help skills are evaluated; this may be included within cognitive, adaptive behavior, or programming assessments. Communication skills are typically evaluated by a speech-language pathologist. Both receptive and

- 90 -

Copyright © Mometrix Media. You have been licensed one copy of this document for personal use only. Any other reproduction or redistribution is strictly prohibited. All rights reserved.

expressive language must be tested and comprehensively rather than simply by single-word vocabulary tests. As indicated, speech articulation is also tested. At least one test of motor skills, typically administered by a physical or occupational therapist, is required. Programming evaluation requires at least one criterion-referenced or curriculum-based measure, typically administered by an educator.

Behavioral variations and characteristics of ADHD

While the chief symptoms associated with ADHD are inattentiveness, impulsive behavior, distractibility, and excessive physical activity, there is considerable variation among individual children having ADHD. For example, the degree of severity of this condition can vary widely from one child to the next. In addition, each child can vary in how much he or she exhibits each of these primary characteristics. Some children might not appear to behave very impulsively but show severe deficits in attention. Some may focus better, but only for short periods, and are very easily distracted. Some display very disruptive behavior, while others do not but may daydream excessively, not attending to programming. In general, children who have ADHD can show deficits in following rules and directions. Also, when their developmental skills are evaluated or observed, they are likely to demonstrate inconsistencies in performance over time. To identify or select specific intervention methods and strategies, professionals should use a comprehensive evaluation to obtain information about the child's specific behaviors in his or her natural environment that need remediation.

Child Find process

Child Find is an ongoing process with the aim of locating, identifying, and referring young children with disabilities and their families as early as possible for service programs. This process consists of activities designed to raise public awareness and screenings and evaluations to identify and diagnose disabilities. The federal IDEA law mandates under Part B that disabled children are guaranteed early childhood special education services and under Part C that infants and toddlers at risk for developmental delays are guaranteed early intervention programs. (Eligibility guidelines vary by U.S. states.) The IDEA requires school districts to find, identify, and evaluate children with disabilities in their attendance areas. School districts have facilitated this Child Find process by establishing community informed referral networks whose members refer children who may have exceptional educational needs (EENs). Network members typically include parents, doctors, birth-to-3 programs, child care programs, Head Start programs, public health agencies, social service agencies, and any other community members with whom the young children come into contact.

Single and multiple risk factors in infants and toddlers

Scientists find that developmental outcomes for children are not reliably predicted by any one risk factor or event. Developmental risk increases with increased biological, medical, or environmental risk factors. However, researchers have found some variables that afford resiliency in children to offset risk factors. These can include the child's basic temperament, the child having high self-esteem, the child having a good emotional relationship with at least one parent; and the child having experiences of successful learning. These findings indicate that assessments should include criteria for multiple biological and environmental risk factors, for cumulative biological and environmental risk factors, and for protective or resilience factors, considering all of these in the context of change occurring over time. Under the IDEA (the Individuals with Disabilities Education Act), U.S. states have the option to provide early intervention services to children considered at risk for adverse developmental outcomes as well as those already identified with them. Some states

Copyright © Mometrix Media. You have been licensed one copy of this document for personal use only. Any other reproduction or redistribution is strictly prohibited. All rights reserved.

apply multiple-risk models, requiring three to five risk factors for service eligibility. Some states also determine eligibility with less DD when biological, medical, or environmental risk factors also exist.

Determining IDEA eligibility in infants and toddlers

The IDEA Part C specifies the areas of development that states must include in defining developmental delays. However, individual states must identify the criteria they use to determine eligibility, including pertinent diagnostic instruments, procedures, and functional levels. States currently use quantitative and qualitative measures. Quantitative criteria for developmental delay include: difference between chronological age and performance level, expressed as a percentage of chronological age; performance at a given number of months below chronological age; or number of standard deviations (SDs) below mean of performance on a norm-referenced test. Qualitative criteria include: development considered atypical or delayed for established norms or observed behaviors considered atypical. At least one state differentially defines delay according to a child's age in months, with the rationale that a 25% delay, for example, is very different for a 1-year-old than a 3-year-old. Quantitative criteria for defining delay and determining eligibility vary widely among states. A 25% or 20% delay; 2 SDs below mean in 1+ areas or 1.5 SD below mean in 2+ areas are some common state criteria.

Sources of information

Military families stationed both in the United States and overseas who have young special needs children can seek information and assistance from the federally funded organization Specialized Training of Military Families (STOMP). The staff of STOMP is composed of parents having special needs children themselves, who also have been trained to work with other parents of special needs children. STOMP staff members are spouses of military personnel who thus understand the unique, specialized circumstances and needs of military families. Another government agency, the U.S. Department of Defense, includes the office of the Department of Defense Education Activity (DoDEA) and provides comprehensive guidance to military families with special needs children who are eligible to receive, or are receiving, free appropriate public education (FAPE) as mandated by the IDEA law (the Individuals with Disabilities Education Act), whether that education is located in the United States or in other countries.

Evaluation of a preschool child aged 3 to 5 years
Under the IDEA (the Individuals with Disabilities Education Act), evaluation information sources include: physicians' reports, the child's medical history, developmental test results, current classroom observations and assessments (when applicable), completed developmental and behavioral checklists, feedback and observations from parents and all other members of the evaluation team, and any other significant records, reports, and observations regarding the child. Under the IDEA, involved in the evaluation are parents, at least one regular education teacher and special education teacher if the child has these, and any special education service provider working with the child—for children receiving early intervention services from birth through age 2 and transitioning to preschool special education, it may be an early intervention service provider; a school administrator knowledgeable about children with disabilities, special education policies, regular education curriculum, and resources available; a psychologist or educator who can interpret evaluation results and discuss indicated instruction; individuals with special expertise or knowledge regarding the child (recruited by school or parents); when appropriate, the child; and other professionals, for example, physical or occupational therapists, speech therapists, medical specialists, and so on.

Copyright © Mometrix Media. You have been licensed one copy of this document for personal use only. Any other reproduction or redistribution is strictly prohibited. All rights reserved.

Providing special education services

If parents observe that their preschooler is not attaining developmental milestones within the expected age ranges or does not seem to be developing in the same way as most other children, they should seek evaluation for possible developmental delay or disability. Although 3- to 5-year-olds are likely not in elementary school yet, the elementary school in a family's school district is still the best first contact because the IDEA law (the Individuals with Disabilities Education Act) specifies that school districts must provide special education services at no family cost to eligible children, including preschoolers. Another excellent source of more information about special education is the National Dissemination Center for Children with Disabilities (NICHCY) of the U.S. Department of Education's Office of Special Education Programs. They partner with nonprofit organizations like the Academy for Educational Development (AED) to produce useful documents for families with special needs children. NICHCY supplies state resource sheets listing main contacts regarding special education services in each U.S. state. Families can obtain these sheets at NICHCY's website or by telephone.

Special education for preschoolers is education specifically designed to meet the individual needs of a child aged 3 to 5 years with a disability or developmental delay. The specialized design of this instruction can include adaptations to the content, to the teaching methods, and the way instruction is delivered to meet a disabled child's unique needs. Special education for preschoolers includes various settings, such as in the home, in classrooms, hospitals, institutions, and others. It also includes a range of related services, such as speech-language pathology services, specialized physical education instruction, early vocational training, and training in travel skills. The school district's special education system provides evaluation and services to eligible preschoolers free of charge. Evaluation's purposes are to determine whether a child has a disability under the IDEA's (the Individuals with Disabilities Education Act) definitions and determine that child's present educational needs.

After the evaluation of a preschool child

After a preschool child is evaluated, the parents and involved school personnel meet to discuss the evaluation results. Parents are included in the group that decides whether the child is eligible for special education services based on those results. For eligible children, the parents and school personnel will develop an IEP. Every child who will receive special education services must have an IEP. The main purposes of the IEP are (1) to establish reasonable educational goals for the individual child and (2) to indicate what services the school district will provide to the child. The IEP includes a statement of the child's present levels of functioning and performance. It also includes a list of more general instructional goals for the child to achieve through school and parental support along with more specific learning objectives reflecting those goals and specifying exactly what the child will be able to demonstrate, under what circumstances, how much of the time—for example, a percentage of recorded instances—and within what time period (e.g., 1 year).

Individualized Education Program

Individualized Education Program goals and objectives
In an IEP, the goals are more global, describing a skill for the child to acquire or a task to master. The objectives are more specific articulations of achievements that will demonstrate the child's mastery of the goal. For example, if a goal is for the child to increase his or her functional communicative vocabulary, a related objective might be for the child to acquire X number of new

Copyright © Mometrix Media. You have been licensed one copy of this document for personal use only. Any other reproduction or redistribution is strictly prohibited. All rights reserved.

words in X length of time; another related objective could be for the child to use the words acquired in 90% of recorded relevant situations. If the goal is for the child to demonstrate knowledge and discrimination of colors, one objective might be for the child to identify correctly a red, yellow, and blue block 95% of the time when asked to point out each color within a group of blocks. Progress toward or achievement of some objectives may be measured via formal tests; with preschoolers, many others are measured via observational data collection.

Procedures and considerations to progress monitoring, updating, and revising IEPs

Once a child has been identified with a disability, determined eligible for special education and related services under the IDEA (the Individuals with Disabilities Education Act), and had an IEP developed and implemented, the child's progress must be monitored. Monitoring methods may be related to evaluation methods. For example, if a child identified with problem behaviors was initially evaluated using a behavioral checklist, school personnel can use the same checklist periodically, comparing its results to the baseline levels of frequency and severity originally obtained. If an affective disorder or disturbance was identified and instruments like the Beck Depression Inventory or Anxiety Inventory were used, these can be used again periodically; reduced symptoms would indicate progress. If progress with IEP goals and objectives is less or greater than expected, the IEP team meets and may revise the program. This can include specifying shorter or longer times to achieve some goals and objectives; lowering or raising requirements proving too difficult or easy; resetting successive objective criteria in smaller or larger increments; changing teaching methods, content, or materials used, and so on.

Copyright © Mometrix Media. You have been licensed one copy of this document for personal use only. Any other reproduction or redistribution is strictly prohibited. All rights reserved.

Literacy Instruction

Phonetics and the speech system

Phonetics is the study of the acoustical and articulatory characteristics of human speech sounds. The first major segment of the human anatomy that is involved in the production of phonemes, or speech sounds, is the subglottal system. This system consists of the structures below the glottis, the opening between the vocal folds. The subglottal system consists of the lungs, the diaphragm, and the trachea. The diaphragm is a muscle just below and attached to the lungs. Lowering the diaphragm fills the lungs with air, or inflates them; raising the diaphragm deflates the lungs, expelling air. Airflow through the nose, throat, and mouth is modified by various parts of the speech system to produce different sounds. Air from the lungs flows up through the airway called the trachea, commonly known as the "windpipe." It travels to the larynx or "voice box," which is found in the second major segment of the speech system.

The second major segment of the human speech system is the larynx, which is commonly known as the "voice box." It is located above the subglottal system, which is the first major anatomical segment of the human speech system. The larynx is composed of cartilage and located above the trachea, commonly called the "windpipe." Within the larynx are muscles known as the vocal folds or vocal cords. The vocal folds are attached at the front by the arytenoid cartilage to the larynx, but the opposite sides of the vocal folds are not attached to anything. The glottis is the space between the vocal folds. When the vocal folds are relaxed, the glottis is open and air flows through it with no resistance. This airflow produces devocalized, or voiceless, sounds. When the vocal folds are partially tensed, the glottis is partly open and the sound produced is a whisper. When the vocal folds are fully tensed, the airflow vibrates against the glottis, causing vocalization and producing voiced sounds.

The upper segment of the speech system is called the supraglottal system because it is located above the glottis, which is the opening between the vocal folds. The supraglottal system is made up of the pharynx, the nasal cavity, and the oral cavity. The pharynx is the region beginning above the larynx ("voice box") and ending below the uvula. The oral cavity contains structures that we use to produce different speech sounds, including the uvula, the velum, the tongue, the hard palate, the alveolar ridge, the teeth, and the lips. The uvula is the appendage of soft tissue hanging down from the top portion of the back of the throat. It is visible when looking at the throat through the mouth. The velum is the soft palate. The alveolar ridge is a line of hard cartilage just behind the upper teeth. People produce varying speech sounds partly by performing such manipulations as touching the tongue to the lips, teeth, alveolar ridge, hard palate, and/or velum.

Place of articulation

Relating to the production of speech sounds
Place of articulation refers to the area of the vocal tract whose shape is changed by speech-producing movements. These changes affect the size of the area through which air flows, varying the frequencies of speech sounds. The production of bilabial phonemes involves both lips touching and then then releasing, as in [b], [m] (voiced), and [p] (voiceless). The production of labiodental phonemes involves the upper teeth touching the lower lip and then releasing, as in [v] (voiced) and [f] (voiceless). Interdental phonemes are pronounced with the tongue between the teeth, as in [ð] (voiced "th" as in "the") and [θ] (voiceless "th" as in "theme"). Dental phonemes are produced by

Copyright © Mometrix Media. You have been licensed one copy of this document for personal use only. Any other reproduction or redistribution is strictly prohibited. All rights reserved.

touching the tip of the tongue to the back of the front teeth. The phonemes [t] and [d] are pronounced dentally in some American English dialects (e.g., in Boston, Massachusetts and in Brooklyn, New York). These are, however, not examples of Standard English pronunciation. Alveolar phoneme pronunciation involves touching the tip of the tongue to the alveolar ridge, as in [t] and [s] (voiceless), and in [d], [z], [n], and [l].

Corresponding speech sounds they produce
Place of articulation refers to the location in the vocal tract that changes shape due to muscular movements, and thereby modifies the sound of the air flowing through the vocal tract. Pronouncing alveopalatal phonemes involves moving the tongue between the alveolar ridge and the hard palate, as in [ʃ]/"sh," [ʧ]/"ch" (voiceless), [ʒ] (as in "meaṣure" or "rou**g**e"), and [ʤ] [as in "judge" (voiced)]. Palatal phonemes are produced by moving the body of the tongue toward the hard palate, as in [j] (i.e. the sound of the "y" in "you"). Velar phonemes are produced by moving the body of the tongue toward the velum/soft palate, as in [k] (voiceless), [g], and [ŋ] ["-ng" (voiced)]. Uvular phonemes, made by moving the back of the tongue toward the uvula, are not found in English, but are used to produce the French "r" sound ([ʁ], which is voiced, and [χ], which is voiceless). Pharyngeal phonemes, produced by articulating the root of the tongue toward the back of the pharynx, are not found in English, but are found in Hebrew, Arabic, and other similar languages. Glottal phonemes, produced at the vocal fold opening/glottis, include the English [h] and the glottal stop [ʔ].

Manner of articulation

Whereas place of articulation refers to the part of the vocal tract we alter to vary phonemes, manner of articulation refers to how the tongue and/or lips control airflow to vary phonemes. Producing plosives involves completely blocking airflow, and then releasing it, as in [p], [b], [t], [d], [k], and [g]. Producing fricatives involves partially blocking airflow, which causes vibration and produces hissing (devocalized) or buzzing (vocalized) sounds, such as [f], [v], [s], [z], [ʃ]/"sh," and [ʒ]/"zh." Affricates are combinations of plosives and fricatives or stops and vibrations, such as [ʧ]/"ch" and [ʤ], as in "judge." Nasals are produced by lowering the velum or soft palate and blocking the vocal tract so that air flows out through the nasal cavity instead of through the oral cavity. American English nasal consonants include [n], [m], and [ŋ]/"ng." While the other consonant phonemes discussed above may be vocalized/voiced or devocalized/voiceless, nasals are always vocalized. Approximants are formed by tightening the vocal tract without blocking airflow, as in [l], [r], [j] (the "y" sound), and [w].

Tap and trill

The tap is produced by quickly touching an articulator to and releasing it from some part of the vocal tract. For example, the tongue quickly touches the alveolar ridge and moves away from it to produce the medial/middle sound [ɾ] in the English words "better," "ladder," etc. The tap is also found in Spanish in short or unrolled "r" sounds. An example is the medial sound in the word *para* (which translates to "for" in English). The trill is produced by rapidly vibrating the tip of the tongue against the roof of the mouth. The trill, also known as a "rolled r," is used in British and Scottish English. It is also used in Spanish for long, trilled, or rolled r's, such as those found in words spelled with double r's. An example of this type of word is the Spanish word meaning "dog": *perro*. The trill is also found in words beginning with r, since initial r's in Spanish are commonly rolled. An example is the Spanish word meaning "rats": *ratones.* To American/English ears, this word sounds like "rrrrratones."

Copyright © Mometrix Media. You have been licensed one copy of this document for personal use only. Any other reproduction or redistribution is strictly prohibited. All rights reserved.

Classification of vowel phonemes

Vowel sounds are phonetically classified according to tongue height, tongue "backness," tension/laxity, and lip rounding/unrounding. The closer to the roof of the mouth the tongue is, the higher the vowel sound. In English, high vowels include [i] ("ee"), [I] as in "it," [u] as in "loot," and [U] as in "look." Middle-height vowels include [e] as in "ray," [E] as in "red," [O] as in "hole," and [Ɔ] as in "haul." Low vowels include [a] as in "father" and [æ] as in "fat." Tongue "backness" refers to how far/near the tongue is from/to the back of the mouth. Front vowels include [i], [I], [e], [ɛ] as in "wet," and [æ]. Central vowels include [a] and [ə] (schwa), which is the sound of the "a" in "about." Back vowels include [u], [U], [O], and [Ɔ]. Vowels using high articulator tension are classified as tense, and include [i] and [e]. Vowels using lower tension are classified as lax, and include [I] and [ɛ]. The lips can be rounded, as with the vowels [u] and [O]; or unrounded, as with [i] or [ɛ].

Phonological awareness, phonemic awareness, and phonics

Phonological awareness refers to the awareness of the sounds that make up a spoken language. This includes being aware of the fact that certain speech sounds rhyme with one another, and that it is possible to break down spoken sentences into individual words, words into individual syllables, and syllables into individual phonemes or speech sounds. Phonological awareness also includes the abilities to talk about speech sounds; to think about them; and to manipulate them into various combinations, sequences, and patterns. The latter includes changing one word into another by inserting, deleting, or exchanging an individual phoneme. Moreover, phonological awareness is an understanding of the relationship between spoken and written language. Typically, children's phonological awareness skills develop continuously and gradually throughout the later preschool years. Children develop phonological awareness through their exposure to language and through direct training, both of which are provided by the adults around them and in their lives.

Phonological awareness focuses on the awareness of speech sounds, which young children typically develop and learn before they learn to read. *Phonemic awareness* refers to awareness of the individual phonemes or speech sounds used in the child's native language, which the child hears in the language spoken by the adults and older children around them in their environment. *Phonological awareness* instruction teaches children to recognize the speech sounds they hear, to identify and differentiate these sounds, to produce them accurately, and to manipulate them. Good phonological awareness facilitates children's ability to make connections between sounds and alphabet letters, hence facilitating phonics. *Phonics* is the instructional method used to establish the Alphabetic Principle (i.e. the concept of sound-to-letter correspondence) and teach skills for decoding (breaking words down to their component sounds/letters) and encoding (blending/combining individual sounds/letters to form words).

Developing phonological and phonemic awareness skills
By developing phonological and phonemic awareness skills, young children develop awareness of the sounds used in their native language. Significantly, they also learn to make the association between the speech sounds (phonemes) they hear and the written/printed letter symbols that represent them. Understanding this connection gives young children the foundation they need for the development of future skills, including word recognition skills and the decoding skills needed to read printed/written language. When young children develop phonological and phonemic awareness, they are less likely to experience deficits or delays in learning to read, and are more likely to achieve success in reading and spelling. The consensus of a great deal of educational research is that strong phonological and phonemic awareness in children is often a predictor of

Copyright © Mometrix Media. You have been licensed one copy of this document for personal use only. Any other reproduction or redistribution is strictly prohibited. All rights reserved.

future long-term success in spelling, reading, and overall literacy performance. Research has also found that this awareness is a more accurate predictor of future success than vocabulary knowledge, intelligence, socioeconomic status, and other related factors.

<u>Skills that should be developed by the later part of early childhood</u>
Young children who have developed phonological awareness can typically recognize the sounds of alliteration in spoken language, which is the repeated use of the same or similar consonants (e.g., "She sells seashells by the seashore"); the sounds of rhyming words; the sounds of words with the same initial sounds (e.g., "Wee Willie Winkie"); and final sounds. They can typically divide words into smaller parts, such as syllables and phonemes (speech sounds). They can usually also count these smaller parts. When given isolated speech sounds, they are typically able to blend these separate phonemes together to form familiar words. Children with good phonemic awareness realize that words are composed of phonemes, and that these individual sounds are symbolically represented by written/printed letters. Hence, they understand the relationship between speech and writing/print. Phonologically aware preschool children can typically also manipulate spoken language by adding, removing, or substituting specific speech sounds to create different words.

Benefits from instruction designed to develop PPA

Phonological and phonemic awareness (PPA) instruction benefits all children learning to read, which includes preschoolers, kindergarteners, and first-graders. In addition, PPA instruction is important for children who are at risk for reading problems. Such children typically have fewer alphabetic skills due to less exposure to and less experience with using the alphabet. This can be because their families have less access to books and/or libraries; their parents have different expectations of reading, or they prioritize reading differently; or their parents do not realize the importance of reading aloud to children to literacy development. Preschoolers with delayed language development, who are more likely to be diagnosed with reading disorders by the time they reach school age, also benefit from PPA instruction. Enhanced PPA enables enhanced awareness of correct speech, so children with articulation disorders also benefit. According to research, children with spelling disorders perform poorly when given PPA tasks. Phonemic instruction improves their understanding of sound-to-letter relationships and their ability to recognize common spelling units found in words, thereby strengthening their spelling skills.

Oral language development

Because of the amount of variation among individual children in the process of normal oral language development, it is neither easy nor accurate to pin down any linguistic developmental milestone to a specific age. Therefore, ranges rather than ages are identified. For example, most normally developing children will utter their first recognizable words sometime between the ages of 12 months and 18 months. However, the progress of normal language acquisition is unpredictable in the individual child, a statement which holds true for other areas of normal growth and development. For example, one child may say his/her first word at the age of 10 months, while another child may begin using words at 20 months. The majority of typically developing children tend to begin speaking in complex sentences around the ages of four to four-and-a-half years. But again, because the pace of normal language development can vary, some children might use complex sentences by three years old, while others only develop this ability by five-and-a-half years old.

Copyright © Mometrix Media. You have been licensed one copy of this document for personal use only. Any other reproduction or redistribution is strictly prohibited. All rights reserved.

<u>Considerations for adults regarding young children's oral language development</u>
The vast majority of children's oral language develops with great natural efficiency. Adults need not try to force it, but can nurture it by providing language-rich environments. Practices that may help include talking to children regularly starting at birth; reading regularly to babies, toddlers, and preschoolers; naming objects, actions, and events children encounter for them; and playing games with speech sounds, words, rhymes, etc. Adults need not be concerned when younger children distort or substitute more difficult phonemes like /r/ and /s/ with easier ones; this is normal. However, if a child still mispronounces such sounds beyond the age of about eight or nine, hearing and speech testing and therapy are indicated. Newborn hearing screenings are vital, as hearing loss is the most common disability in infants. If a child seems not to hear others' speech, a child's closest family/friends have trouble understanding the child's speech, or a child's communication is obviously different from that of same-age peers, adults should consult hearing and speech language specialists.

<u>Genetic and environmental influences on oral language development</u>
As with so many other aspects of human growth and development, oral language development is a product of the combined influences of nature and nurture, and of the interactions between the two. Humans have inborn inclinations to seek out social interaction with other people. Babies communicate their needs and wants through crying and gesturing before acquiring spoken language, and they frequently understand adult communication. Researchers have pointed out that social interactions and oral language development do not take place for the purpose of learning rules, but for connecting with others and making sense of the reality we experience. Children have inherent abilities to decipher linguistic rules through their environmental exposure to spoken language. They can do this without formal instruction. This is evidence of the influence of nature on oral language development, as is over-regularization. An example of the latter includes applying regular verb rules to irregular exceptions (e.g., "tooths," "freezed," "goed," etc.) until exceptions are learned. Adults' constant corrections during this learning stage are typically futile. In addition to natural and environmental influences, children's language development is also influenced by their own cognitive abilities.

<u>Guidelines for supporting the natural development of oral language skills</u>
Teachers should realize that whatever language and/or dialect a child speaks is a reflection of that child's family's and community's values, identity, and experiences. As such, it is a valid communication system that deserves respect. Adults should treat babies and young children as conversationalists even before they begin talking, because they learn conversational rules very early (e.g., attentive gazing, facial expressions, and turn-taking). A significant component of language development is peer learning, particularly in mixed-age child groups. Adults should encourage child interaction by providing activities conducive to talking and using a broad range of materials. Individual and collaborative activities should be balanced. Sharing books, building with blocks, engaging in dramatic play, and taking part in "shop"/carpentry-related activities all stimulate interaction and discussion. While peer learning is important, adults are children's main resources for initiating conversations, questioning, listening, responding, and maintaining language development. Adults should always keep this in mind. Continued interaction into the elementary grades and written language comprehension also support oral language development in children. Language informs all curriculum areas, so active learners in classrooms are always communicating.

Phonology, morphology, semantics, syntax, and pragmatics

Phonology is concerned with the rules for the combinations of speech sounds within a given language. For example, while some African languages include words beginning with the –ng/[ŋ]

Copyright © Mometrix Media. You have been licensed one copy of this document for personal use only. Any other reproduction or redistribution is strictly prohibited. All rights reserved.

phoneme, in English this sound is only word-medial or word-final, never word-initial. Most speakers follow such rules unconsciously. Morphology focuses on the smallest structural/grammatical units that convey or affect meaning. For example, in books, the noun book and the plural –s ending are each morphemes. Semantics focuses on the meanings of morphemes, words, and sentences. Syntax refers to sentence structure and word order, and is related to a language's rules for correctly combining morphemes and words into suffixes/inflections, sentences, questions, imperatives, etc. For example, features like participial modifiers and the verbs they modify are placed in a different order in German and English. The verb-containing phrase "I walked" would follow modifiers like "happily," "down the street," and "on a sunny day" in German, but would precede most if not all modifiers in English. Pragmatics focuses on rules for using language appropriately in various situations. An example of pragmatics would be how to speak at home versus how to speak at school or work.

Common approaches to communicate with young children

Researchers have found that a common practice among teachers when they are using language in their classrooms is to use linear or one-way questions requiring linear/one-way responses. However, experts recommend using reciprocal instructional approaches (e.g., asking open-ended questions that enable two-way/three-way responses). Studies also reveal that teachers are likely to dominate the classroom verbally. Experts believe a better approach would be to encourage and elicit children's conversational language and higher order cognitive skills by deliberately incorporating these into children's play activities. Experts state that teachers should have someone record a video of them during children's play time so they can monitor their own verbal behavior. Teachers should note how many times they verbally describe what the children do, how many times they repeat what a child says and then add some further information to it, how often they comment on and describe the properties of objects, and how often they ask open-ended questions. They should reflect not only on the number and duration of verbal interactions, but also on the quality of each conversation.

Following the CAR teaching strategy

Some researchers recommend using a teaching strategy called "Following the CAR" to engage in conversations with two- to five-year-old children. The C in CAR stands for Comment. In this step, the adult should comment on what a child is looking at, handling, or talking about. The adult should then wait five seconds. Experts find that this interval is important because it gives the young child time to hear and cognitively process the adult's comment, experience a response, formulate that response into verbal form, and then express it orally. The A stands for Ask. To continue the conversation the adult has begun and/or to start a new one, the adult should then ask the child questions about something the child is looking at, handling, or talking about. The adult should again wait five seconds to give the child time to respond. The R stands for Respond. Once the child gives an oral response, the adult should respond to what the child says by repeating the child's response and then adding a bit more information to extend the child's knowledge.

Real conversations

Experts define "real" conversations as those that interest the child and consist of three to four exchanges/"turns" between the child and the adult. Having at least one real conversation with each child on a daily basis is a highly effective way to improve vocabulary development and develop listening comprehension beyond the level of individual words. Teaching strategies that support children's active participation in real conversations include the following: attentively listening to

Copyright © Mometrix Media. You have been licensed one copy of this document for personal use only. Any other reproduction or redistribution is strictly prohibited. All rights reserved.

what the children say; inviting the children to join extended conversations with adults and peers; demonstrating genuine interest in and affection for the children; sending verbal and non-verbal messages that are consistent; avoiding making judgmental comments about children or anybody else to or in front of the children; addressing the children with courtesy; availing oneself of spontaneously occurring opportunities for informal conversations with each child, and/or even planning some opportunities; basing conversations on children's specific interests; and using children's experiences, as well as songs, stories, and books, as topics for conversation.

Stages of English as a second language

For ESL children, the first stage of second language acquisition is preproduction, which takes place during roughly the first six months of learning. Listening comprehension is minimal. The child does not speak in English, but can nod/shake the head "yes/no," draw pictures, and point at things. In the second, early production stage, which lasts from roughly six months to one year into learning, children have limited English comprehension. They can utter one- to two-word answers, essential words, familiar phrases, and present tense verbs. In the third, speech emergence stage, which lasts from about one to three years into learning, children comprehend English well. They can speak in simple sentences, but still make mistakes in pronunciation and grammar. They often misunderstand jokes in English. The fourth stage is intermediate fluency, which begins about three years into the language acquisition process and extends to about the fifth year. By this stage, children have attained excellent English listening comprehension, and do not make many grammatical errors. In the fifth, final stage of advanced fluency, children's English language proficiency is similar to that of a native English speaker. Children typically reach this stage between five and seven years after they start learning English.

Ways in which English as a second language instruction can be improved
Research in the early 1990s found that regardless of the type of bilingual education language programs used (e.g., early-exit, late-exit transitional, or immersion), teachers tended to ask ESL students questions requiring low levels of English language proficiency and lower-order cognitive skills. Teacher knowledge of what stages of second language acquisition students are in, as well as an awareness of the kinds of prompts and questions that are appropriate for each stage both enable teachers to approach children using suitable levels of discourse. Another advantage of knowing the stages is that teachers can assess students' content knowledge as well as their English language proficiency. A third benefit is that knowing language acquisition levels enables teachers to use what Vygotsky termed the zone of proximal development (ZPD), the gap between a learner's current capability and the next level of ability. Vygotsky found that the ZPD can be utilized by providing necessary temporary support—which Bruner called scaffolding—that is gradually withdrawn as students progress.

Stage-appropriate prompts
Children in the preproduction stage of ESL acquisition comprehend little English. They do not speak English, but can nod, point, and draw. Teachers can give prompts like "Where is...?" "Who has...?" "Show me the..." or "Circle the...." In the early production stage, children's comprehension is limited. They can give one- or two-word answers, use some important words and familiar phrases, and use verbs in present tense. Teachers can ask "Yes/No" and "Either/Or" questions and questions requiring short answers consisting of one or two words. They can also use lists and labels to access and expand vocabulary knowledge. In the speech emergence stage, comprehension improves and simple sentences emerge, albeit with grammatical and pronunciation errors. Teachers can now ask children "Why...?" "How...?" and "Explain..." questions, and can expect answers in the form of phrases or short sentences. In the intermediate fluency stage, when students have excellent

Copyright © Mometrix Media. You have been licensed one copy of this document for personal use only. Any other reproduction or redistribution is strictly prohibited. All rights reserved.

comprehension and can use correct grammar more often, teachers can ask children more abstract questions like "What would happen if...?" or "Why do you think...?" During the advanced fluency stage, when students approach native proficiency, teachers can instruct students to retell stories and make decisions.

Scaffolding and the zone of proximal development (ZPD)
Scaffolding, a term coined by Jerome Bruner, involves temporarily providing the support a learner needs to accomplish tasks just above his/her current performance level (i.e. things s/he cannot do independently, but can achieve with assistance). Lev Vygotsky identified the ZPD as the gap between a learner's current ability and the next level. He found that providing scaffolding enables teachers to exploit the ZPD to enhance learning. Teachers can apply this concept to ESL language development through direct instruction, by asking challenging questions, and/or by modeling correct English pronunciation and grammar. For example, a student in the first, preproduction stage of second language acquisition is able to find things, point at objects, and circle pictures, and such tasks are stage appropriate. However, a teacher can promote higher development by providing scaffolding to support students in answering Yes/No questions and/or giving one-word answers. These are tasks associated with the second, early production stage. With teacher support, the student can move to a higher stage of ESL acquisition.

Conversational vs. academic English for ESL learners
Conversational English requires basic skills that are used in interpersonal communication in everyday life, including basic vocabulary, grammar, and pronunciation. Conversational English enables ESL students to comprehend and participate in informal conversations with adults and peers. ESL children generally develop it after living in English-speaking locations for about two years. Conversational English is not particularly difficult cognitively. Children with conversational English skills sound fluent to most people. They converse in English, understand teacher questions, and may even translate for parents. However, their conversational fluency is often not reflected in school homework and tests. Teachers and parents may wrongly assume a child is unmotivated/learning disabled/lazy, when the true reason for the child's academic underachievement is that he or she lacks a knowledge of more cognitively demanding academic English (such as content specific vocabulary in math, science, etc.) and complex-compound sentence syntax. ESL students take at least five to seven years to become fluent in academic English, and take even longer when they lack native language literacy at the time they enroll in an English language school. To understand textbooks, solve word problems, write reports/papers, and develop the problem solving and critical thinking skills needed to comprehend and communicate abstract and novel concepts, students must master academic English.

Word walls
Young ESL children learn English vocabulary words by repeatedly singing the same familiar songs and chants, and by hearing the same stories many times. Such repetition is also favored by young children. While ESL children are involved in activities featuring repeated story readings, rhyme recitations, and/or singing, teachers can supplement these activities to enhance further vocabulary building by providing word walls. A word wall uses visuals to illustrate concepts represented by vocabulary words, as well as by related words. Key characteristics of vocabulary words and related words may also be shown. A word wall can also illustrate concepts like synonyms and subcategories. For example, a word wall for "Chicken Little," "The Little Red Hen," or another poultry-related story could have a picture of a chicken at the top labeled Chicken. Below it on the left might be several related pictures labeled with their names: Rooster, Hen, and Chick. Under the main chicken picture on the right could be several labeled pictures showing chicken characteristics (e.g., Feathers, Beak, and the Eggs that hens lay).

Copyright © Mometrix Media. You have been licensed one copy of this document for personal use only. Any other reproduction or redistribution is strictly prohibited. All rights reserved.

Input hypothesis (Krashen & Terrell)

Krashen and Terrell, who identified the stages of second language acquisition, posited the input hypothesis. This states that when an ESL learner in one stage of acquisition is given instructional input that includes some structures characteristic of the next stage of acquisition, and is also encouraged to use language reflective of that next, higher stage, the learner will advance to that next stage in listening and speaking. The input hypothesis is expressed as i + 1, where i represents the speaker's actual or current level (or stage) of second language acquisition, and i + 1 represents the speaker's potential second language development level. Teachers who know the stages of second language acquisition and the appropriate types of prompts to use for each stage can adapt their prompting so that students respond commensurately with their current stage of English language development and with the next higher stage at the same time.

Jane Hill's Word-MES formula

"Word-MES" is a mnemonic for the key steps in applying the stages of second language development to ESL instruction. Students in the preproduction stage need to learn English vocabulary Words. Teachers should focus on helping students learn and correctly apply basic vocabulary. For example, using the story of "Goldilocks and the Three Bears," teachers can teach words like house, bed, cereal, oatmeal, too, hot, cold, hard, and soft. When working with students in the early production stage, teachers should Model correct English usage. For example, if a child says "Goldie runned," the teacher can respond, "Yes, Goldilocks ran and ran." Teachers should not make explicit corrections. When working with children in the speech emergence stage, teachers can focus on Expanding spoken/written sentences. For example, if a child says, "Bed was too soft," the teacher can expand on this by saying, "Yes, the second bed was too soft," adding the correct article and specifying adjective. Teachers can help students in intermediate and advanced fluency stages to Sound like books by exposing them to words outside their repertoires, repeatedly reading familiar books and singing songs, and using supplementary word walls.

Articulation disorders

Articulation refers to the pronunciation of specific speech sounds and phonemes. Some phonemes are harder to produce than others. Therefore, it is normal for young children not to produce some sounds correctly until they reach a certain level of maturity. For example, children are around seven or eight on average before they can pronounce difficult phonemes like /r/ and /s/. Some children continue to distort, omit, or substitute a certain sound beyond the age norm. Speech therapy can help address these types of issues. If a child mispronounces multiple phonemes beyond the typical age ranges, testing is needed to determine the cause. Multiple factors can affect articulation, including hearing loss, misaligned teeth/jaws, missing teeth, a tongue that is shorter or longer than normal, velopharyngeal insufficiency interfering with complete vocal tract closure, breathing problems, mild cerebral palsy causing neuromuscular weakness and incoordination of the speech mechanisms, mild to moderate intellectual disabilities, and others. Some children's speech is difficult to understand due to multiple misarticulations, which may also be caused by any combination of the factors outlined above.

Aphasia

Aphasia is a language processing deficit caused by neurological damage or deficiency. It may be congenital or incurred during or after birth via accidental injury, including injury due to oxygen loss

Copyright © Mometrix Media. You have been licensed one copy of this document for personal use only. Any other reproduction or redistribution is strictly prohibited. All rights reserved.

(hypoxia or anoxia). Two specific aphasia diagnoses are named after the scientists who identified them. Broca's aphasia has historically been thought to originate in the brain's left hemisphere, and Wernicke's aphasia in the right hemisphere. Recent research, though, suggests that both types involve more numerous, more extensive, and less lateralized damage sites in various locations. Broca's aphasia affects expressive language. A child with Broca's aphasia would exhibit difficulty finding/retrieving words and constructing grammatical spoken sentences at an age when fluent speech is normal. Wernicke's aphasia affects receptive language. A child with Wernicke's aphasia would have difficulty understanding what others say, and may learn to hide this through uttering stock phrases like "I'm fine; how are you?" and "You look pretty today."

Jargon-aphasia

Expressive aphasia and receptive aphasia may be somewhat more familiar to some people than jargon-aphasia. Expressive aphasia impairs an individual's ability to process, formulate, and produce spoken language. Receptive aphasia impairs an individual's ability to process, comprehend, and interpret others' spoken language. Jargon-aphasia is somewhat rare, and is often caused by traumatic brain injury. The injury appears to damage the individual's motor control and coordination of speech mechanisms. The person can mentally formulate thoughts using words, but cannot then express them orally. The patient typically cannot form words, but uncontrollably repeats syllables like "cacacacaca" or "nananananana" when he or she attempts to speak. In early childhood, this should not be confused with normal infant babbling. All babies repeat syllables. It is part of typical speech development. However, if a child is older (three to five years old, for example), cannot form spoken words, and only produces jargon babbling when he or she attempts to speak, speech language pathology and neurological evaluations are indicated.

Voice disorders

Voice disorders can affect various characteristics of a speaker's voice, such as tone, volume, pitch, and nasality. These types of disorders alter the voice's normal quality. For example, some children suffer from birth defects causing cleft lip and/or cleft palate. With the former, the upper lip is split vertically or diagonally, which is visually disfiguring and also interferes with normal speech production. With the latter, the palate or roof of the mouth is split on one or both sides. Causes include parental genetics; genetic and congenital syndromes; multiple birth defects; and prenatal exposure to viruses, drugs, or environmental toxins. Effects include feeding and speech difficulties, ear infections, nasal shape changes, misaligned teeth, and disfigurement. A common symptom of untreated cleft palate is hypernasal speech. Vocal abuse (e.g., excessive screaming/singing/talking) can create vocal cord nodules or polyps. These can result in a hoarse, breathy, or rough voice; reduced pitch range; throat/neck/ear-to-ear pain; and vocal and physical fatigue. Vocal cord paralysis can cause hoarseness/breathiness, vocalization limited to one second, inability to speak loudly/clearly, restricted wind, and choking/aspiration while eating/drinking.

Stuttering

Stuttering is often described by clinicians as a disorder of rate and rhythm. Stutterers may speak faster/slower than normal, or may alternately speed up and slow down their speech without using typical rhythm regulation in their sentences, questions, etc. Common stuttering symptoms include repetitions of individual phonemes ("T-t-t-t-today"), syllables ("To-to-to-to-today"), and/or words ("To-to-to-to do that"); prolongations of consonant or vowel phonemes ("Sssssssssnake" or "Wooooooooould you?"); and blocks, wherein the individual struggles so hard to produce the initial phoneme of a word that the tension causes complete airflow blockage. The individual's face will

Copyright © Mometrix Media. You have been licensed one copy of this document for personal use only. Any other reproduction or redistribution is strictly prohibited. All rights reserved.

often turn red, and he or she may display accompanying learned behaviors like foot-stamping, fist-pounding, and/or facial contortions. Stuttering can be mild, moderate, or severe. Some mild stutterers are "fluent stutterers," demonstrating some repetitions and/or prolongations, but talking right through them without blocking. Some become adept at circumlocution, which describes the practice of "talking around" problematic initial phonemes/words using synonymous words/phrases. Theories of stuttering causes include delayed auditory feedback, which disrupts fluency because stutterers belatedly hear their own speech; anxiety with propositional speech; and lack of self-confidence. Some children simply "grow out of" stuttering.

Delayed language development

Some children develop skills for understanding and using spoken and written language significantly later than normal, even when individual variations are taken into account. This can be due to a number of causes. Children with mild or moderate intellectual disabilities are likely to show delayed language development as well as delayed cognitive development, as these are closely related. Some children do not test with obvious cognitive deficits, but may have minimal neurological damage, which can delay language development. Other children may have no organic basis for the delay, but have been born into environments where they are deprived of adequate environmental stimulation. For example, if a child's parents and/or caregivers/teachers do not routinely talk to them, have limited daily interactions with them, and never read to them, young children are likely to exhibit delayed language development. Some parents who do interact with and talk to their children may still be linguistically, educationally, and culturally deprived themselves. Their children may feel loved and have good self-esteem, but may have a level of language development that is below average for their age.

Alphabetic principle

The concept that written/printed letters and their patterns correspond to speech sounds is called the alphabetic principle. Children's future success with reading is strongly predicted by their early knowledge of the shapes and names of written/printed letters. Children's development of the abilities to view words as series of letters and to remember printed/written word forms is closely associated with their knowledge of letter names. Children cannot learn letter sounds or recognize words without knowing letter names. Being able to recognize and name multiple letters is a prerequisite for comprehending the alphabetic principle, which explains that spoken sounds and printed letters have predictable, systematic relationships. Children follow a sequence of first learning letter names, then learning letter shapes, and finally learning letter sounds. Singing the "ABC" song and reciting rhymes help children learn letter names. Playing with lettered blocks, large 3-D letters, and alphabet books helps them learn letter shapes. Teachers can plan informal instruction so that children are given multiple, varied opportunities to view, compare, and manipulate letters. Relevant activities may include identifying, naming, and writing upper-case and lower-case letters.

Not all children begin preschool or school with good alphabetic knowledge, which refers to an awareness that written letters represent spoken sounds. For those who have not developed this prerequisite skill, educators must provide well-organized instruction to enable students to identify, name, and write the letters of the alphabet. Once they master these skills, they will have the foundation necessary to learn letter sounds and word spellings. A general instructional plan revolving around the alphabetic principle includes several elements. First, teachers should give children explicit instruction in isolated letter-sound correspondences. Second, during each day's lessons and activities, teachers should give children opportunities to practice their developing

Copyright © Mometrix Media. You have been licensed one copy of this document for personal use only. Any other reproduction or redistribution is strictly prohibited. All rights reserved.

knowledge of letter-sound relationships. Teachers should both review children's cumulative learning of letter-sound correspondences already taught and create opportunities for children to practice new letter-sound relationships they are just learning. Finally, to give students opportunities to apply their expanding knowledge of the alphabetic principle early and frequently, teachers can supply phonetic spellings of words with meanings familiar to children for them to read.

Pace and order of lessons

Teaching early literacy skills

There is no expert consensus regarding the speed or sequence that should be used to teach young children letter-to-sound relationships. However, educators generally agree that phonemes and letters with the highest utility—those used most often—should be taught earliest. These include m, a, t, s, p, and h. Conversely, x as in "box," gh as in "through," ey as in "they," and a as in "want" are letter-phoneme relationships that are used less frequently. The letter-sound relationships of consonants least subject to distorted articulation when pronounced in isolation should be taught first. These include f, m, and n. Word-initial or word-medial stops (p, b, t, d, k, and g) are more difficult for young children to combine with other sounds than continuous (fricative/affricate) phonemes are. Sounds that are easily confused (like /b/ and /v/) or letters that look similar (like b and d, or p and g) should be introduced to young children in separate lessons.

Sound-letter correspondences

Early childhood alphabetic principle instruction should be logical and consistent with the rates at which young children are able to learn. Teachers should introduce sound-to-letter relationships that will enable children to work with words as early as possible. According to research findings, direct and explicit instruction controlled by the teacher is more effective for teaching children the alphabetic principle than indirect and implicit methods are. Many teachers also use eclectic approaches, combining multiple teaching methods. Educators should remember that individual children normally learn sound-letter relationships at varying rates. A reasonable rate for introducing sound-letter relationships ranges from two to four relationships weekly. The earliest relationships teachers should introduce are high-utility ones. When introducing consonants and vowels, teachers should present them in an order that facilitates children's reading words readily. Teachers should avoid presenting similar-sounding phonemes and/or similar-looking letters together. They should use separate sessions/lessons to introduce single consonant sounds and consonant blends/clusters. Instruction in blending letters/sounds should use words with letter-sound relationships children have already learned.

Sound-to-alphabet letter relationships instruction

When a teacher is instructing preschoolers on the relationships between spoken sounds and written letters (known as the alphabetic principle), s/he might begin by introducing a few (e.g., two, three, or four) single consonant sounds and one or two short vowel sounds. Once the children have mastered these, the teacher can present some additional new single consonant sounds, present some additional new short vowel sounds, and introduce one long vowel sound in a subsequent lesson. Then, the teacher could introduce consonant blends like st-, cl-, etc. in a separate lesson. Another lesson after the one on consonant blends could focus on digraphs (e.g., ch, sh, and th), which would enable children to read frequently used words like "chair," "she," and "the." A later lesson could introduce consonant clusters such as str-, spl-, etc. Teachers should always teach young children single consonants and consonant blends/clusters in separate lessons to avoid confusion. .

Copyright © Mometrix Media. You have been licensed one copy of this document for personal use only. Any other reproduction or redistribution is strictly prohibited. All rights reserved.

English literacy development in ESL students

To teach ESL students to read English, teachers must know the essential elements of literacy development, the principles of second language acquisition, and the differing conventions of both the students' first (L1) and second (L2) languages. Second language acquisition is an ongoing, lifelong process. In many ways, the process of second language acquisition parallels that of first language acquisition. Regardless of their L1 or their formal L2 instruction, students demonstrate predictable error patterns in learning. Acquiring language is not a linear process. While formal instruction can expand knowledge and inform and ease the process of language acquisition, it cannot accelerate it. Therefore, it is also detrimental to require sequential mastery of each curriculum element before proceeding onto the next element. Activities using language that are meaningful to students within a relevant context and teacher guidance help develop L2 acquisition. Varying language conventions must be kept in mind during instruction. For example, letter-sound correspondences are more consistent in Spanish than in English. Spanish letters are pronounced the same way they are spelled, so Spanish-speaking children can find the multiple pronunciations of the same phoneme in English confusing.

Phonological differences between Spanish and English

Because letter-sound correspondences are more consistent in Spanish than in English, Spanish vowels have fewer possible pronunciations than English vowels. Spanish has fewer total vowel sounds than English, regardless of spelling. This makes learning English more complicated for Spanish-speaking children. In modern Spanish, the pronunciation for the consonants v and b is the same, but these letters have different pronunciations in English. Spanish and English both contain the phoneme /ð/. In Spanish, it is represented by the letter d; in English, it is represented by the letters th. In English, the consonant clusters /sk/, /sp/, and /st/ are word-initial, as in school, special, and star. In Spanish, they are always preceded by /e/, as in escuela (school), especial (special), and estrella (star). Spanish speakers thus have difficulty pronouncing such initial clusters, and often end up using Spanish conventions, saying "estart" for start, "espeak" for speak, etc. Some sounds exist in L2 but not in L1; some L1 sounds transfer to L2; and letter-sound correspondences may differ between languages. Therefore, phonological and phonemic awareness and oral language development are crucial for ELLs.

Phonemic focus of English literacy development vs. the syllabic focus of Spanish literacy development

In English literacy instruction with native English-speaking children, educators teach individual phonemes/speech sounds and their corresponding alphabetic letters (phonics instruction). Spanish, however, is a syllabic language, and Spanish reading is taught using syllables rather than single phonemes. Spanish instruction uses syllables to teach word spellings, word divisions, stressed/accented parts of a word, word reading, and simple sentence construction. English-speaking children are taught to "sound out" a new word they encounter while reading by separating it into individual letters representing individual sounds. Spanish-speaking children are taught to "sound out" words by separating them into their component syllables. For example, in English, children sound out "man" as /m/, /æ/, and /n/. In Spanish, children sound out manzana (apple) as man, za, and na. Teachers must realize that ELLs encounter many phonological, syntactic, and semantic differences between their first and second languages, and that children with less English proficiency depend more on L1 cues. ELLs also expend double the cognitive effort of native

- 107 -

Copyright © Mometrix Media. You have been licensed one copy of this document for personal use only. Any other reproduction or redistribution is strictly prohibited. All rights reserved.

English speakers through their attention to new language sounds, meanings, and structures, as well as their attempts to learn new literacy concepts and skills.

Writing systems of different languages

Not only do different languages have phonological and orthographic differences, but they also use different writing systems. For example, although Spanish is syllabic in phonology and Spanish literacy instruction is syllabic, the Spanish writing system and letter-sound correspondences are (like English) alphabetic. The Chinese writing system is logographic. Rather than using alphabet letters to symbolize speech sounds, Chinese uses ideographs, or characters depicting concepts, to symbolize words. The Japanese language has a combined logographic and syllabic writing system. Directionality can differ, too. In English, Spanish, and other European-based languages, lines of writing/print go from left to right. In Hebrew, they go from right to left; in Chinese, they go from top to bottom. Therefore, children's ESL progress relies on their phonological awareness, their oral language knowledge, their grasp of the alphabetic principle, and their print awareness and book knowledge. These are best developed in purposeful contexts that are relevant to children.

Developing English language literacy

When teaching children learning English as a second language, teachers should make their instruction understandable to them. They can do this by providing visual aids, graphic organizers, and concrete examples of what they are teaching. They should consistently monitor children's language for development levels and use. They can paraphrase to clarify unfamiliar words and the concepts they describe. Teachers should take advantage of every opportunity to establish connections between children's L1 and English. They must repeat things frequently. They can also help ELLs by establishing a safe atmosphere where children receive ongoing support and feel comfortable taking risks. Teachers should adopt and communicate high learning expectations. They should enable children to develop necessary language and literacy skills that are consistent with their current levels of oral English proficiency. Literacy instruction should build upon children's comprehension, the alphabetic principle, and print concepts. Teachers should use language that children understand and find meaningful.

Instructing children to enhance their English language literacy development

Teachers should assess their students' specific needs, and then design instructional programs that address those needs. They should also design instructional plans expressly for new students. They should design instruction so children can understand it. They should assess student progress often. Based on data they collect through assessment and monitoring, teachers should make instructional decisions, including adjusting schedules accordingly. They should create plenty of opportunities for children to participate in extended conversations in English. Teachers should also seek out others in their preschool's community who have expertise in one or more areas, and should use these assets when creating their curriculum. ESL teaching strategies should be integrated into instruction in all content areas. Teachers should activate and access children's background knowledge and connect instructional content to children's real lives. They should give children opportunities to discuss learning materials, topics, and early texts. Teachers must also acknowledge and value diverse cultural patterns of speech and discourse.

Copyright © Mometrix Media. You have been licensed one copy of this document for personal use only. Any other reproduction or redistribution is strictly prohibited. All rights reserved.

Print awareness

Print awareness, also called print literacy, emerges gradually during the preschool years in normally developing children. Print awareness is the understanding that print conveys meaning, and the understanding of print's form and function. Research has found that children typically tend to develop print awareness between three and five years of age. Some researchers have observed that at this age, children go through a significant metamorphosis, wherein they demonstrate exponential increases in self-motivated, independent interactions with print. Such interactions include reciting the alphabet, identifying printed letters, recognizing printed words, and using print as a communicative mechanism.

Many studies have concluded that the development of these print literacy skills by preschool-aged children is a strong predictor of their future achievement in reading. Studies have also shown that while four-year-olds have not mastered either word concepts or print concepts, they may acquire many print concepts sooner than word concepts.

Promoting literacy development and reading comprehension

Instructional strategies designed to promote early literacy development and reading comprehension that are used in many ECE programs (like the EC component of the Partners for Literacy [PfL] Curriculum) include interactive book reading, the 3N strategy, extended teaching, problem solving, and curriculum-embedded assessments. These are also suitable for teaching ESL children. Interactive book reading is a teaching method that should be used at least once per day with each child. Children participate either individually or in pairs. This interactive reading is done in addition to (not instead of) reading in large and small groups. The purpose of interactive book reading is to stimulate responsive, reciprocal instructional conversations between each child and the teacher. Interactive book reading employs three main component strategies: the 3S strategy (3S stands for see, show, and say), wh- questions, and expanded book reading.

3N strategy

In the 3N strategy, the 3 Ns are notice, nudge, and narrate. This teaching strategy involves providing scaffolding. Scaffolding is temporary support that helps a child advance from his or her current skill, knowledge, or competency level to a higher level. Scaffolding permits advancement that the child could not achieve on his or her own. The 3N teaching strategy can be employed to make any activity a learning experience for a young child, because it provides a structure for how teachers should interact with children. First, the teacher notices the level of an individual child's literacy skill(s). Second, the teacher verbally nudges the child to do things that are a step above his or her current skill level. Third, the teacher narrates what the child does, verbally describing and reflecting the child's activities. A number of literacy games designed for young children, including the Partners for Literacy curriculum's LiteracyGames, utilize a 3N instructional strategy.

3S strategy and wh- questions

Interactive book reading is a strategy aimed at generating responsive instructional conversations between the child and teacher. In the 3S strategy, the 3 S's are see, show, and say. First, the teacher asks the child to see/look at a specific feature in a book, such as the main character. If the child succeeds, the teacher then asks him/her to locate an image or a word on a page. If the child does this correctly, the teacher then asks the child to say a word/answer a question. This requires multiple responses, promoting children's attending behavior and building upon each student's

Copyright © Mometrix Media. You have been licensed one copy of this document for personal use only. Any other reproduction or redistribution is strictly prohibited. All rights reserved.

abilities. During the say part of 3S, the teacher asks the child questions beginning with who, what, where, when, and why. These wh- questions help teachers assess children's listening and/or reading comprehension levels, and also encourage ongoing conversations between each child and the teacher.

Activities for expanded book reading instructional strategy

Expanded book reading is an instructional strategy that is part of the interactive book reading teaching format, which is used to promote early childhood literacy development. In expanded book reading, teachers can ask children to predict the possible subject matter of a book. They can give children an overview of a book. They can discuss setting, characters, and events in a book with children. They can help children relate the story in a book to their own lives, thereby making the book meaningful and relevant to children and helping them establish connections between literature and real life. Teachers can enhance the meaning of stories in books by acting them out using puppets and other props. To integrate literacy into all content areas across the curriculum, teachers can design math, science, art, and/or music activities that are related to a book students read. Teachers can ask children to retell the story they read together, which is an excellent way to informally assess their comprehension. This activity also assesses children's receptive and expressive language processing and speech-language production abilities.

Incorporating problem-solving strategies and skills

During each preschool day, teachers can help young children recognize their emotions, identify their own needs and wants, develop empathy for and identify with the emotions of others, recognize situations involving problems, come up with simple solutions to problems, and think about the potential consequences of problem solutions. These activities help children develop age appropriate and developmentally appropriate competencies for solving problems and making decisions. Periods of both formal and informal instruction afford opportunities for children to develop these skills. Developing problem-solving and decision-making skills at an early age has a number of benefits. Young children learn to self-regulate their emotions and behaviors through this development. They develop social skills for interacting with others. Moreover, developing early problem-solving and decision-making skills prepares children for the further development of the higher order cognitive skills they will need to succeed in formal primary, secondary, and higher education settings, as well as in everyday life.

Strategies helping to read new and/or difficult words

Phonics helps children read unknown/difficult words by teaching them how to sound out the phonemes represented by each printed letter. Teachers can help when children mispronounce words that have irregular spellings. They can also confirm children's correct pronunciations of words they have not heard or seen before. Context helps children deduce which of several possible words is most likely to be found in a particular sentence, paragraph, or book by examining its meaning in relation to the overall subject matter. Looking at a word's part of speech and how it fits into the sentence in question is also an example of using context. For example, reed and read have different spellings and meanings, but sound the same (homonyms). After reading the sentence "Reeds grow in marshes," a child knowing the meaning of "reads" can rule this word out even without knowing how it is spelled because it makes no sense in the context of the sentence. Children could also use their knowledge of language structure to analyze the sentence above. Children can ascertain whether a new word is a noun (person/place/thing) or a verb (action/state

Copyright © Mometrix Media. You have been licensed one copy of this document for personal use only. Any other reproduction or redistribution is strictly prohibited. All rights reserved.

of being) by looking at its syntactic placement and its relation to the other words in the sentence that they are familiar with.

Formats used in children's literature and some genres

The picture book is both a genre and a format that encompasses various other genres. It includes wordless storybooks, which contain only pictures. Picture books integrate pictures and text to create a multimodal experience. Text is the most important feature of illustrated story books. Illustrations are secondary but complementary to the text. Poetry books contain poems rather than prose. Poems can use concrete verse, free verse, and rhymed and metered verse. Poetry emphasizes the sounds and meanings of words, and appeals to both readers' emotions and thoughts. Traditional literature is an adapted form of oral storytelling. It includes fairy tales, fables, folklore, epics, and proverbs. "Once upon a time..." introductions and happy endings are common features. Modern fantasy is based on traditional literature, but it is original. It includes modern fairy tales, such as those written by Lewis Carroll and Hans Christian Andersen. White's Charlotte's Web and Milne's Winnie the Pooh are also examples. Fantasy stories are imaginary, and often focus on good vs. evil conflicts, magic, and/or quests. Non-fiction informational books include narrative, how-to, question and answer, activity, life cycle, and concept texts.

Characteristics of good children's literature found in all genres

To select good children's literature, adults should determine whether a book tells an interesting story. The story should be age appropriate. It should also be appealing to a teacher's students. Books should be well-written, and should have original, believable, and well-constructed plots. Story characters should be credible and convincing, and they should grow and change as a result of their experiences. Dialogue should suit the characters, and should sound natural. Stories should have themes that are important to children. Adults should consider whether a book's theme is obviously moralistic. They should consider what the reader can expect based on a book's title and format. Illustrations should contribute to text, and vice versa. Good children's books avoid stereotypes based on race, gender, etc. They should afford pleasant reading/listening experiences. Adults can also read book reviews for guidance. Children's book authors should be knowledgeable about their subject matter, and they should write in a style suitable for the subject being discussed. Informational books should be accurate and well-organized.

Features of children's books that promote early childhood literacy development

Books that some EC educational experts refer to as "predictable books" contain repetitive text throughout. A salient characteristic of young children is their behavior of repeating familiar rhymes/songs/chants/phrases and stories over and over. Children find such repetition enjoyable. They also ask adults to read them the same books repeatedly. In addition to being enjoyable, repetition provides young children with opportunities to practice words and language patterns, and also encourages retention. Children also like repetitive books because they can immediately participate in the reading of the story. Some examples of good "predictable" children's books include the traditional stories "The Three Little Pigs" and "The Little Red Hen." Other examples are Dr. Seuss's "Green Eggs and Ham" and his story "What Was I Scared Of?" found in the compilation Yertle the Turtle. Another feature of children's books promoting early literacy development is pictures. Picture books with equal, interrelated/interdependent pictures and text help young children learn to recognize and begin to read letters and words by relating them to familiar visual images. The pictures in illustrated storybooks inform text, supporting beginning readers' continuing literacy development.

Copyright © Mometrix Media. You have been licensed one copy of this document for personal use only. Any other reproduction or redistribution is strictly prohibited. All rights reserved.

Abilities demonstrating phonological and phonemic awareness

Young children with phonological awareness recognize rhymes they hear, can rhyme words, can "count" the number of syllables in a word by clapping, and can identify words with matching initial sounds (e.g., "mother" and "milk"). Children with phonemic awareness can manipulate individual phonemes in words. For example, they can separate the word "cat" into the sounds /k/, /æ/, and /t/. Children who have problems with phonemic awareness frequently experience reading problems without early intervention. There are several issues teachers may observe in the classroom that can indicate phonological and/or phonemic awareness deficits. Children may not correctly combine individual phonemes to make a word. For example, they may not be able to select and blend the phonemes /k/, /æ/, and /t/ to make "cat." A child may not correctly perform phoneme substitution tasks to make different words. For example, a child may not be able to change the /k/ in "cat" to /m/ to make "mat." A child may have difficulty determining how many syllables are in a word like "paper." A child may also have problems rhyming, syllabicating, or spelling new words based on how they sound.

Word decoding and phonics

Word decoding ability consists of being aware of letter-sound correspondences and letter patterns, and applying them to correctly pronounce the words we read. Phonics is a reading instruction approach that focuses on letter-sound correspondences, exceptions to general rules, and strategies for sounding out new words. In the classroom, if a teacher observes a child is having trouble matching up letters with sounds (or vice versa), this can signal decoding and phonics problems that can interfere with a child's ability to read and spell. Children who can decode words, but must use a great deal of effort to do so, may have decoding and phonics problems. Difficulties with spelling words phonetically and reading are also signs of possible problems. Children who struggle greatly with phonics activities and patterns may have decoding deficits. Children who try to guess words based on the first one or two letters may have problems with decoding and phonics. If after teaching several letter sounds/patterns to a class, a teacher finds that certain children cannot recognize them while reading words and do not include these sounds and patterns in their writing, the teacher should suspect that these children are having problems with decoding and phonics.

Vocabulary frequently identified by educators

Educators frequently divide vocabulary into listening, speaking, reading, and writing vocabulary. These are not necessarily the same. Listening vocabulary refers to the words we must know to understand what we hear others say. Speaking vocabulary refers to the words we use when we talk. Reading vocabulary refers to the words we must know to comprehend what we read. Writing vocabulary refers to the words we use when we write. To read print, children must understand the majority of the words they encounter in a text. Children learn the majority of word meanings indirectly through daily life experiences. Well-designed instruction teaches them additional vocabulary. If a teacher observes that a child has more questions than usual about what words mean in age appropriate/developmentally appropriate texts, the child may have vocabulary issues. A teacher may observe that a child does not use or recognize many words compared to his or her peers, which could also indicate vocabulary issues. A child who cannot see connections/relationships among words in different texts may have vocabulary deficits. If a child frequently cannot find the correct word to express a thought, idea, etc., this could also indicate vocabulary difficulties.

Copyright © Mometrix Media. You have been licensed one copy of this document for personal use only. Any other reproduction or redistribution is strictly prohibited. All rights reserved.

Reading fluency

Reading fluency is the ability to read quickly, accurately, and smoothly both silently and aloud, and to read aloud with appropriate vocal intonations and expression. Children who do not read fluently sound awkward and choppy when they read aloud. Some students who read disfluency have word decoding problems. Others simply need more reading practice to read quickly and smoothly. Reading fluency is important to children's reading motivation. When children find reading laborious or view it as a chore rather than an enjoyable experience, they dislike reading and avoid it. This exacerbates reading problems. Reading fluency becomes more important in upper elementary grades, when the volume of required reading increases exponentially for students. Therefore, younger children with poor reading fluency will also have difficulty meeting academic reading demands in the future. When teachers conduct correct words per minute assessments, children who do not meet the criteria for their grade level may have fluency issues. Struggling and becoming frustrated with speed and/or accuracy while reading aloud may indicate fluency problems. Reading aloud without expression is another sign of fluency issues, as are failing to pause at meaningful breaks in a sentence or a paragraph and failing to "chunk" words into meaningful units.

Abilities necessary for good reading comprehension

To have good reading comprehension, children must be able to (1) decode the words they read, (2) connect what they read to things they already know, and (3) think about what they have read in depth. Knowing enough word meanings (i.e. having enough vocabulary) plays a major role in reading comprehension. Children with good comprehension can make conclusions about what they read, including identifying factual elements, determining the causes of specific events, and identifying comedic characters. Therefore, comprehension involves a combination of reading, thinking, and reasoning. Teachers may observe a number of signs of reading comprehension problems. A child may focus on details/"trees" to the exclusion of the main point/"forest." This child can report how stories end, but cannot explain why. A child may not speculate about characters' motivations or upcoming events when reading a book.

When trying to relate reading to his/her life, a child may choose irrelevant information. A child may not be able to recount logical event sequences in stories or isolate main facts in informational texts. A child may appear to have inadequate vocabulary to understand a text. Finally, a child may be unable to relate details of a story, such as the setting, what the characters look like, etc.

> ➤ **Review Video:** <u>Reading Comprehension Tips</u>
> *Visit* ***mometrix.com/academy*** *and enter* ***Code: 280215***

Reading components of phonological and phonemic awareness

The five basic reading components of phonological and phonemic awareness are word decoding, phonics, fluency, vocabulary, and comprehension. A deficit in any of these components can lead to reading problems. In addition to deficits in one or more of these areas, about two to three percent of children have central auditory processing disorders (CAPDs). Our ears receive environmental sound waves and convert them to acoustic impulses that are carried by nerves to the brain, which interprets these signals as various sounds, including speech. This is auditory processing. Children with CAPD have problems attending to, listening to, and remembering spoken information, and often take longer to process auditory input. They frequently cannot differentiate among sounds in words that sound similar to other phonemes, despite being able to hear them clearly. This causes

Copyright © Mometrix Media. You have been licensed one copy of this document for personal use only. Any other reproduction or redistribution is strictly prohibited. All rights reserved.

decoding difficulties, which interferes with reading. Some children with strong auditory (and language) processing skills have deficits in phonological processing (i.e. processing phonemes/speech sounds specifically). This also typically causes decoding and hence reading difficulties. Language processing problems are broader, including deficiencies in linguistic experiences, vocabulary, comprehension (despite being able to correctly decode words), reading, and writing.

Memory

For children to read, understand what they read, and switch efficiently between the printed language they see and the information they have stored in their memories, children must be able to store information and retrieve it as it is needed. There are three main types of memory. Short-term memory holds small pieces of information for short periods of time. For example, when we hold a phone number in our mind only long enough to dial it, but do not retain it after it is dialed, we use our short-term memory. Working memory holds interim information in the mind for use during calculations. For example, we use our working memory when mentally multiplying double digit numerals or doing long division. Processing new information so that it can be stored for a long period of time, searching for stored information, and retrieving information as it is needed are also functions of working memory. Phonological working memory is a component of phonological processing that is important in reading comprehension, spelling, written expression, and retention. We store enormous amounts of information for many years in our long-term memory. This information influences our differential attention to various environmental factors and our perceptions of the world.

Dyslexia

Preschoolers/kindergarteners who have trouble learning alphabet letters are more likely to have trouble identifying sound-letter correspondences in first grade, and are more likely to have subsequent life-long difficulties with reading. Issues related to children's speech that can indicate dyslexia include mispronouncing unfamiliar, long, or complex words. This may include omitting word parts and/or arranging syllables or word parts in the wrong sequence. Other signs of dyslexia include speech that is not fluent (e.g., speech that is marked by frequent hesitations, "um's," and pauses); speech that uses vague or non-specific wording, such as "things" or "stuff," instead of correct nouns and names of specific objects; speech that suggests the child is having difficulty finding words while speaking, which is indicated when students confuse words that sound similar (e.g., substituting "volcano" for "tornado," substituting "humidity" for "humility," etc.); and speech that shows an inability to generate verbal responses to questions quickly and on demand. Students with dyslexia may also require more time than normal to respond orally to language stimuli; and may also have difficulties with rote memory (e.g., retaining and/or retrieving names, dates, phone numbers, random lists, and other isolated items contained in information presented verbally).

Dyslexic children typically show abnormally slow progress in their acquisition of reading skills. They often lack systematic strategies for reading new words (decoding, sounding out, etc.), and make wild guesses instead. Being unable to read short function words (e.g., "an," "on," and "that") is common, as is stumbling over multisyllabic words. Dyslexic children often miss parts of words when reading and/or fail to decode word parts, and may, for example, read a word aloud with its middle syllable missing (e.g., "imation" for "imagination"). Children with dyslexia tend to fear and hence avoid oral reading because they have made errors in the past and have an expectation that they will make additional errors if they attempt to read aloud again. When they do read aloud, they may omit appropriate inflections; sound like they are reading a foreign language; sound laborious

Copyright © Mometrix Media. You have been licensed one copy of this document for personal use only. Any other reproduction or redistribution is strictly prohibited. All rights reserved.

and choppy, rather than fluent and smooth; mispronounce numerous words; and make numerous omissions and substitutions. While reading, they depend on the context to comprehend meaning, and have more difficulty understanding single/isolated words. Their performance on objective (e.g., multiple choice) tests is typically much poorer than their intelligence and knowledge would predict.

Children who consistently cannot complete written tests in the time allowed may have dyslexia. Children who cannot pronounce more difficult printed words and substitute easier ones for them instead (e.g., "car" for "automobile") may have dyslexia. In math, dyslexia causes difficulty reading word problems. Dyslexic children often misspell words. The spellings are not phonetic, but are often bizarre and wildly different from actual spellings and from native language conventions. Children with dyslexia read very slowly, finding it laborious and exhausting. Reading is such a chore to dyslexic children that they do not enjoy it, do not read for pleasure, and will avoid reading whenever possible. Such children have a lot of trouble learning foreign languages. Despite good fine motor skills and word processing abilities, they often have poor handwriting. Homework seems to take forever for dyslexics. Some students ask parents to read so they don't have to. Dyslexics' reading becomes more accurate with time and practice, but still remains labored and dysfluent. Dyslexic children often have family histories of problems with reading, spelling, and learning foreign languages. Dyslexia can cause low self-esteem. This is not always obvious, but can be detected by sensitive, skilled professionals.

Learning to spell

Children must understand the alphabetic principle—the concept that words are comprised of individual phonemes/speech sounds, and that the letters of our alphabet represent those sounds in writing/print—in order to learn how to spell. They must also develop a knowledge of specific letter-to-sound correspondences. As children gain more experience hearing, understanding, and using words, they start to observe patterns in the ways in which letters are combined. They also notice repeated series of letters that create syllables, common roots for many related words, prefixes, suffixes, word endings, and other word features. When children know these basic patterns and have also learned their language's basic spelling principles and rules, they can usually figure out how to spell new words they hear. Moreover, children can usually read words that they can spell. Therefore, children's development of good spelling skills promotes the development of good reading and writing skills as well.

Stages (Gentry, 1982) of children's spelling development

(1) Precommunicative stage: Children use alphabet letters, but may not know the whole alphabet, may not differentiate between upper case and lower case letters, or may not know that English is written from left to right. They do not demonstrate knowledge of letter-to-sound correspondences.

(2) Semiphonetic stage: Children begin to comprehend letter-to-sound correspondences. They frequently use simple logic to symbolize words with single letters. A good example is using "U" for "you" (early texting potential!).

(3) Phonetic stage: Children use letters to represent all speech sounds they hear in words. These representations may not always be correct, but are systematic and understandable (e.g., writing "kom" instead of "come").

Copyright © Mometrix Media. You have been licensed one copy of this document for personal use only. Any other reproduction or redistribution is strictly prohibited. All rights reserved.

(4) <u>Transitional stage:</u> Children begin the transition from phonetically spelling words according to their sounds to visually and structurally learning conventional word spellings. They still make errors as they assimilate this new knowledge (e.g., writing "highked" instead of "hiked").

(5) <u>Correct stage:</u> Children know fundamental English orthographic rules, including silent letters, irregular and alternative spellings, prefixes, suffixes, and other word features. They have learned many word spellings, and recognize misspellings. Their knowledge of exceptions to spelling rules and the generalizations they make about spelling are usually correct.

Invented spelling

When young children have not yet learned how to spell many (or any) words, they commonly "invent" spellings for spoken words they hear. They do this by identifying letters that correspond to the separate phonemes (speech sounds) they hear and arranging them in a sequence that matches the word's sounds. Linguistic researchers (e.g., Read, 1975) studying preschoolers have found that different children choose the same phonetic spellings. These children have developed phonemic and phonetic awareness, enabling them to invent spellings before they have actually learned to spell. This skill is a prerequisite to learning how to read, spell, and write. Researchers observe that neither adult influence nor chance could explain diverse children's high incidence of selecting the same phonetic spellings. Therefore, even at young ages, children can identify the phonetic properties of English words that are symbolized by their real spellings. Experts conclude from these observations that spelling is a developmental process rather than merely a word memorization process, and that it results in comprehension that goes beyond understanding simple sound-to-letter correspondences.

Writing skills development

(1) <u>Scribbling and drawing:</u> Young children grasp crayons/pencils with their fists, exploring form, space, and line. As their fine motor skills and cognitive understanding of symbolic representation develop concurrently, they progress to (2) <u>letter-like forms and shapes</u>. They comprehend that written symbols represent meanings. They start including shapes like circles and squares into their drawing and writing, but they are randomly located without much spatial orientation. Children in this stage commonly write figures and ask parents, "What does this say?" (3) <u>Letters:</u> Children can form letters, and start writing them randomly. They usually write consonants first. They do not initially possess a knowledge of symbol-to-sound correspondence; this develops gradually. Children tend to favor writing their own initials. (4) <u>Letters and spaces:</u> Children realize that printed/written words are separated by spaces, develop an understanding of the concept of a word, use 1:1 word correspondence, and write correctly spaced words. They write initial and final word sounds and vowels, correct the spelling of some high frequency words, and experiment with sentence construction and punctuation. (5) <u>Conventional writing and spelling:</u> Children write, spell, and punctuate correctly most of the time. They view various forms of purposeful writing as more important.

<u>Writing relative to purposes, audiences, and other aspects</u>
According to the National Institute for Literacy, writing is defined as "the ability to compose text effectively for various purposes and audiences." We use writing as a tool to help us collect detailed information, document it, and disseminate it to widespread audiences. We use writing to express our ideas, thoughts, and feelings, and to persuade our readers to believe or agree with what we write. Researchers have also found that the learning capacity of an individual increases when his or her writing skills improve. This aspect of writing skills mirrors that of reading skills in that the

Copyright © Mometrix Media. You have been licensed one copy of this document for personal use only. Any other reproduction or redistribution is strictly prohibited. All rights reserved.

development of both improves learning ability. Students need instruction to learn to write well. Reading skills have been found both to be reinforced by and to reinforce important writing skills like spelling and grammar. Thus, when teachers help children improve their writing, they are contributing to the improvement of their reading abilities as well.

POWER strategy

One popular model of the writing process proposed by experts, the POWER strategy, has five steps. In planning, student and teacher ask and select Yes/No on a checklist to decide whether the student selected a good topic, researched/read about the topic, considered what information readers would want to know, and wrote down all of his/her ideas.

In organization, the student and teacher ascertain if the student grouped similar ideas together, selected the best ideas for the composition, and arranged the ideas in a logical sequence.

In writing, the student and teacher decide whether the student wrote down his/her ideas in sentences. They also decide whether the student did his/her best to get help when it was required. To get the necessary information and assistance, the student may have consulted a text, asked a learning partner/classmate for assistance, and/or asked the teacher for help.

In editing, the student and teacher consider whether the student read his/her first draft to himself/herself, marked the parts s/he liked and those that might need changing, read the first draft to his/her partner/classmate, and listened to the other student's input.

In rewriting, the student and teacher look at whether the student made changes in his/her composition, edited it for correct mechanics, and wrote the final draft using his/her best handwriting.

Rating a child's early writing efforts to assess emerging writing skills

One easy rating scale (Clay, 1993) focuses on three areas: language level, message quality, and directional principles. Each category has six progressive levels.

For language level, the categories are (1) alphabetical (writes letters), (2) word (writes any recognizable word), (3) word group (writes any two-word phrase), (4) sentence (writes any simple sentence), (5) punctuated story (writes two or more related sentences), and (6) paragraphed story (includes two themes).

The levels for message quality are as follows: (1) Student has a concept of signs/symbols. (2) Student has a concept that a message is communicated. (3) Student copies a message. (4) Student repeats sentence patterns like "This is a..." (5) Student tries to record his/her own ideas in writing. (6) Student writes a successful composition.

The levels for directional principles are as follows: (1) Student does not demonstrate knowledge of directionality. (2) Student exhibits partial directional knowledge (e.g., left to right or start at the top left or return from top right down to the left). (3) Student reverses the direction. (4) Student follows the correct directional pattern. (5) Student uses correct directionality and spacing between words. (6) The student writes extensively without problems related to arranging and spacing text.

Copyright © Mometrix Media. You have been licensed one copy of this document for personal use only. Any other reproduction or redistribution is strictly prohibited. All rights reserved.

Standard conventions of written English

Written English should meet the standard conventions of correct spelling, capitalization, punctuation, grammar, and handwriting. Traditionally, teachers have paid more attention to a composition's appearance, length, word usage, and spelling than to how well-organized it is or how appropriate its content is. This habit can cause a superficial focus on imperfect form, while essentially ignoring the fact that the function is effective and meaningful. Other readers also form negative first impressions of writing when its appearance and/or format are less than acceptable, even if it otherwise effectively conveys its message. One type of common spelling error is vowel combination reversals (e.g., writing "siad" instead of "said," writing "freind" instead of "friend," etc.).

Capitalization errors include failing to capitalize words at the start of sentences, months of the year, and proper nouns/names. Another type of capitalization error is incorrectly capitalizing words/letters within words. Punctuation errors include omitting commas in dates, omitting commas before conjunctions in compound sentences, omitting/substituting semicolons in complex sentences, and adding extraneous punctuation marks. Grammatical errors include incorrect/conflicting verb tenses, subject-verb disagreement, missing articles, misplaced modifiers, and dangling participles. Handwriting errors/problems include illegible writing, poor alignment, and incorrect/poor spacing.

Motivating young children to write

Experts note that like adults, children prefer participating in activities they find exciting rather than ones they find unexciting/uninteresting. To motivate students to write, teachers can share personal journals and other samples of their own writing, post e-mailed/handwritten letters/notes in classrooms, display favorite magazines and books, and show children fun greeting cards/invitations. They should also invite children to bring writing samples from home. Teachers can create classroom "writing corners" that contain varied writing examples contributed by children and teachers. Diverse writing activities help children stay enthusiastic about writing. Children can take turns contributing a sentence for a daily class newsletter/journal/newspaper, and teachers can have students practice sounding out and spelling words as they dictate their sentences. Teachers can deliberately make some transcribing errors and have children correct them. Daily pages can be compiled into monthly class books. Connecting writing subjects to people/things that are familiar and exciting to children, and guiding students in how to write and ask classmates "interview" questions using modeling and other techniques both help motivate students. Encouraging/guiding children to evaluate and record their comments about authors, illustrators, and books can also be a motivational tool. Ultimately, children will learn to write their own critiques.

Copyright © Mometrix Media. You have been licensed one copy of this document for personal use only. Any other reproduction or redistribution is strictly prohibited. All rights reserved.

Mathematics

Problem solving skills

Being able to solve problems is fundamental to all other components of mathematics. Children learn the concept that a question can have more than one answer and a problem can have more than one solution by participating in problem solving activities. To solve problems, a child must be able to explore a problem, a situation, or a subject; think through the problem, situation, or subject; and use logical reasoning. These abilities are needed to not only solve routine/everyday problems, but also novel/unusual ones. Using problem solving skills not only helps children think mathematically, but also promotes their language development and their social skills when they work together. Children are naturally curious about how to solve everyday problems. Adults can take advantage of this inherent curiosity by discussing everyday challenges, asking children to propose ways to solve them, and asking them to explain how they arrived at their solutions. Adults can also invite children to propose problems and ask questions about them. This helps them learn to analyze different types of problems and realize that many problems have multiple possible solutions.

Steps preparing young children to learn

The process of solving problems often involves the following steps: understanding the problem; coming up with a plan to solve the problem; putting that plan into action; and, finally, observing the outcome and reflecting on whether the solution was effective, and whether the answer arrived at makes sense. Solving problems not only involves learning this series of steps, but also requires children to develop the qualities needed to solve problems. Children who are able to solve problems have a number of characteristics. For example, children who are effective problem solvers are able to focus their attention on the problem and its individual component parts. They can formulate hypotheses about the problem/situation, and then test them for veracity. They are willing to take risks within reason. They are persistent if they do not solve a problem right away, and do not give up if their first attempt at solving a problem is unsuccessful. They maintain flexibility, and experiment with alternate methods. They also demonstrate self-regulation skills.

Using problem solving skills in daily life

Young children continually explore their environments to unravel mysteries about how things work. For example, preschoolers use math concepts to understand that they have three toys, to comprehend that three fingers equals three toys, or to understand that two cookies plus one more equals three cookies. To do abstract mathematics in the future, young children will need two major skills that are also used to solve problems: being able to visualize a scenario, and being able to apply common sense thinking. Thinking and planning to achieve goals within the constraints of the properties of the surrounding environment is a natural behavior for young children. They will persist in their efforts to get an older sibling to stop another activity to play with them, to repair broken toys with tape or chewing gum, to manipulate a puzzle or plastic building blocks to get one uncooperative piece to fit, etc. The great 20th century mathematician and teacher George Polya stated that problem solving is "the most characteristically human activity." He pointed out that problem solving is a skill learned by doing, and that developing this skill requires a great deal of practice.

Games/activities

One method that has been found to enhance children's reasoning skills is using adult-child conversations to play mental mathematics games. For example, once children are able to count

Copyright © Mometrix Media. You have been licensed one copy of this document for personal use only. Any other reproduction or redistribution is strictly prohibited. All rights reserved.

beyond five, adults can give them basic oral story problems to solve (e.g., "If you have two plums and I give you two more, how many will you have?"). Using children's favorite foods in story problems, which takes advantage of their ready ability to envision these foods, is a good place to start. Thereafter, adults can add story problems involving pets, toys, cars, shopping, and other familiar objects/animals/activities. Experts advise adults not to restrict the types of problems presented to a child based solely on the child's grade level. Children can work with any situation if they can form mental imagery. Adults can sometimes insert harder tasks (e.g., problems involving larger numbers, problems involving division with remainders, or problems with negative number answers). Even toddlers can solve problems such as how to divide three cookies between two people. The division may not be fair, but it will likely be efficient. Adults should use the Socratic method, asking guiding questions to allow children to arrive at a solution to a problem themselves, rather than telling them a "right" answer.

Mental math games

Adults can use children's favorite foods and toys to pose story problems to children that involve addition and subtraction. For example, they can ask them questions like "If I give you [this many] more, how many will you have?" or "If we take away [this many], how many are left?" It is better to ask children questions than to give them answers. It is important to use turn taking. In this method, the adult poses a story problem to the child, and then the child gets to pose one to the adult. Adults must try to solve the problem, even if the child makes up numbers like "bazillion" or "eleventy." Games should be fun, not strictly factual like math tests. Adults can introduce age-appropriate story topics as children grow older. At the end of early childhood/around school age, children can handle the abstract algebraic concept of variables/unknown numbers (which some experts call "mystery numbers") and use this concept in games. Adults can pose riddles where "x" or "n" is the unknown number, and children must use an operation (e.g., $x + 4 = 7$) to solve the riddle.

Communicating with children to promote mathematical reasoning skills

Adults reciprocally talk to and listen to children during communication that is focused on using mathematical skills like problem solving, reasoning, making connections, etc. To promote young children's understanding, adults can express mathematical concepts using pictures, words, diagrams, and symbols. Encouraging children to talk with their peers and adults helps them clarify their own thoughts and think about what they are doing. Communicating with children about mathematical thinking problems also develops their vocabularies and promotes early literacy and reading skills. Adults should listen to what children want to say, and should have conversations with them. Communicating about math can also be accomplished through reading children's books that incorporate numbers and/or repetition or rhyme. In addition to talking, adults can communicate math concepts to children by drawing pictures or diagrams and using concrete objects (e.g., blocks, crayons, pieces of paper, fingers, etc.) to represent numbers and/or solve problems. Children also share their learning of math concepts through words, charts, drawings, tallies, etc. Even toddlers hold up fingers to tell others how old they are.

Reasoning skills appling early mathematical and scientific concepts

A major component of problem solving is reasoning. Children reason when they think through questions and find usable answers. They use reasoning skills to make sense of mathematical and scientific subject matter. Children use several abilities during the reasoning process. For example, they use logic to classify objects or concepts into groups. They follow logical sequences to arrive at conclusions that make sense. They use their analytical abilities to explain their own thought

- 120 -

Copyright © Mometrix Media. You have been licensed one copy of this document for personal use only. Any other reproduction or redistribution is strictly prohibited. All rights reserved.

processes. They apply what they have learned about relationships and patterns to help them find solutions to problems. They also use reasoning to justify their mental processes and problem solutions. To support children's reasoning, adults can ask children questions, give them time to think about their answers, and listen to their answers. This simple tactic helps children learn how to reason. Adults can also ask children why something is as it is—letting them think for themselves rather than looking for a particular answer—and listen to the ideas they produce.

Making connections in children's early mathematical development

Children informally learn intuitive mathematical thinking through their everyday life experiences. They naturally apply mathematical concepts and reasoning to solve problems they face in their environment. However, one frequent problem among children when they begin formal education is that they can come to see academic mathematics as a collection of procedures and rules, instead of viewing it as a means of finding solutions to everyday, real-life problems. This view will interfere with children's ability to apply the formal mathematics they learn to their lives in a practical and useful way. Teachers can help prevent this outcome by establishing the connection between children's natural intuitive math and formal mathematics. They can do this by teaching math through the use of manipulative materials familiar to children. They can use mathematics vocabulary words when describing children's activities, which enables children to develop an awareness of the natural mathematical operations they use in their daily lives. When a teacher introduces a new mathematical concept to children, s/he can give illustrative examples that draw upon the children's actual life experiences.

Mathematics and everyday life and other academic subjects

We use math throughout our lives during everyday activities. There are countless examples and combinations of various mathematical concepts in the real world. Additionally, math concepts inform other academic content areas, including music, art, and the sciences. Therefore, it is important for children not to view math as an isolated set of procedures and skills. Children comprehend math more easily when they can make connections, which involve applying common mathematical rules to multiple, varied functions, processes, and real-life activities. For example, adults can ask children to consider problems they encounter daily and solve them. When a parent asks a child to help put away groceries, the child practices sorting categories of foods and packages, and they experiment with comparative package sizes and shapes. Parents need not be concerned with what specific mathematical processes are involved, but should simply look for examples of math in everyday life and expose children to these examples on a regular basis. For example, pouring liquid into containers of various sizes and speculating which one will hold the most is an easy, fun activity that incorporates a number of skills and concepts, including estimation, measurement, spatial sense, and conservation of liquid volume.

Integrating math into everyday activities

Integrating math into the context of everyday activities has been the philosophy of early childhood math education until recently. For example, when teachers have children line up, they ask them who is first, second, third, etc. to practice counting. When children play with blocks, teachers ask them to identify their shapes and whether one block is larger/smaller than another. During snack times, teachers help children learn 1:1 correspondence by having them place one snack on each plate. These activities are quite valuable. However, some educators maintain that they are insufficient when used on their own, because in larger classes it is not always possible to take advantage of "teachable moments" with every child. Therefore, this educational approach cannot be applied systematically. These educators recommend that in addition to integration strategies, EC

Copyright © Mometrix Media. You have been licensed one copy of this document for personal use only. Any other reproduction or redistribution is strictly prohibited. All rights reserved.

teachers should use a curriculum. The HighScope curriculum, the Creative Curriculum, and Big Math for Little Kids are just a few examples. Many teachers combine several curricula, selecting parts of different programs. Using a curriculum allows teachers to use a more planned approach to integrate math into all activities.

Representation skills

Young children develop an understanding of symbolic representation—the idea that objects, written letters, words, and other symbols are used to represent other objects or concepts—at an early age. This is evident in their make-believe/pretend play, and in their ability to learn written language and connect it to spoken language. As children develop early math skills, representing their ideas and information they acquire helps them organize, document, and share these ideas and facts with others. Children may count on their fingers; create tallies using check marks/tick marks and/or words; draw pictures or maps; and, as they grow older, make graphs. Teachers must help children apply mathematical process skills as they use learning center materials. For example, when a child enjoys sorting rocks by color, the teacher can state that the child is classifying them, bridging informal math activities with math vocabulary. Asking the child how s/he is categorizing the rocks emphasizes math vocabulary. Asking the child after s/he finishes what other ways s/he could classify the rocks encourages problem solving.

Patterns and relationships

Patterns are generally defined as things that recur or are repeated regularly. Patterns can be found in images, sounds, numbers, events, actions, movements, etc. Relationships are generally defined as connections or associations between things that are identified and/or described using logic or reasoning. Being aware of patterns and relationships among aspects of the environment helps us comprehend the fundamental structure of these aspects. This awareness enables us to predict what will occur next in a series of events, even before it actually happens. This gives us more confidence in our environment and in our ability to interact with it. We find patterns and relationships in such areas of life as art, music, and clothing. Math-specific activities like counting numbers and working with geometrical shapes, lines, arcs, and curves also involve patterns and relationships. When children understand patterns and relationships, they can understand repetition; rhythm; categorization; and how to order things from smallest to biggest, from shortest to longest, etc.

Adults can help young children develop their understanding of patterns and relationships in life by looking at pictures and designs with them, encouraging and guiding them to identify patterns within drawings, paintings, and abstract designs such as prints on fabrics and other decorative designs. When children participate in movement activities, including dancing to music, running, skipping, hopping, playing simple musical instruments, etc., adults can help them identify patterns in their own and others' movements. Adults can encourage young children to participate in hands-on activities, such as stringing wood, plastic beads, or penne and other hollow dry pasta tubes onto pieces of string to make necklaces with simple patterns (e.g., blue-yellow-blue-yellow). As children grow older, adults can encourage them to create more complicated patterns. They can alternate a larger number of colors, and they can vary the numbers of each color in more complex ways (e.g., three blue, two yellow, one red, etc.).

Number sense and number operations

Counting is one of the earliest numeracy skills that young children develop. Even before they have learned the names of all the numbers, young children learn to count to three, then to five, etc.

Copyright © Mometrix Media. You have been licensed one copy of this document for personal use only. Any other reproduction or redistribution is strictly prohibited. All rights reserved.

However, number sense involves a great deal more than just counting. Number sense includes understanding the various applications of numbers. For instance, we use numbers as tools for conveying and manipulating information, as tools for describing quantities, and as tools for characterizing relationships between or among things. Children who have developed number sense are able to count with accuracy and competence. Given a specific number, they can count upwards from that number. They can also count backwards. They are able to break down a number and then reassemble it. They are able to recognize relationships between or among different numbers. When children can count, are familiar with numbers, and have good number sense, they can also add and subtract numbers. Being familiar with numbers and being able to count easily helps young children understand all other areas of mathematics.

Developing number sense and numeracy skills
As children complete their daily activities, it is beneficial for adults to count real things with children and encourage them to count as well. This helps children understand numbers by using their own experiences with objects in the environment, and gives them practice counting and using numbers. To help children understand that we use numbers to describe quantities and relationships, adults can ask children to sort objects by size, shape, or color similarity. They can also ask children to sort objects according to their differences (e.g., which object is bigger/smaller). Adults can also discuss with children how numbers are used to find street addresses and apartment numbers, and to keep score during games. To help children count upwards and downwards with efficiency and accuracy, adults can point out that counting allows us to determine how many items are in a group. Adults should point to each object as they count it. They can count on their fingers and encourage young children to do the same. Adults should also help children count without repeating or skipping any numbers.

Spatial sense and geometry

Spatial sense is an individual's awareness of one's own body in space and in relation to the objects and other people around the individual. Spatial sense allows young children to navigate environmental spaces without colliding with objects and other people; to see and hear adequately, and to be aware of whether others can see and hear them; and to develop and observe a socially and culturally appropriate sense of their own and others' personal space. Geometry is the area of mathematics involving space, sizes, shapes, positions, movements, and directions. Geometry gives descriptions and classifications of our physical environment. By observing commonplace objects and spaces in their physical world, young children can learn about solid objects and substances, shapes, and angles. Adults can help young children learn geometry by identifying various shapes, angles, and three-dimensional figures for them; asking them to name these shapes, angles, and figures when they encounter them in the future; and asking them to describe different shapes, draw them in the air with their fingers, trace drawings of the shapes with their fingers, and then draw the shapes themselves.

Because it involves many physical properties like shape, line, and angle, as well as abstract concepts, young children learn geometry most effectively via hands-on activities. Learning experiences that allow them to touch and manipulate concrete objects, such as boxes, containers, puzzles, blocks, and shape sorters, usually work best. Everyday activities can also help children learn geometry concepts. For example, adults can cut children's sandwiches into various geometrical shapes and let children fit them together and/or rearrange them into new patterns. Children become better able to follow directions and navigate through space when they develop geometric knowledge and spatial sense. Adults can provide activities that promote the development of geometric knowledge and spatial sense. For example, they can let children get into and out of big

Copyright © Mometrix Media. You have been licensed one copy of this document for personal use only. Any other reproduction or redistribution is strictly prohibited. All rights reserved.

appliance boxes; climb over furniture; and go into, on top of, out of, under, around, over, and through different objects and structures to allow children to experience the relationship between their bodies and space and solids. As they mature, children can play games in which they search for "hidden" shapes. Such shapes may be irregular, may lack flat bases, or may be turned in various directions.

Measurement

Measurement is the process of determining how long, wide, and tall something is physically and how much it weighs by using measuring units such as inches, feet, yards, square feet, ounces, and pounds. Measurement is also used to quantify time using units like seconds, minutes, hours, days, weeks, months, years, centuries, millennia, etc. Measurement is not just a formal means of quantifying size, area, and time. It is also an important method for young children to seek and identify relationships between and among things they encounter outside of school in everyday life. When young children practice measuring things, they are able to understand not only the sizes of objects and beings, but also their comparative sizes (i.e., how large or small something is compared to another object used as a reference). Furthermore, they are able to figure out how big or little something is on their own.

While it is obviously important for children to eventually learn standardized measurement units like inches, feet, yards, etc., adults can facilitate early development of measurement skills by letting children choose their own measurement units. For example, they might use their favorite toy to describe a playmate or sibling as "three teddy bears tall"; or they might describe a room as "seven toy cars long." Similarly, when children are too young to know formal time measurements like minutes and hours, adults can support children's ability to quantify time using favorite TV shows. For example, four-year-olds can often relate to the idea of one episode of a show (whether it is 30 minutes or 60 minutes long) as a time measurement. Adults can apply this with statements like, "Daddy will be home in one episode." Numerous everyday activities, including grocery shopping, cooking, sewing, gardening, woodworking, and many others, involve measurement. Adults can ask children to help with these tasks, and then discuss measuring with children as they participate.

Measurement of time

Younger children typically do not have an understanding of the abstract concept of time. However, adults can still help children understand that time elapses, and that we count/measure this process. For example, adults can ask younger children simple questions, such as "Who can stand on one foot longer?" This comparison strategy helps children figure out which of two or more actions/activities takes a longer/the longest period of time. Even when children do not yet understand what "five minutes" means, adults should still make such references (e.g., "You can play for five minutes longer, and then we must leave."). Repeating such references will eventually help children understand that time passes. Adults can time various everyday activities/events and tell children how long they took. They can also count the second hand's ticks on a watch/clock (e.g., "one second...two seconds...three seconds..."). This familiarizes children with counting, and with using counting to track the passage of time. Until children are old enough to understand abstractions like today/yesterday/tomorrow, adults can use concrete references like "after lunch" or "before bedtime."

Copyright © Mometrix Media. You have been licensed one copy of this document for personal use only. Any other reproduction or redistribution is strictly prohibited. All rights reserved.

Fractions

Fractions are parts or pieces of a whole. While adults understand this and do not remember ever not understanding it, very young children think differently in this regard. As Piaget showed, children in the preoperational stage of cognitive development cannot perform logical or mathematical mental operations. They focus on one property of an object rather than all of its properties, a practice he called centration. Hence, if you cut an apple into pieces, very young children see that there are more pieces than there were before, and they believe that several apple pieces are more than one apple. They cannot yet comprehend the logical sequence of dividing an apple into fractions. To comprehend fractions, children must know what a whole unit consists of, how many pieces the unit is divided into, and whether the pieces are of equal size. Adults can help children understand fractions through informal sharing activities, such as slicing up a pizza or a pan of brownies, and/or equally dividing household/preschool chores and play materials.

> ➢ **Review Video: Fractions**
> *Visit **mometrix.com/academy** and enter **Code: 262335**

Estimation

Estimation is making an educated or informed guess about a measurement when no actual measurement is available. As adults, we often make estimates about the sizes of objects when we do not know their exact measurements, about the amounts of substances we have not actually measured, and about the numbers of small objects in large collections when we have not actually counted the objects. However, young children are in the process of learning the concepts of sizes and numbers. Children must comprehend concepts of comparison and relativity (e.g., larger, smaller, more, less, etc.) before they will be able to make accurate estimates. When children start to develop the ability to estimate amounts or sizes, this process helps them learn related math vocabulary words, such as "about" or "around," and "more than" and "less than" [something else]. Through estimating, they also learn how to make appropriate predictions and arrive at realistic answers. It is important for young children to learn how to make estimates, to recognize when it is appropriate to apply the estimation method, and to recognize when their estimates are reasonable.

To accustom young children to the idea of estimating, adults should regularly use words related to estimation in their conversations with children (e.g., "around," "about," "approximately," "near," "more than [some other amount or number]," "less than [some other amount or number]," "between [two numbers or amounts]," etc.). During everyday activities like shopping or eating, adults can ask children to estimate amounts of foods, numbers of items, or lengths of time. Later, adults can help children compare the actual outcome with their original estimate. This process helps children learn to make realistic/reasonable estimates. Activities promoting estimation skills can be very simple. Adults can ask children, for example, to guess which of their friends is tallest, and then test the accuracy of the guess using real measurements. When children grow older, adults can write down estimates and real measurements, and can then repeat the exercise described above or present a similar one. With repetition, children will eventually begin making more accurate estimates. The goal is not for children to come up with exact measurements, but ones that are close to actual amounts/numbers. Giving children opportunities to practice improves their estimating skills.

Copyright © Mometrix Media. You have been licensed one copy of this document for personal use only. Any other reproduction or redistribution is strictly prohibited. All rights reserved.

Probabilities and statistics

In general, when people work with statistics, they present them in graphs or charts to organize them, interpret them, and make it easier to see relationships among individual statistics. Graphs are a visual alternative that depict mathematical information and show relationships among individual statistics, especially changes over time. Graphs also allow for the comparison of different groups. Probabilities indicate the likelihood that something will happen. Adults use probabilities to predict things, such as people's risks of developing or dying from various diseases or medical conditions; the chances of accidents; children's risks of experiencing academic difficulties, dropping out, or developing emotional and behavioral disorders; and the chances that a certain area will receive rain or snow. Scientists use probabilities to predict the likelihood of various behaviors or outcomes they are studying. They use statistics to show the numbers and proportions of responses or results obtained in research studies. Calendars are one type of chart. Adults can help children use them to organize daily and weekly activities, and to understand how we organize information.

Charts and graphs

According to experts, almost every daily activity can be charted in some way. For example, adults can help children peel the little stickers off of plums, bananas, etc. and stick them to a piece of paper/poster board divided into columns. After a week, they can count each column to determine how many pieces of each kind of fruit they ate. Similarly, adults can show children how to use removable stickers or color forms to document the number of times they performed any daily activity. For example, children could place a color form near the telephone every time it rings and/or every time somebody picks it up to make a call. They could also place a color form near the front door every time somebody comes in, goes out, and/or rings the doorbell/knocks. This enables children to count the number of times given events occur by recording them. Some children are better able to understand math by viewing and making graphs. This is because creating graphs involves representing quantities visually instead of just listing numbers.

Mathematical milestones

Counting is considered a math skill milestone for young children. Typical four-year-olds enjoy counting aloud. Experts identify three levels of counting. The first is counting from 1 to 12, which requires memorization. The second level is counting from 13 to 19, which requires not only memorization, but also an understanding of the more unusual rules for "teen" numbers. The third level is counting from 20 on. This process is very consistent, and the numbers are ordered according to regular rules. Experts in math education believe that at this level of counting, children are discovering a regular mathematical pattern for the first time, which is base ten (i.e. 20, 30, 40, 50, etc. are 2 tens, 3 tens, 4 tens, 5 tens, etc., and after the base a number between 1 and 9 is added). Researchers and educators in early childhood mathematics programs recommend encouraging children as young as four years old to learn to count up to 100. They find that doing this helps young children learn about and explore patterns in depth.

Clinical interview

Clinical interviews have long been used by individual and family therapists, as well as by researchers. Piaget used them along with observations and case histories to understand young children's thinking as he formulated his cognitive developmental theory. Interviewers ask structured/semi-structured/open-ended questions and listen to the responses, often recording them for accuracy. This method gives the interviewer a way to find out what the respondent is

Copyright © Mometrix Media. You have been licensed one copy of this document for personal use only. Any other reproduction or redistribution is strictly prohibited. All rights reserved.

thinking and feeling inside, which cannot be determined by observing outward behaviors alone. In educational settings, a teacher might ask a child questions like, "How did you do this?" "What is happening now?" "Can you tell me more about this?" "Why are you doing this?" "What are you thinking about now?" etc. Flexible questioning helps uncover the child's thought process, which is what is leading him/her to engage in specific behaviors. Just observing the behaviors alone does not allow the child to express his/her knowledge. While fully interviewing each child in a classroom is not practical, teachers can adapt this method by asking clinical interview-type questions as part of their instruction.

Teachers can gain a lot of information and insight about how children are learning math concepts by observing their behaviors. For children to actually express their knowledge and thinking processes, however, teachers must ask them questions. For example, when a teacher introduces new shapes to young children, s/he can ask them the shapes' names, how they differ from one another, and why they think the shapes differ. Teachers can then use children's various responses to elicit further responses from them. This technique requires children to use language in significant ways during math activities. Therefore, these activities not only teach math skills, but also promote literacy development. Asking clinical interview-type questions promotes children's development of math communication skills, one of the essential components of math education. Additionally, being able to put one's knowledge and thoughts into words is a skill that is very important in all areas of education, not just math education. Using clinical interview-type questions helps children learn to use language to explain their thinking, share ideas, and express themselves, promoting and strengthening children's awareness of the functions of mathematical language.

Young children's thinking and learning

Young children think in concrete ways and cannot understand abstract concepts, so effective EC math curricula typically use many concrete objects that children can see, feel, and manipulate to help them understand math concepts. Young children also naturally learn through exploring their environments, so good EC math curricula have many exploration and discovery activities that allow and encourage hands-on learning. In everyday life, young children start to observe relationships as they explore their surroundings. They match like objects, sort unlike objects, categorize objects, and arrange objects in simple patterns based on shared or contrasting properties. They start to understand words and phrases like "a little," "a lot," "more," "less," and "the same [as...]." Preschoolers use available materials such as sticks, pieces of string, their feet, their hands, their fingers, etc. as tools to measure objects. They also use rulers, measuring cups, and other conventional tools. They use their measurements to develop descriptions, sequences, and arrangements, and to compare various objects.

Spatial awareness

When preschool children build structures with blocks and put together pieces of puzzles during play, they are not only having fun, but are also developing spatial awareness. The relationships of objects to each other and within space are important concepts for children to learn, and serve as a foundation for the principles of geometry and physics that children will learn later. When they are moving around, preschoolers begin to notice how other people and objects are positioned in space, and how their own bodies move through space in relationship to objects and other people.

This type of spatial awareness supports children's developing gross motor skills, coordination, and social skills. Young children can and should learn a number of math concepts and skills, such as the ones recommended by preschool math curricula like the HighScope program's "Numbers Plus"

Copyright © Mometrix Media. You have been licensed one copy of this document for personal use only. Any other reproduction or redistribution is strictly prohibited. All rights reserved.

preschool mathematics curriculum. These concepts and skills include number symbols and names, counting, shapes, spatial awareness, relationships of parts to the whole, measurement, units, patterns, and analyzing data.

Rational numbers and irrational numbers

In mathematics, rational numbers are numbers that can be written as ratios or fractions. In other words, a rational number can be expressed as a fraction that has a whole number as the numerator (the number on top) and the denominator (the number on the bottom). Therefore, all whole numbers are automatically rational numbers, because all whole numbers can be written as fractions with a denominator of 1 (e.g., 5 = 5/1, 68 = 68/1, 237 = 237/1, etc.). Even very large, unwieldy fractions (e.g., 9,731,245/42,754,021) are rational numbers, because they can be written as fractions.

> ➤ **Review Video: Rational Numbers**
> *Visit **mometrix.com/academy** and enter **Code: 280645***

Irrational numbers can be written as decimal numbers, but not as fractions, because the numbers to the right of the decimal point that are less than 1 continue indefinitely without repeating. For example, the value of pi (π) begins as 3.141592…, and continues without end. The square root of 2 ($\sqrt{2}$) = 1.414213…. There are an infinite number of irrational numbers between 0 and 1. However, irrational numbers are not used as commonly in everyday life as rational numbers.

> ➤ **Review Video: Irrational Numbers**
> *Visit **mometrix.com/academy** and enter **Code: 433866***

Cardinal, ordinal, nominal, and real numbers

Cardinal numbers are numbers that indicate quantity. For example, when we say "seven buttons" or "three kittens," we are using cardinal numbers. Ordinal numbers are numbers that indicate the order of items within a group or a set. For example, when we say "first, second, third, fourth, fifth, etc.," we are using ordinal numbers. Nominal numbers are numbers that name things. For example, we use area code numbers along with telephone numbers to identify geographical calling areas, and we use zip code numbers to identify geographical mailing areas. Nominal numbers, therefore, identify categories or serve as labels for things. However, they are not related to the actual mathematical values of numbers, and do not indicate numerical quantities or operations. Real numbers include all rational and irrational numbers. Rational numbers can always be written as fractions that have both numerators and denominators that are whole numbers. Irrational numbers cannot, as they contain non-repeating decimal digits. Real numbers may or may not be cardinal numbers.

Button board

By gluing buttons of various sizes and colors to a piece of cardboard, teachers can initiate a number of activities that help preschoolers learn math concepts while having fun. Preschoolers are commonly learning shapes and how to draw them. Teachers can give children lengths of string/twine/yarn or long shoelaces and show them how to wrap them around different buttons to form shapes like rectangles, triangles, and squares. To practice counting and 1:1 correspondence, teachers can ask children to wrap their string around a given number of buttons. Preschoolers need to learn the concept that spoken number words like "five" can equate to a group of five concrete

Copyright © Mometrix Media. You have been licensed one copy of this document for personal use only. Any other reproduction or redistribution is strictly prohibited. All rights reserved.

objects (such as buttons), and this activity promotes that learning. The button board is also useful for giving preschool children practice with sorting or classifying objects into groups based on a common characteristic. For example, the teacher can ask children to wrap their pieces of string around all the big buttons, all the little buttons, only the red buttons, only the blue buttons, etc.

Making mathematics fun

Teachers can encourage preschool children's counting and number development by creating a grid on the floor with the numbers 1 to 10 using masking tape, construction paper, and markers. Teachers could also draw the grid outdoors by drawing on pavement with chalk. The teacher arranges the numbers in ascending order within the grid of 10 squares/rectangles. S/he asks the children if they can name these numbers. The teacher provides beanbags. Each child gets a chance to throw a beanbag into any one of the numbered squares. Children can see how far they can throw and/or practice their aim. Each child names the number inside the square/rectangle where his/her beanbag lands. The children then play a version of hopscotch by hopping from numbered square to square, collecting their beanbags, and then hopping back. If desired, the teacher can write the number each child's beanbag lands on onto a "scoreboard" graph. Children will observe his/her writing the same numbers found on the floor/ground onto a "scoreboard." Teachers can review learning after the game to assess whether children can count using number words, name selected numbers, and throw accurately with consistency.

Reusing sectioned plastic trays from the grocery store

A teacher can wash and reuse the compartmentalized plastic trays from the grocery store that are used for vegetable and fruit to create a preschool counting activity. The teacher supplies beads, pennies, erasers, or other small objects, as well as about a dozen sticky notes. S/he writes a number on each note. For older preschoolers, the teacher can write the numeral and the word (e.g., "7" and "seven"). For younger children, the teacher can write the numeric symbol ("7," for example) plus seven dots or other marks as a clue to that number symbol. The teacher puts one numbered note in each compartment and the supply of small objects in the central dip compartment. Then, s/he guides each child to transfer the correct number of each small object to the correct compartment. The child should count aloud while transferring each small object, and should repeat this process until all compartments with a numbered sticky note have the correct number of objects. Children can then repeat the process to practice and perfect their counting, or the teacher can place notes with different numbers in the tray's compartments.

Game that teachers can create for the practicing of practice number recognition

Teachers can help preschoolers practice identifying numbers and counting by creating a fun "fishing for numbers" game. Teachers cut 10 fish shapes that are about 6 inches long from pieces of construction paper that are different colors. Teachers then write a single number between 1 and 10 on each "fish." Near each fish "mouth," the teacher punches a hole and inserts a paper clip through it. The teacher makes "fishing rods" by tying strings to dowels and gluing a magnet to each string. After spreading out the fish so the children can easily see the numbers, the teacher assigns each child a number and they "fish" for it, picking up the fish by bringing the magnet close to the paper clip. The children then "reel in" their catches. This gives children practice correctly identifying number names. The game can be adapted for more advanced math concepts as well. For example, the teacher can cut out fish shapes of various sizes and have children "fish" for larger/smaller fish. The activity can also be adapted to promote literacy development. The teacher can write letters instead of numbers on the fish to give students practice with alphabet recognition, or s/he can write a Dolch word/sight word on each fish to give students practice recognizing and identifying important vocabulary words.

Copyright © Mometrix Media. You have been licensed one copy of this document for personal use only. Any other reproduction or redistribution is strictly prohibited. All rights reserved.

Creating collages

Fundamental math skills that prepare preschoolers for kindergarten include shape recognition. To introduce children to an activity they will view as fun rather than as work, teachers can show children how to make a collage of a familiar figure. This will also give children the opportunity to experiment with an artistic process. For example, they can create a Santa Claus or an Easter Bunny as a holiday art project. They can make collages of other imaginary/real people for various events/seasons/topics. Teachers cut out paper templates, including circles for heads, triangles for hats, squares for bodies, and narrow rectangular strips for limbs. First, they help children name each shape. They have each child trace the template shapes onto paper and cut them out with child-safe scissors. The teacher then instructs children to arrange their cutout shapes on a piece of cardboard/construction paper. Once they are in the correct positions, the children glue the shapes in place. Teachers can subsequently teach additional shapes (octagons, ovals, etc.), challenging children to make new, different collages.

Red Rover game

Red Rover is a good game for groups of children who are attending parties or playing outdoors at parks/playgrounds. Two teams take turns calling and roving. The child called runs to the other team and tries to fit into its line. If successful, s/he gets to call another player to bring back to his/her home team. If not, s/he joins the opposite team. The game continues until one team has no more members. Teachers can adapt this game to teach shape recognition by cutting out various shapes from construction paper of different colors and pinning a shape to each child's shirt. In large groups, more than one child can have the same shape or color. Instead of children's names, the teacher instructs players to use shapes and colors when calling (e.g., "Red Rover, Red Rover, blue circles come over!"). This supports the development of shape and color recognition skills. Teachers can vary action verbs (e.g., "....hop over/jump over/skip over") to support vocabulary development and comprehensive skills. When children perform such movements, they are also practicing and developing gross motor skills.

Cookie baking activity

Young children are typically curious about adult activities like baking. They usually want to know more about the process, and often ask many questions. They also love to be included and to participate, frequently offering/asking to help. Letting them help builds their self-esteem and self-efficacy (i.e. their confidence in their competence to accomplish a task). Adults can allow children to help while also providing instruction and practice with shape recognition, measurement, sorting, and categorization. The adult prepares a favorite cookie recipe. Some children can help measure ingredients, which helps develop the math skill of measurement. With the dough rolled out, children use cookie cutters of various shapes. Recognizing, naming, and selecting the shapes promote the development of shape recognition skills. Adults "shuffle"/mix the baked cookie shapes and have children separate cookies with like shapes into groups, which promotes sorting skills. Having children identify similar/different shapes, sizes, and colors promotes categorization skills. Arranging cookie shapes into patterns for children to identify promotes pattern recognition skills, which are necessary to the development of math skills and many other skills. Giving each child a cookie to eat afterward is naturally reinforcing.

Pasta necklace making as a learning activity

Stringing beads/noodles is an activity that helps young children develop hand-eye coordination, which they will need for writing and other everyday activities that require fine motor coordination. Noodles are typically the perfect size for young children's hands. They are inexpensive, usually costing less than comparably-sized beads. Moreover, pasta is non-toxic, an advantage when

Copyright © Mometrix Media. You have been licensed one copy of this document for personal use only. Any other reproduction or redistribution is strictly prohibited. All rights reserved.

working with little persons who put things in their mouths. Hollow, tubular noodles like penne, ziti, wagon wheels, etc. are ideal. Fishing line/craft beading string/other stiff string is best; soft, limp string/yarn is harder for young children to manipulate. Using multicolored vegetable pasta removes the need to use markers or dye to add color. If using white pasta, children can color the noodles with markers, but adults should keep in mind that the ink can bleed onto skin/clothes even when it is dry. Adults should cut pieces of string that are long enough to allow children to easily slip the necklaces on and off after they are tied. Adults should also use a knot to secure a noodle to one end of the string. By providing more than one noodle shape, adults can invite children to string the noodles to create patterns, which develops pattern recognition and pattern creation abilities. These abilities also inform repetition, rhythm, categorization, and sequencing skills, which are important in math, music, art, literature, clothing design, etc.

<u>Learning game that involves writing numbers, identifying numbers, and running</u>
A game for young children that some educators call "Number Dash" (Miller, ed. Charner, 2009) builds foundational math concepts and skills, while providing physical activity. It can involve small or large groups (the referenced authors say "the more the merrier"). Help children write large numbers on a paved area with sidewalk chalk. Make sure numbers are spread far enough apart so children will not collide while running. There should be one of each number for each child (e.g., six "1s," "2s" "3s," etc. if there are six children). Use chalk colors that contrast with the pavement color to ensure the numbers will be highly visible. Tell children to run ("dash") to whichever number you call out and stand on it until you call another number. Call out numbers randomly. Encourage children who have located the number to help their classmates/playmates. This game develops gross motor skills, number writing skills, and number recognition skills. It also provides experience with playing organized games, following rules, following directions, and cooperating with and helping others. This game can also be played with letters, colors, and/or shapes.

Knowing number names and understanding 1:1 correspondence

Young children learn to name numbers in a way that is similar to how they learn to recite alphabet letters. However, learning to associate number symbols with concrete objects in the real world environment is a major advance in their cognitive development. The concept of 1:1 correspondence entails matching number symbols to the quantities they represent, an essential early math skill. Teachers can support the development of this math skill with a simple "grab bag" game youngsters enjoy. The teacher writes a number from 1 to 10 on each of ten cards, folding each card in half and putting them into a paper lunch bag. The teacher provides each child with a handful of pennies/play coins/buttons/little blocks to use as counting tokens. Each child takes a turn closing his/her eyes and pulling a card out of the bag. The child reads the number on the card, counts out the corresponding number of pennies/tokens, and puts them with the card. As children learn, teachers can place additional and/or different numbers (e.g., 11 to 20) in the grab bag. To promote the development of early literacy skills, teachers can also include the name of the number on each card.

Early math skills and sequencing/ practice fine motor skills

In hot weather, making ice cube necklaces is a fun activity that helps young children cool off while learning to sequence objects. The activity also helps children develop their manual motor skills and learn about liquid and solid states of matter. Regular ice cube trays are fine; those with "fun-shaped" compartments are even better. The teacher cuts plastic drinking straws so that they will fit into each ice cube compartment. The children participate, watching and/or helping pour water into trays and adding various food colorings/fruit juices. The teacher places one straw clipping into each

Copyright © Mometrix Media. You have been licensed one copy of this document for personal use only. Any other reproduction or redistribution is strictly prohibited. All rights reserved.

compartment. While putting the trays into the freezer, the teacher tells children that 32° Fahrenheit/0° Celsius is the temperature at which water freezes.

Children practice making scientific observations by noting how long the water takes to freeze. They empty the cubes into a big bowl. The children put on bathing suits or other clothing that can get wet, and the class goes outdoors. The teacher provides strings that are knotted at one end, and calls out a color pattern (e.g., one blue cube, then a yellow cube, etc.). Children follow the teacher's instructions to create color-patterned necklaces they can tie, wear, and watch melt.

Identifying shapes

The three levels of perceiving shapes that children typically move through sequentially are seeing, naming, and analyzing. Very young children recognize simple shapes like circles, squares, and triangles. As their cognitive and language skills develop, they learn the names for these shapes, and use these names to identify single shapes. The third level is analyzing each shape to understand its properties. Whereas identifying shapes visually is intuitive and based on association, analyzing their properties is more abstract, since a shape can have a number of different appearances. For example, three-year-olds can differentiate a triangle from other shapes. However, if you show them a very tall, skinny/short, wide/lopsided/crooked triangle, they will have trouble identifying it as a triangle. At the analysis level, children realize that a triangle has three sides, which are not necessarily equal in length. An activity that young children enjoy is closing their eyes, reaching into a bag of assorted shapes, finding a triangle by touch, and explaining why it is a triangle. This involves both the second and third levels of naming and analysis.

A significant mark of progress in early math skills development is the ability to not only identify various shapes, but also to draw them. Once young children develop this ability, they typically want to practice it all the time. Teachers can encourage this by helping children make pattern resist paintings. The teacher tapes white paper to children's tables/trays, gives them crayons, and invites them to fill the paper with drawings of different shapes of various sizes and colors. Teachers can introduce young children to new shapes (e.g., ovals, stars, crescent moons, etc.) by drawing them on separate pieces of paper for children to look at and copy. Then, the teacher replaces the crayons with water, watercolor paints, and brushes; shows the children how to dip brushes into paint and water to dilute the colors; and allows them to paint over their crayoned shapes, covering all the white paper with color. The children see the shapes show through the paint, creating the pattern resist. Dipping brushes and diluting various colors also develop children's color recognition skills and their hand-eye coordination.

Counting

A common practice among preschool children is counting on their fingers. Young children learn concretely before they develop abstract thought, so they must have concrete objects to work with to understand abstract mathematical concepts. They use their fingers to count because fingers are concrete. A simple activity that allows children to continue finger counting while removing additional visual support is "blind finger counting." Using eyesight to count objects we can see is relatively easy.

However, when children cannot see objects, they must learn to count mentally instead. This allows them to take another step in their progress from concrete to abstract thinking. To count mentally without visual reinforcement takes practice. Teachers can tape a shoebox lid to the box and cut a small hole in it. Children can fit a hand through the hole, but cannot see inside. Children close their

- 132 -

Copyright © Mometrix Media. You have been licensed one copy of this document for personal use only. Any other reproduction or redistribution is strictly prohibited. All rights reserved.

eyes; the teacher drops several small objects into the box; and each child reaches in, counting the objects using only touch. Varying objects and quantities maintains the fun of this activity.

Sorting and categorization

One of the major learning accomplishments of young children is being able to identify similarities and differences among objects. Developing this ability enables children to sort like objects into groups, and to place objects into categories based on their differences. When preschoolers compare and contrast objects, they demonstrate an important early step in the development of critical thinking, analytical, and problem solving skills. For an easy, entertaining guessing game, adults can select assorted household items familiar to children and put them into a bag/pillowcase. They then give children various clues (e.g., "I stir lemonade with this...," "It's made of wood," "We keep it in the kitchen drawer...," etc.) and ask them to guess which items are in the bag. It is important to give young children one to two minutes to consider each clue before they make a guess. Adults repeat clues when children guess incorrectly. If children guess correctly, they are allowed to look inside the bag. Youngsters greatly enjoy seeing that the object they guessed is actually inside the bag. Adults can gradually make the game more challenging by beginning with very common objects, and then eventually progressing to more unusual ones.

According to the U.S. Department of Agriculture, preschoolers need three 1/2-cup servings of fruit and three 1/2-cup servings of vegetables daily. However, many young children are picky/resistant. Adults can motivate them to eat produce with a "food rainbow" project. Adults show children a picture of a rainbow, and discuss its colors and their sequence (teaching some earth science, optics, and color theory!). A fun art project is allowing students to color their own rainbows, which improves fine motor skills. Then, adults can have children cut out pictures from grocery circulars and name each food. The adult can help children find one healthy fruit/vegetable for each color, gluing each food to its corresponding stripe on the rainbow. Adults can then help children pull apart cotton balls and glue them to their rainbow pictures to represent clouds. Children can then post their food rainbows on refrigerators as artwork and as healthy eating reminders. At the bottom, children can draw and color one box (bottom-up) for each food they eat (e.g., blue = blueberries, orange = carrots, red = apples, etc.) to create a bar graph. Children should try to "eat" the entire rainbow every week. This activity gives children the opportunity to produce colorful art, eat better, track and document their diets and develop graphing skills.

Prerequisite abilities

Prerequisite abilities that young children need in order to develop early math skills include the ability to identify, copy, expand, and create patterns; as well as the ability to count. Adults can promote the development of these skills by giving children a craft project and introducing them to an interactive game they can play using their crafts. First, the children paint six ping pong balls red on one side to make red-and-white balls. Then, the children paint six ping pong balls blue on one side to make blue-and-white balls. Once the paint dries, the adult puts several balls into an egg carton so that one color is face up. The adult starts making a simple pattern (e.g., two white, then two red, then two blue), and asks each child to continue the pattern. Then, the adult allows each child to create his or her own original color patterns. Once a child masters creating patterns using solid colors, he or she can then use both the white and colored sides of the balls to create more complex patterns. Children can design an infinite number of patterns, which are often quite artistic.

Copyright © Mometrix Media. You have been licensed one copy of this document for personal use only. Any other reproduction or redistribution is strictly prohibited. All rights reserved.

Developing counting skills, numeracy skills, and motor skills

Young children enjoy tossing objects and practicing their aim. Adults can make a beanbag game that helps children learn numbers and identify sets, while also allowing them to construct their own game rules. First, the adult should cover five big, equally-sized coffee (or similar) cans with paper that is adhesive on one side. The adult should then use markers to write a number from 1 to 5 and draw the corresponding number of dots on each can. The next step is to fill 15 tube socks with beans and knot/tie/sew them shut. The following numerals and the corresponding number of dots should be written on each homemade beanbag using markers: the number 1 on five beanbags, the number 2 on four beanbags, the number 3 on three beanbags, the number 4 on two beanbags, and the number 5 on one beanbag. Next, the adult should attach the cans to the floor with tape or Velcro. Then, the adult should mark a line on the floor that children must stand behind, and should direct children ONLY to toss the beanbags into the cans. Children will devise various games/rules. First, they may simply toss the beanbags into the cans; then, some may try to toss beanbags into a can that has the same number as the one marked on the beanbag. Eventually, some may throw three beanbags into the "3" can. They may/may not keep score. Allowing children to determine the details and rules gives them an opportunity to develop their imagination and decision making skills, and to create their own games while learning number and set identification.

Developing shape recognition skills, fine motor skills, creativity, observational skills, and general and early math vocabulary skills

In one type of shape matching game, EC teachers help children make a game board out of construction paper that is shaped like a tree. Teachers first help the children cut a treetop and leaf shapes from green paper. They discuss children's preferences for tall/short and thick/thin trunks, giving them practice using descriptive vocabulary words, particularly ones related to size. This step builds both general and math concept vocabulary. Children cut trunks from brown paper and paste/glue them on the treetops. While out of the children's sight, the teacher cuts 5 to 10 (or more) pairs of shapes per child/tree from different colors of construction paper. Pairs should not match exactly (e.g., a blue square can be paired with a red square). The teacher glues one of each pair of shapes to each child's tree while the child is not looking. The teacher then gives each child the rest of the shapes, and invites children to see how quickly they can match each shape to its "partner" on the tree. The teacher can provide "warmer/cooler" distance clues, and should provide reinforcement each time a child correctly matches a pair of shapes. Teachers can make this activity more challenging by using more shapes and/or getting students to match shapes that are different sizes (e.g., children can be asked to match smaller diamonds to larger diamonds).

Copyright © Mometrix Media. You have been licensed one copy of this document for personal use only. Any other reproduction or redistribution is strictly prohibited. All rights reserved.

Strengthening numeracy skills

Adults can adapt the format of "20 Questions," "I Spy," and other similar guessing games to focus on numbers and help children learn number concepts. For example, adults could say, "I'm thinking of a number from 1 to 10...." and then give children 10 guesses. Adults give children cues as they guess, such as "higher" and "lower," to help them narrow down the number of possible correct answers. As children improve, adults can increase the number range (e.g., from 0 to 50) or use larger numbers (e.g., from 20 to 40). As children's skills and self-confidence develop, adults can reverse roles, having children think of numbers and give clues while adults guess. Young children enjoy the fun of guessing, getting closer using clues, deducing correct answers, and fooling adults with their own clues. Concurrently, they learn to describe numbers, compare them, and sequence them. Adults can make the game more difficult by limiting the number of guesses allowed and/or setting time limits. They can make it easier by providing a written number line for children to reference. This game requires no materials (or just a basic number line), is a great way to pass time, and entertains children while helping to develop numeracy skills.

Promoting pattern recognition skills, imagination, an understanding of symbolic representation, and map reading skills

A treasure hunt is an ideal outdoor activity for young children, and can also be adapted for indoor fun. The treasure can be anything (e.g., a small toy/play money/chocolate "coins"/rocks spray painted gold or silver, etc.). The adult should put the treasure in a paper bag marked with a large X. The adult should hide it somewhere where it is not visible, but will not be overly difficult for children to find. Then, the adult should make a treasure map, using few words and many pictures, sketching landmark objects in the area (trees, houses, etc. if the activity will be done outdoors, and furniture, walls, etc. if the activity will be done indoors). The adult should ensure the map is developmentally appropriate for young children, and that they will be able to read it independently. Adults with time and motivation can make the map look authentic by soaking it in tea/coffee, drying it in a 200° oven, or even charring its edges. Adults should include a dotted line on the map that reinforces the simple directions and indicates the path to the treasure, which is indicated on the map by a large X. Children have fun, use their imaginations, make connections between symbols and images to corresponding real-world physical objects, and begin learning to read maps.

Concept of starting at zero rather than one

A teacher is introducing standard measures to her class as part of a unit on measurement, one of the early math skills. She shows the children a ruler, explaining that it is one foot long, and that we can use it to measure inches and parts of inches. She demonstrates placing the ruler on paper to measure a given length, explaining that the ruler can also be used as a straight edge for drawing lines. One child asks, "How come you started with zero? Why don't you start with one like when we count?" The teacher responds, "That's a very good question! Zero means none/nothing. When we count, we start with one because we already have at least one of something. When you were born, you were not one year old; your age began at zero. After a year, on your first birthday, you were one year old. We also begin measuring distances at zero/none/nothing. The first piece/unit of measurement is one, not two. The distance from zero to one is equal to one. To get to one inch, for example, we need to start at zero."

Copyright © Mometrix Media. You have been licensed one copy of this document for personal use only. Any other reproduction or redistribution is strictly prohibited. All rights reserved.

Geometric shapes and their properties

A teacher has been working with students to help them develop their shape identification skills. They can recognize shapes by sight, and have also learned the defining properties of different shapes (number of sides, etc.). The teacher shows the class this figure:

She asks how many rectangles they can find in the figure. One student answers, "There is one rectangle," which is incorrect because a square is a rectangle; this figure has four rectangles that are squares. Moreover, the entire figure is itself a rectangle. Another student therefore says, "There are five rectangles." This response is also incorrect. Two adjacent squares also form a rectangle; this means there are three additional rectangles. Three adjacent squares also form a rectangle; this means there are two additional rectangles. Thus, the figure has a total of 10 rectangles. Solving this puzzle requires the use of many skills, including analyzing visual information, synthesizing visual information, recognizing patterns, recognizing shapes, and identifying the properties of shapes.

Collecting, organizing, and displaying data

A preschool teacher is teaching her group of ten children about basic data collection, data arrangement, and data display. She shows children yellow, blue, and green sticky notes, and has each child select his/her favorite color. Five children choose yellow notes, three select blue, and two choose green. By choosing one of three colors, each child has participated in data collection. The teacher draws lines to divide a sheet of paper into three columns, and labels each column with one of the colors. She helps the children place their chosen sticky notes in the correct columns. By arranging the colored sticky notes into columns, the teacher and children have organized the data they gathered. Once all notes are in their proper color columns, the completed chart is an example of how collected, organized data can be displayed.

Selecting one of three colors of sticky notes, organizing them, and displaying them
The teacher had ten children each choose one of three colors of sticky notes, an example of basic data collection. She used a chart with three columns to organize the children's choices as follows:

BLUE	YELLOW	GREEN
blue sticky note	yellow sticky note	green sticky note
blue sticky note	yellow sticky note	green sticky note
blue sticky note	yellow sticky note	
	yellow sticky note	
	yellow sticky note	

The chart displays the collected and organized data. The teacher asks the children which color was chosen the most. Seeing five yellow notes, they answer, "yellow." She asks which color was chosen the least, and they say, "green." She asks them to use numbers to arrange the color choices from most popular to least popular. They arrive at, "five yellow, three blue, and two green." Together, the teacher and the children point to and count ten children. She tells them five equals half of ten, and asks which color half of the children chose. Together, they figure out it was yellow. These are examples of analyzing and interpreting data.

Copyright © Mometrix Media. You have been licensed one copy of this document for personal use only. Any other reproduction or redistribution is strictly prohibited. All rights reserved.

Science

Fundamental science concepts

Science entails asking questions, conducting investigations, collecting data, and seeking answers to the questions asked by analyzing the data collected. Natural events that can be examined over time and student-centered inquiry through hands-on activities that require the application of problem solving skills are most appropriate for helping young children learn basic science. In their everyday lives, young children develop concepts of 1:1 correspondence through activities like fitting pegs into matching holes or distributing one item to each child in a class. They also develop counting concepts by counting enough items for each child in the group or counting pennies in a piggy bank. They develop classification concepts when they sort objects into separate piles according to their shapes or some other type of category (e.g., toy cars vs. toy trucks). When children transfer water, sand, rice, or other substances from one container to another, they develop measurement concepts. As they progress, children will apply these early concepts to more abstract scientific ideas during grade school.

Learning science as normal developmental processes

Infants use their senses to explore the environment, and are motivated by innate curiosity. As they develop mobility, children gain more freedom, allowing them to make independent discoveries and think for themselves. Children learn size concepts by comparing the sizes of objects/persons in the environment to their own size, and by observing that some objects are too large to hold, while others are small enough to hold. They learn about weight when trying to lift various objects. They learn about shape when they see that some objects roll away, while others do not. Babies learn temporal sequences when they wake up wet and hungry, cry, and have parents change and feed them. They also learn this concept by playing, getting tired, and going to sleep. As soon as they look and move around, infants learn about space, including large/small spaces. Eventually, they develop spatial sense through experiences like being put in a playpen/crib in the middle of a large room. Toddlers naturally sort objects into groups according to their sizes/shapes/colors/uses. They experiment with transferring water/sand among containers of various sizes. They learn part-to-whole relationships by building block structures and then dismantling them.

Naturalistic, informal, and structured learning experiences

Children actively construct their knowledge of the environment through exploring it. Young children's learning experiences can be naturalistic (i.e. spontaneously initiated by the child during everyday activities). During naturalistic learning, the child controls his/her choices and actions. Informal learning experiences also allow the child to choose his or her actions and activities, but they include adult intervention at some point during the child's engagement in naturalistic pursuits. In structured learning experiences, the adult chooses the activities and supplies some direction as to how the child should perform the associated actions. One consideration related to EC learning that teachers should keep in mind is that within any class or group of children, there are individual differences in learning styles. Additionally, children from different cultural groups have varying learning styles and approaches. EC teachers can introduce science content in developmentally appropriate ways by keeping these variations in mind.

Copyright © Mometrix Media. You have been licensed one copy of this document for personal use only. Any other reproduction or redistribution is strictly prohibited. All rights reserved.

Naturalistic learning experiences

Motivated by novelty and curiosity, young children spontaneously initiate naturalistic experiences during their everyday activities. Infants and toddlers in Piaget's sensorimotor stage learn by exploring the environment through their senses, so adults should provide them with many objects and substances they can see, hear, touch, smell, and taste. Through manipulating and observing concrete objects/substances, preschoolers in Piaget's preoperational stage begin learning concepts that will enable them to perform mental operations later on. Adults should observe children's actions and progress, and should give positive reinforcement in the form of looks, facial expressions, gestures, and/or words encouraging and praising the child's actions. Young children need adult feedback to learn when they are performing the appropriate actions. For example, a toddler/preschooler selects a tool from the toolbox, saying, "This is big!" and the mother responds, "Yes!" A four-year-old sorting toys of various colors into separate containers is another example of a naturalistic experience. A five-year-old who observes the mixing of two colors that yields a third color is another example.

Informal learning experience

Informal learning experiences involve two main components. First, the child spontaneously initiates naturalistic learning experiences during everyday activities to explore and learn about the environment. Second, the adult takes advantage of opportunities during naturalistic experiences to insert informal learning experiences. Adults do not plan these in advance, but take advantage of opportunities that occur naturally. One way this happens is when a child is on the right track to solve a problem, but needs some encouragement or a hint from the adult. Another way is when the adult spots a "teachable moment" during the child's naturalistic activity, and uses it to reinforce a basic concept. For example, a three-year-old might hold up three fingers, declaring, "I'm six years old." The parent says, "Let's count fingers: one, two, three. You're three years old." Or, a teacher asks a child who has a box of treats if s/he has enough for the whole class, and the child answers, "I don't know." The teacher then responds, "Let's count them together," and helps the child count.

Structured learning experiences

Naturalistic learning experiences are spontaneously initiated and controlled by children. Informal learning experiences involve unplanned interventions by adults during children's naturalistic experiences, which is when adults offer suitable correction/assistance/support. Structured learning experiences differ in that the adult pre-plans and initiates the activity/lesson, and provides the child with some direction. For example, a teacher who observes a four-year-old's need to practice counting can give the child a pile of toys, and then ask him/her how many there are. To develop size concepts, a teacher can give a small group of children several toys of different sizes, and then ask the children to inspect them and talk about their characteristics. The teacher holds up one toy, instructing children to find one that is bigger/smaller. If a child needs to learn shape concepts, the teacher might introduce a game involving shapes, giving the child instructions on how to play the game. Or, a first grade teacher, recognizing the importance of the concept of classification to the ability to organize scientific information, might ask students to bring in bones to classify during a unit on skeletons.

Activity collecting and organizing data

Preschoolers and kindergarteners continue their earlier practices of exploration to learn new things, and they apply fundamental science concepts to collect and organize data in order to answer questions. To collect data, children must have observation, counting, recording, and organization skills. One activity kindergarteners and teachers enjoy is growing bean sprouts. For example, the teacher can show children two methods: one using glass jars and paper towels saturated with

Copyright © Mometrix Media. You have been licensed one copy of this document for personal use only. Any other reproduction or redistribution is strictly prohibited. All rights reserved.

water, the other using cups of dirt. The children add water daily as needed, observe developments, and report to the teacher, who records their observations on a chart. The teacher gives each child a chart that they add information to each day. The children count how many days their beans took to sprout in the glass jars and in the cups of dirt. They then compare their own results for the two methods, and they compare their results to those of their classmates. The children apply concepts of counting, numbers, time, 1:1 correspondence, and comparison of numbers. They also witness the planting and growing process.

Science process skills

Science process skills include observation (using the senses to identify properties of objects/situations), classification (grouping objects/situations according to their common properties), measurement (quantifying physical properties), communication (using observations, classifications, and measurements to report experimental results to others), inference (finding patterns and meaning in experiment results), and prediction (using experimental experience to formulate new hypotheses). Inferences and predictions must be differentiated from objective observations. Classification, measurement, and comparison are basic math concepts which, when applied to science problems, are called process skills. The other science process skills named, as well as defining and controlling variables, are equally necessary to solve both science and math problems. For example, using ramps can help young children learn basic physics concepts. Teachers ask children what would happen if two balls were rolled down a ramp at the same time, if two balls were rolled down a ramp of a different height/length, if two ramps of different heights/lengths were used, etc. In this activity, children apply the scientific concepts of observation, communication, inference, and prediction, as well as the concepts of height, length, counting, speed, distance, and comparison.

> ➤ **Review Video: Science Process Skills**
> *Visit **mometrix.com/academy** and enter **Code: 601624***

Scientific method

Children are born curious, and naturally engage in problem solving to learn. Problem solving and inquiry are natural child behaviors. EC teachers can use these behaviors to promote children's scientific inquiry. Scientific inquiry employs the scientific method. The first step in the method is to ask a question, which is another natural child behavior. Just as adult scientists formulate research questions, the first step of the scientific method for children is asking questions they want to answer. Next, to address a question, both adults and children must form a hypothesis (i.e. an educated guess about what the answer will be). The hypothesis informs and directs the next steps: designing and conducting an experiment to test whether the hypothesis is true or false. With teacher instruction/help, children experiment. For example, they might drop objects of different weights from a height to see when each lands, as Galileo did. Teachers help record outcomes. The next steps are deciding whether the results prove/disprove the hypothesis and reporting the results and conclusions to others.

> ➤ **Review Video: The Scientific Method**
> *Visit **mometrix.com/academy** and enter **Code: 191386***

Copyright © Mometrix Media. You have been licensed one copy of this document for personal use only. Any other reproduction or redistribution is strictly prohibited. All rights reserved.

Physical science and matter

Physical science is the study/science of the physical universe surrounding us. Everything in the universe consists of matter (i.e., anything that has mass and takes up space) or energy (i.e., anything that does not have mass or occupy space, but affects matter and space). Three states of matter are solid, liquid, and gas. Solids preserve their shape even when they are not in a container. Solids have specific, three-dimensional/crystalline atomic structures and specific melting points. Liquids have no independent shape outside of containers, but have specific volumes. Liquid molecules are less cohesive than solid molecules, but more cohesive than gas molecules. Liquids have flow, viscosity (flow resistance), and buoyancy. Liquids can undergo diffusion, osmosis, evaporation, condensation, solution, freezing, and heat conduction and convection. Liquids and gases are both fluids, and share some of the same properties. Gases have no shape, expanding and spreading indefinitely outside of containers. Gases can become liquid/solid through cooling/compression/both. Liquids/solids can become gaseous through heating. Vapor is the gaseous form of a substance that is solid/liquid at lower temperatures. For example, when water is heated it becomes steam, a vapor.

Solids

Solids are one of the three forms of matter. The other two are liquids and gases. *Solids* maintain their shape when they are not inside of containers, whereas liquids and gases acquire the shapes of containers holding them. Containers also prevent liquids and gases from dispersing. Of the three forms of matter, solids have the most cohesive molecules. Solid molecules are most attracted to each other, and solid molecules are held together most strongly. Solid atoms are organized into defined, three-dimensional, lattice-shaped patterns (i.e., they are crystalline in structure). Solids also have specific temperatures at which they melt. Some substances that seem solid, such as plastic, gel, tar, and glass, are actually not true solids. They are amorphous solids because their atoms do not have a crystalline structure, but are amorphous (i.e., the positions of their atoms have no long-range organization). They also have a range of melting temperatures rather than specific melting points.

Liquids

Of the three states of matter—solid, liquid, and gas—*liquids* have properties that fall somewhere in between those of solids and gases. The molecules of solids are the most cohesive (i.e. they have the greatest mutual attraction). Gas molecules are the least cohesive, and liquid molecules are in between. Liquids have no definite shape, while solids do. Liquids have a definite volume, whereas gases do not. The cohesion of liquid molecules draws them together, and the molecules below the surface pull surface molecules down, creating surface tension. This property can be observed in containers of water. Liquid molecules are also attracted to other substance's molecules (i.e. adhesion). Surface tension and adhesion combined cause liquids to rise in narrow containers, a property known as capillarity. Liquids are buoyant (i.e. they exert upward force so objects which have more buoyancy than weight float in liquids, while objects which have more weight than buoyancy sink in liquids). Liquids can be made solid by freezing, and can be made gaseous by heating/evaporation. Liquids can diffuse, which means they can mix with other molecules. Liquid diffusion across semi-permeable membranes is known as osmosis.

> ➤ **Review Video:** Properties of Liquids
> *Visit* **mometrix.com/academy** *and enter* **Code: 802024**

Copyright © Mometrix Media. You have been licensed one copy of this document for personal use only. Any other reproduction or redistribution is strictly prohibited. All rights reserved.

Gases

Gas, liquid, and solid are the three states of matter. *Gases* have the least cohesive (i.e. mutually attracted) molecules of the three states of matter, while solids have the most cohesive molecules. Gases do not maintain a defined shape, while solids do. If not contained within a receptacle, gases spread and expand indefinitely. Gases can be elementary or compound. An elementary gas is composed of only one kind of chemical element. At normal temperatures and pressures, 12 elementary gases are known: argon*, chlorine, fluorine, helium*, hydrogen, krypton*, neon*, nitrogen, oxygen, ozone, radon*, and xenon*. Compound gases have molecules containing atoms of more than one kind of chemical element. Carbon monoxide (which contains one carbon and one oxygen atom) and ammonia (which contains nitrogen and hydrogen atoms) are common compound gases. Heating gas molecules/atoms charges them electrically, making them ions. Plasma combines positive gas ions and electrons. Some gases are colorless and odorless, while others are not. Some burn with oxygen, while others do not. *Noble/inert gases have single atoms that do not normally form compounds with other elements.

> ➢ **Review Video:** Basic Properties of Gas
> *Visit* ***mometrix.com/academy*** *and enter* ***Code:*** **105199**

Light

When a beam of light hits a smooth surface like a mirror, it bounces back off that surface. This rebounding is reflection. In physics, the law of reflection states that "the angle of incidence equals the angle of reflection." This means that when light is reflected, it always bounces off the surface at the same angle at which it hit that surface. When a beam of light hits a rough rather than a smooth surface, though, it is reflected back at many different angles, not just the angle at which it struck the surface. This reflection at multiple and various angles is scattering. Many objects we commonly use every day have rough surfaces. For example, paper may look smooth to the naked eye, but actually has a rough surface. This property can be observed by viewing paper through a microscope. Because light waves striking paper are reflected in every direction by its rough surface, scattering enables us to read words printed on paper from any viewing angle.

> ➢ **Review Video:** Light
> *Visit* ***mometrix.com/academy*** *and enter* ***Code:*** **900556**

When light strikes a medium, the light wave's frequency is equal or close to the frequency at which the electrons in the medium's atoms can vibrate. These electrons receive the light's energy, making them vibrate. When a medium's atoms hang on tightly to their electrons, the electrons transmit their vibrations to the nucleus of each atom. This makes the atoms move faster and collide with the medium's other atoms. The energy the atoms got from the vibrations is then released as heat. This process is known as absorption of light. Materials that absorb light, such as wood and metal, are opaque. Some materials absorb certain light frequencies but transmit others. For example, glass transmits visible light (and therefore appears transparent to the naked eye), but absorbs ultraviolet frequencies. The sky looks blue because the atmosphere absorbs all colors in the spectrum except blue, which it reflects. Only blue wavelengths/frequencies bounce back to our eyes. This is an example of subtractive color, which we see in paints/dyes and all colored objects/materials. Pigments absorb some frequencies and reflect others.

Copyright © Mometrix Media. You have been licensed one copy of this document for personal use only. Any other reproduction or redistribution is strictly prohibited. All rights reserved.

When light moves from one transparent medium to another (e.g., between water and air/vice versa), the light's speed changes, bending the light wave. It bends either away from or toward the normal line, an imaginary straight line running at right angles to the medium's surface. We easily observe this bending when looking at a straw in a glass of water. The straw appears to break/bend at the waterline. The angle of refraction is the amount that the light wave bends. It is determined by how much the medium slows down the light's speed, which is the medium's refraction index. For example, diamonds are much denser and harder than water, and thus have a higher refraction index. They slow down and trap light more than water does. Consequently, diamonds sparkle more than water. Lenses, such as those in eyeglasses and telescopes, rely on the principle of refraction. Curved lenses disperse or concentrate light waves, refracting light as it both enters and exits, thus changing the light's direction. This is how lenses correct (eyeglasses) and enhance (telescopes) our vision.

> ➤ **Review Video: <u>Reflection, Transmission, and Absorption of Light</u>**
> *Visit **mometrix.com/academy** and enter **Code: 109410**

Magnetism

Magnetism is the property some objects/substances have of attracting other materials. The form of magnetism most familiar to us is certain materials attracting iron. Magnets also attract steel, cobalt, and other materials. Generators supplying power include magnets, as do all electric motors. Loudspeakers and telephones contain magnets. Tape recorders use magnets. The tape they play is magnetized. Magnets are used in compasses to determine the location of north and various corresponding directions. In fact, the planet Earth is itself a giant magnet (which is why compasses point north). Hence, like the Earth, all magnets have two poles: a north/north-seeking pole and a south/south-seeking pole. Opposite poles attract, and like poles repel each other. Magnets do not need to touch to attract/repel each other. A magnet's effective area/range is its magnetic field. All materials have some response to magnetic fields. Magnets make nearby magnetic materials into magnets, a process known as magnetic induction. Materials that line up parallel to magnetic force field lines are paramagnetic, while materials that line up perpendicular to magnetic force field lines are diamagnetic.

Scientists have known about the effects of magnetism for hundreds of years. However, they do not know exactly what magnetism is, or what causes it. French physicist Pierre Weiss proposed a theory of magnetism in the early 20th century that is widely accepted. This theory posits that every magnetic material has groups of molecules—domains—that function as magnets. Until a material is magnetized, its domains have a random arrangement, so one domain's magnetism is cancelled out by another's. When the material comes into a magnetic field—the range/area wherein a magnet is effective—its domains align themselves parallel to the magnetic field's lines of force. As a result, all of their north-seeking/north poles point in the same direction. Removing the magnetic field causes like poles to repel one another as they normally do. In easily magnetized materials, domains revert to random order. In materials that are harder to magnetize, domains lack sufficient force to disassemble, leaving the material magnetized. Later versions of Weiss's theory attribute domain magnetism to spinning electrons.

Electrical properties of insulation and conduction in terms of atomic structure

The smallest units of all matter are atoms. The nuclei of atoms are orbited by negatively charged electrons. Some materials have electrons that are strongly bound to their atoms. These include air, glass, wood, cotton, plastic, and ceramic. Since their atoms rarely release electrons, these materials have little or no ability to conduct electricity, and are known as electrical insulators. Insulators

Copyright © Mometrix Media. You have been licensed one copy of this document for personal use only. Any other reproduction or redistribution is strictly prohibited. All rights reserved.

resist/block conduction. Metals and other conductive materials have free electrons that can detach from the atoms and move around. Without the tight binding of insulators, materials with loose electrons enable electric current to flow easily through them. Such materials are called electrical conductors. The movements of their electrons transmit electrical energy. Electricity requires something to make it flow (i.e., a generator). A generator creates a steady flow of electrons by moving a magnet close to a wire, creating a magnetic field to propel electrons. Electricity also requires a conductor (i.e., a medium through which it can move from one place to another).

Electrical current and current/amperage and voltage

Magnetism and electricity are related, and they interact with each other. Generators work by using magnets near conductive wires to produce moving streams of electrons. The agent of movement can range from a hand crank, to a steam engine, to the nuclear fission process. However, all agents of movements operate according to the same principle. A simple analogy is that a generator magnetically pushes electrical current the way a pump pushes water. Just as water pumps apply specific amounts of pressure to specific numbers of water molecules, generator magnets apply specific amounts of "pressure" to specific numbers of electrons. The number of moving electrons in an electrical circuit equals the current, or amperage. The unit of measurement for amperage is the ampere, or amp. The amount of force moving the electrons is the voltage. Its unit of measurement is the volt. One amp equals 6.24×10^{18} electrons passing through a wire each second. For example, a generator could produce 1 amp using 6 volts when rotating 1,000 times per minute. Today's power stations rely on generators.

Heat

Heat is transmitted through conduction, radiation, and convection. Heat is transmitted in solids through conduction. When two objects at different temperatures touch each other, the hotter object's molecules are moving faster. They collide with the colder object's molecules, which are moving slower. As a result of the collision, the molecules that are moving more rapidly supply energy to the molecules that are moving more slowly. This speeds up the movement of the (previously) slower moving molecules, which heats up the colder object. This process of transferring heat through contact is called thermal conductivity. An example of thermal conductivity is the heat sink. Heat sinks are used in many devices. Today, they are commonly used in computers. A heat sink transfers the heat building up in the computer processor, moving it away before it can damage the processor. Computers contain fans, which blow air across their heat sinks and expel the heated air out of the computers.

Vibrations and sound

When any physical object moves back and forth rapidly, this is known as vibration. The movements that occur during vibration disturb the surrounding medium, which may be solid, liquid, or gaseous. The most common sound conducting medium in our environment is gaseous: our atmosphere (i.e. the air).

An object's vibratory movements represent a form of energy. As this acoustic energy moves through the air, it takes the form of waves, sound waves specifically. The outer ear receives and amplifies the sound and transmits it to the middle ear, where tiny bones vibrate in response to the sound energy and transmit it to the inner ear. The inner ear converts the acoustic energy into electrical energy. The electrical impulses are then carried by nerves to the brain. Structures in the brain which are associated with hearing receive these electrical signals and interpret them (i.e.

Copyright © Mometrix Media. You have been licensed one copy of this document for personal use only. Any other reproduction or redistribution is strictly prohibited. All rights reserved.

make sense of them) as sounds. The reception of sound waves in the ear is auditory sensation, and the brain's interpretation of them is auditory perception.

> **Review Video: Sound**
> *Visit **mometrix.com/academy** and enter **Code: 562378***

Positions and motions of objects in space in the physical world

Moving physical objects changes their positions. According to Newton's first law of motion, an object at rest tends to stay at rest and an object in motion tends to stay in motion, unless/until an opposing force changes the object's state of rest/motion. For example, an object at rest could be a small rock sitting on the ground. If you kick the rock into the air, it moves through the air. The rock will continue to move, but when a force like gravity acts on it, it falls/stops moving. The resulting motion from kicking the rock illustrates

> **Review Video: Newton's First Law of Motion**
> *Visit **mometrix.com/academy** and enter **Code: 590367***

Newton's second law of motion states that F = ma (force equals mass times acceleration). Thus, moving objects maintain their speeds unless some force(s) cause acceleration or slowing/stopping, as frictional forces do.

> **Review Video: Newton's Second Law of Motion**
> *Visit **mometrix.com/academy** and enter **Code: 737975***

Newton's third law of motion: for every action there is an equal and opposite reaction. The acceleration or increase in velocity (a) of an object depends on its mass (m) and the amount of force (F) that is applied to the object.

> **Review Video: Newton's Third Law of Motion**
> *Visit **mometrix.com/academy** and enter **Code: 838401***

Solar system's location and components

The universe is composed of an unknown (possibly infinite) number of galaxies or star systems, such as the Spiral Nebula, the Crab Nebula, and the Milky Way. Our sun, Sol, is one of billions of stars in the Milky Way. The solar system's planets are held in position at varying distances (according to their size and mass) from the Sun by its gravitational force. These planets orbit or revolve around the Sun. From the closest to the Sun to the farthest away, the solar system's planets are Mercury, Venus, Earth, Mars, Jupiter, Saturn, Uranus, and Neptune. Pluto was historically included as the ninth planet, but was demoted to a "dwarf planet" by the International Astronomical Union in 2006.

Due to angular momentum, planets rotate on their axes, which are imaginary central lines between their north and south poles. One complete Earth rotation equals what we perceive as one 24-hour day. As the Earth turns, different portions face the Sun. These receive daylight, while the portions turned away from the Sun are in darkness. One complete revolution of the Earth around the Sun represents one calendar year.

> **Review Video: Solar System**

Copyright © Mometrix Media. You have been licensed one copy of this document for personal use only. Any other reproduction or redistribution is strictly prohibited. All rights reserved.

Pluto

Since more powerful observatories have enabled greater detection and measurement of celestial objects, the International Astronomical Union has defined three criteria for defining a planet. First, it must orbit the Sun. Pluto meets this criterion. Second, it must have enough gravitational force to shape itself into a sphere. Pluto also meets this criterion. Third, a planet must have "cleared the neighborhood" in its orbit. This expression refers to the fact that as planets form, they become the strongest gravitational bodies within their orbits. Therefore, when close to smaller bodies, planets either consume these smaller bodies or repel them because of their greater gravity, clearing their orbital area/"neighborhood." To do this, a planet's mass must sufficiently exceed the mass of other bodies in its orbit. Pluto does not meet this criterion, having only 0.07 times the mass of other objects within its orbit. Thus, astronomers reclassified Pluto as a "dwarf planet" in 2006 based on its lesser mass and the many other objects in its orbit with comparable masses and sizes.

Earth

Earth is roughly spherical in shape. Its North and South Poles at the top and bottom are farthest away from and least exposed to the Sun, so they are always coldest. This accounts for the existence of the polar ice caps. The Equator, an imaginary line running around Earth at its middle exactly halfway between the North and South Poles, is at 0° latitude. Sunrises and sunsets at the Equator are the world's fastest. Days and nights are of virtually equal length at the Equator, and there is less seasonal variation than in other parts of the world. The equatorial climate is a tropical rainforest. Locations close to the North Pole, like Norway, are at such high latitudes that their nights are not dark in summertime, hence the expression "Land of the Midnight Sun." They also have very little light in wintertime. As Earth revolves around the Sun over the course of a year, the distance and angle of various locations relative to the Sun change. Thus, different areas receive varying amounts of heat and light. This is what accounts for the changing seasons.

Rocks found on the Earth's surface

Earth's rock types are sedimentary, igneous, and metamorphic. These categories are based on the respective processes that form each type of rock. Igneous rocks are formed from volcanoes. Metamorphic rocks are formed when igneous and sedimentary rocks deep inside the Earth's crust are subjected to intense heat and/or pressure. Sedimentary rocks are formed on Earth's surface, and characteristically accumulate in layers. Erosion and other natural processes deposit these layers. Some sedimentary rocks are held together by electrical attraction. Others are cemented together by chemicals and minerals that existed during their formation. Still others are not held together at all, but are loose and crumbly. There are three subcategories of sedimentary rock. Clastic sedimentary rocks are made of little rock bits—clasts—that are compacted and cemented together. Chemical sedimentary rocks are frequently formed through repeated flooding and subsequent evaporation. The evaporation of water leaves a layer of minerals that were dissolved in the water. Limestone and deposits of salt and gypsum are examples. Organic sedimentary rocks are formed from organic matter, such as the calcium left behind from animal bones and shells.

> ➤ **Review Video:** <u>Igneous, Sedimentary, and Metamorphic Rocks</u>
> *Visit* **mometrix.com/academy** *and enter* **Code: 689294**

Copyright © Mometrix Media. You have been licensed one copy of this document for personal use only. Any other reproduction or redistribution is strictly prohibited. All rights reserved.

Earth's metamorphic rocks

Sedimentary rocks are formed on the Earth's surface by layers of eroded material from mountains that were deposited by water, minerals like lime, salt and gypsum deposited by evaporated floodwater, and organic material like calcium from animal bones and shells. Igneous rocks are formed from liquid volcanic rock—either magma underground or lava on the surface—that cools and hardens. Metamorphic rocks are formed from sedimentary and igneous rocks. This happens when sedimentary and/or igneous rocks are deep inside the Earth's crust, where they are subjected to great pressure or heat. The process of metamorphism does not melt these rocks into liquid, which would happen inside a volcano. Rather, the pressure and/or heat change the rocks' molecular structure. Metamorphic rocks are thus more compact and denser than the sedimentary or igneous rocks from which they were formed. They also contain new minerals produced either by the reconfiguration of existing minerals' structures or by chemical reactions with liquids infiltrating the rock. Two examples of metamorphic rocks are marble and gneiss.

Igneous rocks

Igneous or volcanic rocks are formed from the magma emitted when a volcano erupts. Magma under the Earth's surface is subject to heat and pressure, keeping it in liquid form. During a volcanic eruption, some magma reaches the surface, emerging as lava. Lava cools rapidly in the outside air, becoming a solid with small crystals. Some magma does not reach Earth's surface, but is trapped underground within pockets in other rocks. Magma cools more slowly underground than lava does on the surface. This slower cooling forms rocks with larger crystals and coarser grains. The chemical composition and individual cooling temperatures of magma produce different kinds of igneous rocks. Lava that cools rapidly on the Earth's surface can become obsidian, a smooth, shiny black glass without crystals. It can also become another type of extrusive rock, such as andesite, basalt, pumice, rhyolite, scoria, or tuff (formed from volcanic ash and cinders). Magma that cools slowly in underground pockets can become granite, which has a coarse texture and large, visible mineral grains. It can also become another type of intrusive rock, such as diorite, gabbro, pegmatite, or peridotite.

Erosion

Erosion is a natural process whereby Earth's landforms are broken down through weathering. Rain, wind, etc. wear away solid matter. Over time, rain reduces mountains to hills. Rocks break off from mountains, and in turn disintegrate into sand. Weathering and the resulting erosion always occur in downhill directions. Rain washes rocks off mountains and down streams. Rains, rivers, and streams wash soils away, and ocean waves break down adjacent cliffs. Rocks, dirt, and sand change their form and location through erosion. They do not simply vanish. These transformations and movements are called mass wasting, which occurs chemically (as when rock is dissolved by chemicals in water) or mechanically (as when rock is broken into pieces). Because materials travel as a result of mass wasting, erosion can both break down some areas and build up others. For example, a river runs through and erodes a mountain, carrying the resulting sediment downstream. This sediment gradually builds up, creating wetlands at the river's mouth. A good example of this process is Louisiana's swamps, which were created by sediment transported by the Mississippi River.

Copyright © Mometrix Media. You have been licensed one copy of this document for personal use only. Any other reproduction or redistribution is strictly prohibited. All rights reserved.

Basic physical characteristics of living organisms

All living organisms have fundamental needs that must be met. For example, plants that grow on land need light, air, water, and nutrients in amounts that vary according to the individual plant. Undersea plants may need less/no light. They need gases present in the water, but not in the air above the water. Like land plants, they require nutrients. Like plants, animals (including humans) need air, water, and nutrients. They do not depend on light for photosynthesis like most plants, but some animals require more light than others, while others need less than others or none at all. Organisms cannot survive in environments that do not meet their basic needs. However, many organisms have evolved to adapt to various environments. For example, cacti are desert plants that thrive with only tiny amounts of water, and camels are desert animals that can also go for long periods of time with little water. Penguins and polar bears have adapted to very cold climates. Internal cues (e.g., hunger) and external cues (e.g., environmental change) motivate and shape the behaviors of individual organisms.

Animal life cycles

Most animals, including mammals, birds, fish, reptiles, and spiders, have simple life cycles. They are born live or hatch from eggs, and then grow to adulthood. Animals with simple life cycles include humans. Amphibians like frogs and newts have an additional stage involving a metamorphosis, or transformation. After birth, they breathe through gills and live underwater during youth (e.g., tadpoles). By adulthood, they breathe through lungs and move to land. Butterflies are examples of animals (insects) that undergo complete metamorphosis, meaning they change their overall form. After hatching from an embryo/egg, the juvenile form, or larva, resembles a worm and completes the majority of feeding required. In the next stage, the pupa does not feed, and is typically camouflaged in what is called an inactive stage. Mosquito pupae are called tumblers. The butterfly pupa is called a chrysalis, and is protected by a cocoon. In the final stage, the adult (imago) grows wings (typically) and breeds. Some insects like dragonflies, cockroaches, and grasshoppers undergo an incomplete metamorphosis. There are egg, larva, and adult stages, but no pupa stage.

Reproduction

A few examples of the many ways in which organisms reproduce include binary fission, whereby the cells of prokaryotic bacteria reproduce; budding, which is how yeast cells reproduce; and asexual reproduction. The latter occurs in plants when they are grafted, when cuttings are taken from them and then rooted, or when they put out runners. Plants also reproduce sexually, as do humans and most other animals. Animals, including humans, produce gametes (i.e. sperm or eggs) in their gonads through the process of meiosis. Gametes are haploid, containing half the number of chromosomes found in the body's cells. During fertilization, the gametes combine to form a zygote, which is diploid. It has the full number of chromosomes (half from each gamete), which are arranged in a genetically unique combination. Zygotes undergo mitosis, reproducing their gene combination with identical DNA sequences in all new cells, which then migrate and differentiate into organizations of specialized organs and tissues. These specialized organs in biologically mature organisms, alerted by signals such as hormonal cues, undergo meiosis to create new haploid gametes, beginning the cycle again.

Plant reproduction

Most plants can reproduce asexually. For example, cuttings can be rooted in water and planted. Some plants put out runners that root new growths. Many plants can be grafted to produce new

Copyright © Mometrix Media. You have been licensed one copy of this document for personal use only. Any other reproduction or redistribution is strictly prohibited. All rights reserved.

ones. Plants also reproduce sexually. Plants' sexual life cycles are more complex than animals', since plants alternate between haploid form (i.e. having a single set of chromosomes) and diploid form (i.e., having two sets of chromosome) during their life cycles. Plants produce haploid cells called gametes* (equivalent to sperm and egg in animals) that combine during fertilization, producing zygotes (diploid cells with chromosomes from both gametes). Cells reproduce exact copies through mitosis (asexual reproduction), becoming differentiated/specialized to form organs. Mature diploid plants called sporophytes—the plant form we usually see—produce spores. In sporophytes' specialized organs, cells undergo meiosis. This is part of the process of sexual reproduction, during which cells with half the normal number of chromosomes are produced before fertilization occurs. The spores produced by the sporophyte generation undergo mitosis, growing into a haploid plant of the gametophyte generation that produces gametes*. The cycle then repeats.

Ecology

Ecology is defined as the study of interactions between organisms and their environments. Abiotic factors are the parts of any ecosystem that are not alive, but which affect that ecosystem's living members. Abiotic factors also determine the locations of particular ecosystems that have certain characteristics. Abiotic factors include the sunlight; the atmosphere, including oxygen, hydrogen, and nitrogen; the water; the soil; the temperatures within a system; and the nutrient cycles of chemical elements and compounds that pass among living organisms and their physical environments. Biotic factors are the living organisms within any ecosystem, which include not only humans and animals, but also plants, microorganisms, etc. The definition of biotic factors also includes the interactions that occur between and among various organisms within an ecosystem. Sunlight determines plant growth and, hence, biome locations. Sunlight, in turn, is affected by water depth. Ocean depths where sunlight penetrates, called photic zones, are where the majority of the photosynthesis on Earth occurs.

Ecological relationship

Organisms interact, both with other organisms and their environments. Relationships wherein two differing organisms regularly interact so that one or both of them benefit are known as ecological relationships. In mutualistic relationships, both organisms benefit. For example, bacteria live in termites' digestive systems. Termites eat wood. However, they cannot digest the cellulose (the main part of plant cell walls) in wood. The bacteria in termites' guts break down the cellulose for them, releasing the wood's nutrients. Reciprocally, the termites as hosts give the bacteria a home and food. In commensalistic relationships, one organism benefits and the other one is unaffected. One example is barnacles attaching to whales. Barnacles, which are filter feeders, benefit from the whales' swimming, which creates currents in the water that bring the barnacles food. The whales are not disturbed by the barnacles. In parasitic relationships, the parasite benefits, but the host suffers. For example, tapeworms inside animals' digestive tracts get nutrients. The hosts lose the nutrients stolen by the worms, and can sustain tissue damage because of the presence of the tapeworms.

Copyright © Mometrix Media. You have been licensed one copy of this document for personal use only. Any other reproduction or redistribution is strictly prohibited. All rights reserved.

Social Studies

Levels of self-awareness

Even newborns demonstrate differentiation of body through rooting and orienting responses, which are triggered by touching the cheek. (1) <u>Differentiation</u>: At this level, children recognize correspondence between their movements and those in the mirror, and differentiate their mirror images from other individuals. They differentiate the self. (2) <u>Situation</u>: At this level, beyond matching the surface properties of what they feel and what they see in the mirror, and beyond differentiating the self, children realize that their reflection is unique to their self. They also realize that their body/self and other things are situated in space. (3) <u>Identification</u>: At this level, beyond differentiating and situating the self, children now identify their reflection as "me." When psychologists place a dot/sticky note on a child's face before s/he looks in a mirror, the child reaches toward his or her own face to touch/remove it, demonstrating self-recognition and an emerging self-concept. (4) <u>Permanence</u>: At this level, children identify a permanent self across time and space, recognizing themselves in photos and home movies regardless of year/age/clothing/location/setting, etc. (5) <u>Self-consciousness/"meta" self-awareness</u>: At this level, children recognize their self from others' perceptions/perspectives as well as their own. They experience pride, shame, and other "self-conscious" feelings.

Highlights in the progression of children's self-awareness

From birth, infants differentiate their bodies from the environment, and differentiate internal from external stimuli (i.e., self-touch/stimulation vs. non-self/others' touch/stimulation). From two months old, babies show a sense of their body's position relative to other things in their environment. They systematically imitate others' facial expressions and movements. They also explore and consider the environment's responses to their own actions. Additionally, they smile and socially interact face-to-face with others, showing a new sense of shared experiences. By four months, infants systematically reach for and touch objects they see, showing hand-eye coordination. From four to six months, they regulate their reaching based on their sitting/posture and balance. By six months, babies can differentiate video of themselves from that of other, identically dressed babies. Babies between the ages of four and seven months can differentiate live video of themselves from that of experimenters imitating the same behaviors. By two years, children develop an understanding of symbolic representation, and know that mirror images and pictures of themselves stand for themselves. They also start to develop language skills and develop the ability to engage in pretend play.

Contributing factors to children's early development of interpersonal relationships

The first basic factor that contributes to the development of interpersonal relationships in early childhood is child-adult relationships. These are the earliest interpersonal interactions, and start to develop at birth. When children's needs are consistently met by adults, children learn to trust adults. In his famous theory of development, Erikson called the first stage of psychosocial development and the central conflict of infancy basic trust vs. mistrust. The second factor is autonomy, which refers to making decisions and doing things for oneself. Toddlers develop autonomy. Erikson called his second stage of psychosocial development and the central conflict of toddlerhood autonomy vs. shame and self-doubt. Children who are consistently given developmentally appropriate autonomy are more likely to respect others' autonomy, a key feature

Copyright © Mometrix Media. You have been licensed one copy of this document for personal use only. Any other reproduction or redistribution is strictly prohibited. All rights reserved.

of interpersonal development. The third basic factor is pretend play, which emerges as children's understanding of symbolic representation develops and they begin to use things to stand for other things. Pretending to be grown-ups engaging in adult activities helps children learn about adult skills and roles. Interacting with peers in make-believe scenarios prepares children for real-life adult interactions. Constructive ECE approaches do not involve punishing children who have not developed sufficient interpersonal relationship awareness. Instead, they encourage adults to teach children socially acceptable behaviors and reward positive interpersonal interactions.

Developmental milestones

By the time they are a year old, most babies have begun to interact with their peers, particularly when it comes to activities involving concrete objects. The development of walking and talking abilities in normally developing toddlers by the time they are two years old enables them to coordinate their behavior when playing with peers. They can imitate one another's behaviors, and can alternate roles during play, as they understand symbolic representation and can create make-believe scenarios. Pretend play increases from the ages of three to five years, as do prosocial behaviors, which include helping and caring for others. At the same time, egocentrism and aggressive behaviors decrease, as children are more able to consider others' viewpoints and feelings. Emergent social interaction skills such as these form the foundation for children's early peer relationships. When children demonstrate preferences for certain peers and choose to play and otherwise interact with them over others, this is the beginning of what will develop into preschool friendships, which are based mostly upon mutual play activities and exchanges of concrete things. Children tend to form daycare friendships with members of their own sex only over time.

ECE views regarding conflict resolution processes

ECE experts find that while many elementary and secondary schools have implemented conflict resolution programs, children should start learning how to resolve conflicts at younger ages. For example, experts associated with the successful HighScope EC curriculum have designed an approach to conflict resolution for children from 18 months to six years old. The steps in EC conflict resolution are similar to those used to resolve adult conflicts in education, law, labor relations, and diplomacy. Such problem solving steps have also been found to be effective in daycares, Head Start programs, preschools, nursery schools, and kindergartens. While the steps are the same regardless of the age of the children, they are applied differently according to children's developmental levels. Adults supply much of the language to describe problems and solutions for toddlers; preschoolers can often do this themselves. After experiencing the conflict resolution process, elementary school students can frequently function as mediators for classmates. Even very young children with limited language skills should be encouraged to agree and participate through nodding, pointing, and answering yes/no questions. Conflict mediation and resolution skills help children develop lifelong problem solving and social skills.

The steps used to mediate EC conflicts resemble the steps used in adult mediation. For example, EC experts at the HighScope Educational Research Foundation designed a conflict resolution approach for children aged 18 months to 6 years that consists of these six steps:
1. Calmly approach the children who are in conflict and stop any harmful behaviors.
2. Acknowledge what the children are feeling.
3. Collect information about the conflict.

Copyright © Mometrix Media. You have been licensed one copy of this document for personal use only. Any other reproduction or redistribution is strictly prohibited. All rights reserved.

4. Restate what the problem is.
5. Ask children to suggest possible solutions, and help them choose one together.
6. Follow up by providing support as needed.

Experts find that children as young as 18 months demonstrate emergent problem solving skills. They observed young children's abilities to immediately and honestly express emotions. They noted that with adult support, children can frequently generate simple and creative problem solutions. While school conflict resolution is typically aimed at preventing violence, teaching conflict resolution skills can also help children develop the social skills needed to grow into independent, productive members of society.

Parenting styles identified by psychologists

Psychologists (Baumrind, 1967; Maccoby & Martin, 1983) have identified four parenting styles:

(1) <u>Authoritarian</u> These parents are strict, punitive, demanding, and unresponsive. They do not explain reasons for their rules to children. Their children are obedient and proficient at completing academic/technical tasks, but they are less competent socially and less happy. They also have lower self-esteem.

(2) <u>Authoritative</u> This is the ideal parenting style. These parents are responsive, nurturing, and forgiving. They are assertive without being restrictive or intrusive. They set rules, but explain them. They are democratic, address children's questions and input, and use supportive rather than punitive discipline. Their children tend to be competent, successful, and happy.

(3) <u>Permissive</u> These parents are indulgent, lenient, nontraditional, and undemanding. They are nurturing, responsive, and communicative with children, but do not expect their children to show much maturity and/or self-control. They avoid confrontation and seldom use discipline, often acting more like friends than parents. Their children's self-regulation skills are deficient and they are not as happy as many of their peers. They tend to have difficulty with authority and perform poorly in school.

(4) <u>Uninvolved</u> These parents are undemanding, unresponsive, and uncommunicative. They meet their children's basic needs, but are relatively detached from their children's lives. In extreme cases, these parents may neglect/reject children. Their children have low self-esteem and lack self-control.

Family systems theory

Family systems theory studies the behavior of the family unit rather than the behavior of individual family members. Family behavior includes the interactions among family members and how the family unit responds to stress. Some family characteristics have been identified as particularly pertinent to ECE (Christian/NAEYC, 2006). They are boundaries, roles, rules, hierarchy, climate, and equilibrium. Hierarchy is a family's balance of power, control, and decision making. Culture, religion, age, gender, and economic status influence the family hierarchy, which shifts whenever changes occur in the family's composition. Climate refers to a family's emotional quality, and includes the physical and emotional environments in which families raise children. These environments reflect a family's belief about families and children. Family climate determines whether a child feels safe/loved/supported or frightened/rejected/unhappy in his/her family.

Copyright © Mometrix Media. You have been licensed one copy of this document for personal use only. Any other reproduction or redistribution is strictly prohibited. All rights reserved.

Equilibrium refers to the family's balance and consistency. It is disrupted by stress and change, and is maintained or protected by family traditions, customs, and rituals.

Family systems theory examines not individual behavior but family behavior, including communication, interaction, connection/separation, loyalty/autonomy, and responses to stress within the context of the family unit. Family system components particularly influential in early childhood development include the following:

(1) <u>Boundaries:</u> This refers to limits, separateness, and togetherness (i.e. what/whom the family includes/excludes). "Disengaged" families value independence over belonging, and are open to new input. "Enmeshed" families value togetherness over autonomy, and have more closed/restrictive boundaries.

(2) <u>Roles:</u> Each family member has a role (e.g., helper, clown, peacemaker, victim, rescuer, etc.). Family members also tend to assume these roles in social, school, and work contexts.

(3) <u>Rules:</u> Family interaction rules have long-term influences (e.g., parents who view life as predictable are likely to plan ahead, while those who view life as less controllable may not prevent/avoid problems, but rather address them as they occur). Family rules can be unspoken. Also, the rules of family cultures and school cultures can conflict. The other three of the six prominent influences on EC are hierarchy, climate, and equilibrium.

Human socialization

Socialization is the process by which individuals learn their society's norms, values, beliefs, and attitudes; and what behaviors society expects of them relative to those parameters. This learning is imparted by agencies of socialization. The family, peer groups, and leaders of opinion are considered primary socializing agencies. The family is probably the most important because it has the most significant influence on individual development. Families influence the self-concept, feelings, attitudes, and behaviors of each individual member. As children grow, they encounter peer groups throughout life, which also establish norms and values to which individual group members conform. Schools, workplaces, religions, and mass media are considered secondary socializing agencies. Schools dictate additional academic and behavioral norms, values, beliefs, and behaviors. Workplaces have their own cultures that continue, modify, and/or add to the values and behaviors expected of their members. Religions also regulate members' behavior through beliefs, values, goals, and norms that reflect moral principles within a society. Mass media communicate societal conventions (e.g., fashion/style), which enables individuals to learn and adopt new behaviors and/or lifestyles.

Institutions that function as socializing agents

Family is the first and most important socializing agent. Infants learn behavioral patterns from mothers. Their primary socialization is enabled through such early behaviors as nursing, smiling, and toddling. Babies soon interact with other family members. All the infant's physiological and psychological needs are met within the family. Babies learn their sleeping, eating, and toileting habits within the family environment. Babies' personalities also develop based on their early experiences, especially the amounts and types of parental love and affection they receive. School is also a critical socializing agent. Children extend family relationships to society when they go to school. Cognitive and social school experiences develop children's knowledge, skills, beliefs, interests, attitudes, and customs, and help determine the roles children will play when they become

Copyright © Mometrix Media. You have been licensed one copy of this document for personal use only. Any other reproduction or redistribution is strictly prohibited. All rights reserved.

adults. In addition to family relationships, receiving reinforcements at school and observing and imitating teachers influence personality development. Peer groups that are based on friendships, shared ideas, and common interests in music, sports, etc. teach children/teens about conforming to rules and being rejected for not complying with these rules. Mass media like TV profoundly influence children, both negatively and positively.

Culture

While no single definition of culture is universally embraced, one from the cultural anthropology perspective is "…a system of shared beliefs, values, customs, behaviors and artifacts that members of society use to cope with their worlds and with one another, and that are transmitted from generation to generation through learning." (Bates and Fratkin, 2002) Cultural groups are based on a wide range of factors, including geographic location, occupation, religion, sexual orientation, income, etc. Individuals may follow the beliefs and values of more than one culture concurrently. For instance, recent immigrants often espouse values and beliefs from both their original and adopted countries. Traditionally, social systems like education and healthcare have approached cultural diversity by focusing on race/ethnicity and common beliefs about various racial/ethnic group customs. These are frequently generalizations (e.g., lumping Mexican, Cuban, and Puerto Rican cultures together and describing them as "Latino" culture). This type of practice can lead to oversimplified stereotypes, and therefore to unrealistic behavioral expectations. Service professionals need more detailed knowledge of cultural complexities and subtleties to effectively engage and interact with families.

Cultural paradigms of collectivism and individualism
Certain world cultures are oriented more toward collectivism, while others are oriented more toward individualism. Native American, Latin American, Asian, and African cultures are more often collectivistic, focusing on interdependence, social interactions, relationships, and connections among individuals. North American, Canadian, European, and Australian cultures are more commonly individualistic, focusing on independence, uniqueness, self-determination, and self-actualization (realizing one's full potential). Individualism favors competition and distinguishing oneself as an individual, while collectivism favors cooperation that promotes and contributes to the harmony and well-being of the group. Individualist cultures value teaching young children object manipulation and scientific thinking, while collectivist cultures value social and relational behaviors. For example, adults in collectivist cultures may interpret a child's first steps as walking toward the adult, while adults in individualist cultures interpret them as developing motor skills and autonomy. These interpretations signify what each culture values most, forming the child's cultural orientation early in life. The planning and design of educational and other programs should be informed by a knowledge of these and other cultural differences.

Acculturation and assimilation

Acculturation describes the process whereby people adapt or change their cultural traditions, values, and beliefs as a result of coming into contact with and being influenced by other cultures over time. Some cultures adopt certain characteristics from other cultures they are exposed to, and two or more separate cultures may sometimes virtually fuse. However, assimilation, wherein various ethnic groups unite to form a new culture, is different from acculturation. One dominant culture may assimilate others. A historical example is the Roman Empire, which forced many members of ancient Greek, Hebrew, and other cultures to abandon their own cultures and adopt Roman law, military allegiance, traditions, language, religion, practices, and customs (including dress). The extent of a diverse cultural group's acculturation influences how it interacts with social

Copyright © Mometrix Media. You have been licensed one copy of this document for personal use only. Any other reproduction or redistribution is strictly prohibited. All rights reserved.

systems like education and healthcare. Groups that are strongly motivated to maintain their cultural identity may interact less with mainstream systems that significantly conflict with or vary from their own cultural beliefs.

Measuring the acculturation

Social scientists currently use indices such as people's country of birth, how long they have lived in America, their knowledge of the English language, and their level of English language use to study acculturation. However, these factors are measured not because they are the core elements of acculturation, but because they are easier to validly and reliably measure than the underlying cultural beliefs, attitudes, and behaviors they reflect, which are harder to quantify. The interactions between American educators and culturally diverse families can be problematic on both sides. Educators have difficulty interacting, communicating, and collaborating with families that come from a variety of other countries, speak various other languages, and differ in their degree of acculturation to American culture.

On the other hand, immigrant and culturally diverse families encounter a foreign language, different cultural customs and practices, and an unfamiliar educational system with different methods of assessment, placement, curriculum planning and design, instruction, and evaluation—not to mention different special education laws and procedures. Thus, the acculturation challenges related to interactions between American educators and culturally diverse families are bilateral.

Aspects of cultural competence at the system level within service systems

It is important for educational professionals to acquire and demonstrate cultural competence at the individual level to effectively interact with individual children and their families. Moreover, cultural competence is also important at the program level, the school level, and the system level. According to the National Center for Cultural Competence (NCCC), system level cultural competence is a continuing process that includes "...valuing diversity, conducting self-assessments (including organizational assessments), managing the dynamics of differences, acquiring and institutionalizing cultural knowledge, and adapting to the diversity and cultural contexts of the individuals and communities served." (Goode, 2001) Individual educational interactions are informed by a knowledge of cultural diversity and of the importance of such diversity in educational settings, an ability to adapt to the population's cultural needs, and a willingness to engage in ongoing self-reflection. This same set of knowledge and skills is also applied at the system level. Family engagement is important in EC care and education. This includes understanding the developmental needs of families as well as their children, especially when families and/or children speak different languages.

Culturally competent professional

A culturally competent professional demonstrates the ability to enable "...mutually rewarding interactions and meaningful relationships in the delivery of effective services for children and family whose cultural heritage differs from his or her own." (Shonkoff, National Research Council and Institute of Medicine, 2000) Providing interpreters and/or translators does not on its own constitute cultural competence. Hiring racially diverse educational staff in schools is also not enough. Culturally competent educators demonstrate highly developed self-awareness of their own cultural values and beliefs. They must also have and/or develop communication skills that allow them to elicit information from students and families regarding their own cultural beliefs. Further, they must be able to understand how diverse cultural views may affect a child's education, as well

Copyright © Mometrix Media. You have been licensed one copy of this document for personal use only. Any other reproduction or redistribution is strictly prohibited. All rights reserved.

as how parents/families receive, comprehend, interpret, and respond to educators' communications. Therefore, educators must develop communication skills to meet educational goals.

Cultural differences in parents' goals for raising their children

Depending on their cultural group, parents have varying goals for their children, and use different practices to achieve those goals. For example, research on four different cultural groups in Hawaii found the following differences related to what parents visualized when they pictured their children as successful adults: Native Hawaiians most wanted their children to have social connections, be happy in their social networks, and demonstrate self-reliance as adults. Caucasian American parents most valued self-reliance, happiness, spontaneity, and creativity as developmental outcomes for their children. Filipino American parents most valued the development of traits related to obedience, citizenship, respect for authority, and good conduct and manners in their children. Japanese American parents placed priority on their children's achievement, as well as their ability to live well-organized lives, stay in contact with family, and master the demands of life. Such distinct, significant differences imply that these parent groups would vary in how they would respond to young children's assertive behaviors, in their disciplinary styles (e.g., permissive, authoritative, authoritarian), and in the emphasis they would place on activities focusing on physical and cognitive skill mastery vs. social competence and connection.

Differences in American parents

Parents in America have been found to show distinct preferences for the kinds of care and educational services they access for their children. For example, Caucasian parents in America are more likely to turn to preschool centers for help with their young children's care and instruction. This preference is influenced not only by custom, but also by scientific evidence that center-based preschool experience improves children's skills and prepares them for school. Hispanic parents in America are more likely to use home-based and/or family-based care settings. This preference probably reflects the more collectivist Hispanic perspective, which places more importance on social relationships than on structured learning in early childhood. Educators can take a culturally competent approach to such cultural diversity by looking for ways in which young children's school readiness skills can be promoted in family and home-based child care settings.

Depending on their native culture, parents vary in terms of the early experiences they select for their young children. For example, Latino parents tend to prefer family-based/home-based care. White parents tend to prefer center-based daycare and education designed to promote school readiness. Another cultural difference is parental beliefs about children's learning capacities. For example, research in California found that the majority of Latino parents believed their children's learning capacity is set at birth; only a small minority of white parents held this belief. Parents subscribing to a transactional child development model view the complex interaction between child and environment as creating a dynamic developmental process. These parents are more likely to value the stimulation of early childhood development, seek/implement activities that will provide such stimulation, and access early intervention services for children with developmental delays/difficulties. Parents subscribing to a view of fixed, innate cognitive capacity are less likely to believe their children's cognitive abilities can be influenced by educational experiences, and may not see the benefits of or seek out early learning stimulation and intervention.

Copyright © Mometrix Media. You have been licensed one copy of this document for personal use only. Any other reproduction or redistribution is strictly prohibited. All rights reserved.

Variations in reading to young children

Researchers analyzing national early childhood surveys have identified significant variations in how often white, Asian, and Hispanic parents read to their young children. This variation is not solely due to varying cultural values. Additional factors include parents' financial limitations; time limitations; familiarity and comfort with accessing libraries and other government resources, websites, etc.; and literacy levels in both English and their native languages. Educators must realize that trying to encourage or even teach parents to read to their children earlier and/or more often is unlikely to be successful if parents do not place value or priority on the benefits of being read to, or do not view the outcomes of reading aloud to children as benefits. Reading to children is known to promote school readiness and academic success. Educators should also understand that some children, despite not being read to in early childhood, become successful adults. Additionally, some cultures, including African Americans, emphasize oral learning traditions more than written ones, developing different skills, such as the basic understanding of story flow.

Developmental milestones and their associated ages that vary according to culture

Research has found that different cultures have different age expectations for many early childhood developmental milestones. For example, Filipinos expect children to eat using utensils at 32.4 months. Anglo families expect children to do this at 17.7 months, and Puerto Ricans expect children to reach this milestone at 26.5 months. Filipino cultures expect children to sleep all night by 32.4 months; Puerto Rican and Anglo cultures expect this at 14.5 and 14.4 months, respectively. Similarly, while Anglos expect children to sleep by themselves at around 13.8 months and Puerto Ricans at around 14.6 months, Filipinos do not expect this until 38.8 months. Filipinos expect children to eat solid food by 6.7 months; Anglos by 8.2 months; and Puerto Ricans by 10.1 months. In Anglo families, an 18-month-old not drinking from a cup could indicate developmental delay if parents introduced the cup when s/he was one year old and regularly continued encouraging cup use. But, Filipino parents of an 18-month-old have likely not even introduced the child to a cup yet, so the fact that the child is not using a cup would not be cause for concern from a development standpoint.

<u>Early milestones that have varying age expectations among different cultural groups</u>
When EC researchers investigated the average expectations of different cultural groups of when children would reach various developmental milestones, some of the milestones they examined included: eating solid food, weaning from nursing, drinking from a cup, eating with the fingers, eating with utensils, sleeping alone, sleeping through the night, choosing one's own clothes, dressing oneself, and playing alone. They also looked at daytime and nighttime toilet training. Educators must become aware of different cultures' different socialization goals before assuming culturally diverse children have developmental delays. On the other hand, they must also avoid automatically attributing variations in milestone achievement to cultural child rearing differences when full developmental assessments might be indicated. Family expectations and values influence the complex process of developmental assessment. When families and assessors share common cultures, it is more likely that valid data will be collected and interpreted. When their cultures differ, however, it is more likely that the assessment information will be misinterpreted. Employing EC teachers/care providers who are familiar with the child, family, and assessment setting as mediators can make developmental assessments more culturally competent.

Copyright © Mometrix Media. You have been licensed one copy of this document for personal use only. Any other reproduction or redistribution is strictly prohibited. All rights reserved.

Factors affecting parents who are immigrants to America

Parents educated in other countries may not know a great deal about the American educational system, and may not be aware of the educational demands made on their children, even in early childhood. Educators need to work with these parents to find common ground by identifying shared goals for children. While culturally diverse parents may disagree with some educators' goals, they can collaborate with educators to promote those on which they do agree. Immigrant parents may also be unaware of additional services available in America for children with developmental and/or learning problems. Educators can help parents by providing this information. Another consideration is that some other cultures have more paternalistic educational systems. Parents from such cultures, rather than vocally advocating for their children who need services, tend to wait for teachers/specialists to voice concerns before communicating any problems they have observed. Thus, they could miss out on the chance to obtain helpful services. Even worse, educators could misconstrue their behavior as a lack of interest in children's progress, or as resistance to confronting problems.

Essential concepts in geography

(1) Location: This concept identifies "where" a place is and examines the positive and negative properties of any place on the surface of the Earth. Absolute location is based upon latitude and longitude. Relative location is based upon changing characteristics of a region, and is influenced by surrounding areas. For example, urban areas have higher land prices than rural ones.

(2) Distance: This identifies "how far" a place is, and is often described in terms of location. It is also related to the effort required to meet basic life needs. For example, the distance of raw materials from factories affects transportation costs and hence product prices. In another example, land costs less the farther it is from highways.

(3) Achievability: The conditions on the Earth's surface dictate how accessible a geographic area is. For example, villages on beaches are easier to reach. Villages surrounded by forests or swamps are harder to reach. As its economy, science, technology, and transportation develop, a region's level of dependency on other areas changes.

(4) Patterns: These are found in geographical forms and in how geographical phenomena spread, which affect dependency on those phenomena. For example, in fold regions (areas where the folding of rocks forms mountains), the rivers typically form trellis patterns. Patterns are also seen in human activity that is based on geography. For example, in mountainous regions, settlements predominantly form spreading patterns.

(5) Morphology: This is the shape of our planet's surface resulting from inner and outer forces. For example, along the northern coast of Java, sugarcane plantations predominate on the lowlands.

(6) Agglomeration: This is defined as collecting into a mass, and refers to a geographic concentration of people, activities, and/or settlements within areas that are most profitable and relatively narrow in size.

(7) Utility value: This refers to the existence and relative usefulness of natural resources. For example, fishermen find more utility value in the ocean than farmers do, and naturalists perceive more utility value in forests than academics would.

Copyright © Mometrix Media. You have been licensed one copy of this document for personal use only. Any other reproduction or redistribution is strictly prohibited. All rights reserved.

(8) Interaction: This is the reciprocal and interdependent relationship between two or more geographical areas, which can generate new geographical phenomena, configurations, and problems. For example, a rural village produces raw materials through activities like mining ores or growing and harvesting plant crops, while a city produces industrial goods. The village needs the city as a market for its raw materials, and may also need the city's industrial products. The city needs the village for its raw materials to use in industrial production. This interdependence causes interaction.

(9) Area differentiation: This informs the study of variations among regional geographical phenomena. For example, different plants are cultivated in highlands vs. lowlands due to their different altitudes and climates. Area differentiation also informs the study of regional variations in occupation (farming vs. fishing, etc.).

(10) Spatial interrelatedness: This shows the relationship between/among geographic and non-physical phenomena, like rural and urban areas. The example above of village-city interaction also applies here.

Graphs

Graphs display numerical information in pictorial forms, making it easier to view statistics quickly and draw conclusions about them. For example, it is easier to see patterns/trends like increases/decreases in quantities using visual graphs than columns of numbers. Line graphs, bar graphs, and pie charts are the most common types of graphs. Line graphs depict changes over time by plotting points for a quantity measured each day/week/month/year/decade/century etc. and connecting the points to make a line. For example, showing the population of a city/country each decade in a line graph reveals how the population has risen/fallen/both. Bar graphs compare quantities related to different times/places/people/things. Each quantity is depicted by a separate bar, and its height/length corresponds to a number. Bar graphs make it easy to see which amounts are largest/smallest within a group (e.g., which of several cities/countries has the largest population). Pie charts/circle graphs divide a circle/"pie" into segments/"slices" showing percentages/parts of a whole, which also facilitates making comparisons. For example, the city/country with the largest population is the largest segment on a pie chart or circle graph.

> ➤ **Review Video: Bar Graph**
> *Visit **mometrix.com/academy** and enter **Code: 226729***

Grid on a geographical map
Maps show absolute geographic location (i.e. the precise "address" of any place on the planet) using a grid of lines. The lines running from east to west are called parallels or latitudes, and they correspond to how many degrees away from the equator a place is located. The lines running from north to south are called meridians or longitudes, and they correspond to how many degrees away from the prime meridian a place is located. To determine the absolute location of a place, we find the spot on the map where its latitude and longitude intersect. This intersection is the place's absolute location. For example, if we look at Mexico City on a map, we will find that its latitude is 19° north and its longitude is 99° west, which is expressed in cartography as 19° N, 99° W. Numbers of latitudes and longitudes like these are also referred to as coordinates.

Tools that cartographers supply on maps
On maps depicting local, national, and world geography, cartographers supply tools for navigating these maps. For example, the compass rose indicates the directions of north, south, east, and west.

Copyright © Mometrix Media. You have been licensed one copy of this document for personal use only. Any other reproduction or redistribution is strictly prohibited. All rights reserved.

By looking at the compass, people can identify the locational relationships of places (e.g., in South America, Chile is west of Argentina). The scale of miles indicates how distances on a map correspond to actual geographical distances, enabling us to estimate real distances. For example, the scale might show that one inch is equal to 500 miles. By placing a piece of paper on the map, we can mark it to measure the distance between two cities (e.g., Washington, DC, in the USA and Ottawa in Canada) on the map, and then line the paper up with the scale of miles to estimate an actual distance of approximately 650 miles between the two cities. Map keys/legends identify what a map's symbols and colors represent.

Categories of features that can be displayed on maps
Maps can be drawn to show natural or man-made features. For example, some maps depict mountains, elevations (altitudes), average rainfall, average temperatures, and other natural features of an area. Other maps are made to depict countries, states, cities, roads, empires, wars, and other man-made features. Some maps include both natural and man-made features (e.g., a map showing a certain country and its elevations). Different types of maps are described according to their purposes. For example, political maps are made to depict countries, areas within a country, and/or cities. Physical maps are drawn to display natural features of the terrain in an area, such as rivers, lakes, and mountains. Thematic maps are drawn to focus on a more specific theme or topic, such as the locations and names of battles during a war or the average amounts of rainfall a country, state, or region receives in a given year or month. Some maps are made for more than one purpose, and indicate more than one of the types of information described above.

Reading and analyzing the information on a special purpose map
First, read a map's title and look at the overall map. This provides a general idea of what the map shows. For example, a map entitled "Battles of the Punic Wars" would not be a good choice if someone was looking for the political boundaries of modern day Greece, Italy, and Spain. Next, read the map's legend/key to see what symbols and colors the map uses, and what each represents. For example, some lines represent divisions between countries/states; some, roads; some, rivers; etc. Different colors can indicate different countries/states, elevations, amounts of rainfall, population densities, etc. These are not uniform across all maps, so legends/keys are necessary references. Use the legend/key to interpret what the map shows. For example, by looking at colors representing elevations, one can determine which area of a country has the highest/lowest altitude. Draw conclusions about what the map displays. For example, if a country map mainly has one color that indicates a certain elevation range, it can be concluded that this is the country's most common elevation.

Chronological thinking and understanding history

To see cause-and-effect relationships in historical events and explore and understand relationships among those events, students must have a solid grasp of when things happened and in what time sequence (chronology). Teachers can help students develop chronological thinking by using and assigning well-constructed/well-written narratives. These include histories written in the same style as stories, works of historical literature, and biographies. These hold students' attention, allowing them to focus on authors' depictions of temporal relationships among antecedents, actions, and consequences; of historical motivations and deeds of individuals and groups; and of the time structure of sequential occurrences. By middle school, students should have the skills needed to measure time mathematically (e.g., in years/decades/centuries/millennia), interpret data displayed in timelines, and calculate time in BCE and CE. High school students should be able to analyze patterns of historical duration (e.g., how long the U.S. Constitutional government has lasted) and patterns of historical succession (e.g., the development of expanding trade and

- 159 -

Copyright © Mometrix Media. You have been licensed one copy of this document for personal use only. Any other reproduction or redistribution is strictly prohibited. All rights reserved.

communication systems, from Neolithic times through ancient empires and from early modern times to modern global interaction).

Students should be able to differentiate among past, present, and future. They should be able to identify the beginning, middle, and end/outcome of historical narratives/stories. They also should be able to construct their own historical narratives, including working forward and backward in time from some event to explain causes and temporal development of various events, issues, etc. Students should be able to calculate and measure calendar time, including days/dates, weeks, months, years, centuries, and millennia. They should be able to describe time periods using BCE/BC and CE/AD. They should be skilled at comparing calendar systems (e.g., Roman, Gregorian, Julian, Hebrew, Muslim, Mayan, and others) and at relating the calendar years of major historical events. They should be able to look at timelines and interpret the information they contain, and make their own timelines using equidistant time intervals and recording events sequentially. Students should be able to explain change and continuity in history through reconstructing and applying patterns of historical duration and succession. They should be able to identify the structural principles that are the bases of alternative periodization models, and to compare these models.

Our country's laws and rules

Young children must understand the purposes of rules/laws: They identify acceptable/unacceptable citizen behaviors; make society and life predictable, secure, and orderly; designate responsibilities to citizens; and prevent persons in authority positions from abusing their roles by limiting their power. Understanding these functions of laws/rules enables children to realize that our government consists of individuals and groups authorized to create, implement, and enforce laws and manage legal disputes. Some creative EC teachers have used children's literature to illustrate these concepts. Children can relate personally to stories' characters, and story situations make the concepts real and concrete to children. Stories can be springboards for discussing rules and when they do/do not apply. One activity involves children in small groups making class rules (e.g., "No talking" and "Stay in your seat"), and then rewriting these to be more realistic (e.g., "Talk softly in class; listen when others talk" and "Sit down and get right to work"). Children consider issues of safety and fairness, and develop an understanding of judicial and legislative roles.

Copyright © Mometrix Media. You have been licensed one copy of this document for personal use only. Any other reproduction or redistribution is strictly prohibited. All rights reserved.

Practice Test

Practice Questions

1. A teacher asks her students to compare and contrast two animals they saw at the zoo. This is an example of what level of Bloom's taxonomy?
    A. Knowledge
    B. Comprehension
    C. Application
    D. Analysis

2. Students studying fractions manipulate "fraction blocks," blocks cut to represent fractional parts, to learn the concept of adding and subtracting fractions. Which level of development as described by Piaget does this activity demonstrate?
    A. Sensory-motor stage
    B. Pre-operational stage
    C. Concrete operational stage
    D. Formal operations stage

3. According to Kohlberg, at which developmental level do children understand that good behavior is expected?
    A. Post-Conventional
    B. Conventional
    C. Pre-Conventional
    D. Adolescent

4. Erikson's stages of development include all of the following except
    A. Young childhood
    B. Middle adulthood
    C. Adolescence
    D. Late childhood

5. In Bronfenbrenner's organization of child development, the family or classroom is considered a
    A. Chronosystem
    B. Microsystem
    C. Macrosystem
    D. Mesosystem

6. One of Vygotsky's major contributions to the field of early childhood development is the concept of
    A. Punishment/obedience
    B. A taxonomy of learning skill levels
    C. The importance of play as a learning activity
    D. The formal operations stage of development

Copyright © Mometrix Media. You have been licensed one copy of this document for personal use only. Any other reproduction or redistribution is strictly prohibited. All rights reserved.

7. Which of the following is a component of the Constructivist learning theory?
    A. Students, teachers, and classmates establish knowledge cooperatively every day
    B. Students are taught to develop skills in problem solving and critical thinking
    C. Children only learn language and culture through interaction with adults and other children
    D. It is important to help the learner gain an understanding of how knowledge is constructed

8. Social and behavioral theories of learning stress the importance of
    A. Good behavior on the part of students
    B. The social interactions of students that aid or inhibit learning
    C. A reward system for good behavior or growth in skills
    D. The direct connection between thoughts and speech

9. A teacher becomes aware that a certain student's family is in a crisis situation. What is his or her best course of action?
    A. Counsel the child on how best to handle the situation at home
    B. Contact the parents with a direct offer to help with their problems
    C. Report the crisis situation to school or civil authorities
    D. Attempt to deal with the student as well as possible despite the situation

10. Which of the following is the best way to assist children from families with limited incomes?
    A. Lower expectations for these children's achievements in the classroom
    B. Cooperate with school administrators and public officials to provide such assistance as a free lunch program and/or some academic assistance
    C. Counsel parents on ways to economize with their limited financial resources
    D. Provide the best possible instruction without any need for intervention or public assistance

11. The teacher notices that a student's attention in the classroom is decreased. The student seems restless and unable to concentrate. Which of the following may be the cause of this change in behavior?
    A. The child is coming down with an illness, such as the flu
    B. A problem has developed at home, such as divorce or abuse
    C. The child has entered a period of rapid physical growth which distracts him or her from cognitive activity
    D. All or any of the above

12. Which of the following is a symptom of an emotionally-neglected child?
    A. Extreme focus on school activities, seeking self-esteem
    B. Acts of jealousy or aggression toward other children
    C. Cooperative attitude in the classroom and on the playground
    D. Initiating social interaction with other students in the class at inappropriate times

13. Which of the following is an important aspect of allowing and encouraging children's play?
    A. Children need frequent opportunities to rest and relax
    B. Play teaches children cooperation and sharing
    C. Play encourages competition and opposition
    D. Play time gives the teacher a much needed rest period

Copyright © Mometrix Media. You have been licensed one copy of this document for personal use only. Any other reproduction or redistribution is strictly prohibited. All rights reserved.

14. What personal benefits can a young child obtain from play?
    A. Development of motor skills, such as hand-eye coordination
    B. Development of personal interests
    C. The ability to entertain himself or herself when alone
    D. All of the above

15. Social development and cognitive development often progress together because
    A. The more knowledge a child has, the more social he becomes
    B. As children are developing physically, they lose interest in social interactions
    C. Children develop the dexterity to show their cognitive development
    D. All areas of development—physical, social, and cognitive—are interrelated

16. The concept of latent development is important for teachers because:
    A. Teachers can be more patient with students if they understand their latency
    B. Teachers can wait until a student demonstrates complete ability in a certain skill area
    C. Teachers will be able to instruct the class as a whole group if they understand the stage at
       which everyone in the classroom is developing
    D. Developing skills may give clues for the next stage of instruction a student will need

17. A flat or agitated expression coupled with incoherent speech is a major symptom of
    A. Autism
    B. Drug or alcohol abuse
    C. Schizophrenia
    D. Intellectual disabilities

18. Which of the following actions are important for a teacher to do to create learning conditions for
students with disabilities?
    A. Use a child-centered approach to instruction
    B. Help students identify their own learning needs
    C. Structure learning experiences appropriate to the needs of the disabled student
    D. All of the above

19. When a child begins to act violently, breaking things and quarreling with other students,
teachers should see this change in behavior as a
    A. Sign of intellectual disabilities
    B. Sign of emotional difficulties
    C. Sign the child is becoming autistic
    D. Sign the child is abusing drugs or alcohol

20. If a child exhibits loss in cognitive thinking, social behavior, and usual academic progress, the
teacher should suspect that the child
    A. May be developing schizophrenia
    B. May be having emotional problems at home
    C. May be epileptic
    D. May be abusing drugs

Copyright © Mometrix Media. You have been licensed one copy of this document for personal use only. Any other reproduction or redistribution is strictly prohibited. All rights reserved.

21. What makes a child eligible for special education services?
   A. Falling behind academically and refusing to do any work at school
   B. Having a diagnosed physical or emotional disability that has been evaluated professionally
   C. Recommendation by the classroom teacher that the child needs additional help
   D. Request by parents for the child to be given special education services

22. If a child demonstrates a lack of concentration in the classroom and also becomes easily agitated, he or she may be suffering from
   A. Lack of sleep and/or nutrition
   B. Little verbal interaction at home
   C. A significant mental or emotional disability
   D. Severe physical abuse

23. At what age do children normally demonstrate a speech pattern that is 90% intelligible?
   A. Two years
   B. Three years
   C. Four years
   D. Five years

24. If a child appears delayed in speech development, which of the following is the best course to follow?
   A. Take a wait-and-see approach, as there are wide variations in patterns of speech development
   B. Use in-depth evaluations and early intervention to assist the child with language delays
   C. Help the child with common developmental speech problems, such as saying "w" for "r"
   D. Have the child repeat common words and phrases after an adult pronounces them

25. Which of the following is NOT a characteristic of a child with emotional disturbance?
   A. Lower academic performance
   B. Social skills deficits
   C. Aggressive behaviors
   D. Exaggerated efforts to make friends

26. How should the teacher best deal with an academically talented student who typically finishes work ahead of other students and tends to get into mischief while waiting for others to finish?
   A. Reprimand the student and remind him or her that his talents require setting a good example.
   B. Assign the student an appealing task related to the subject area that requires creativity, research, and/or in-depth study of the subject, such as creating a play or making a collage
   C. Permit the early finisher to have additional play time or extended recess as a reward for rapid completion of assignments
   D. Have the student tutor or help those who are not finished because they are having difficulty with the assignment

27. The most important factor for the teacher to keep in mind when teaching students with disabilities is
   A. Vary instructional pace and content to meet the specific needs of disabled students
   B. Slow the pace of classroom instruction to give the disabled students time to catch up
   C. Group the disabled students into a special section set apart from the regular students
   D. Insist that disabled students remain in their seats and focus on instruction

Copyright © Mometrix Media. You have been licensed one copy of this document for personal use only. Any other reproduction or redistribution is strictly prohibited. All rights reserved.

28. Seeking the appropriate method for meeting the needs of a disabled student is most often initiated by
    A. Parents
    B. A school's Child Study Team
    C. Community agencies
    D. The student's classroom teacher

29. Involvement of parents in developing a student's IEP (individualized education program) is essential because:
    A. An IEP must be approved by a parent before it can be enacted
    B. Parents know their children's needs, and an IEP must be tailored to those needs
    C. Teachers do not have the legal rights to discuss student needs with community representatives
    D. Students will not be willing to follow an IEP unless they have parental support

30. What is meant by the "least restrictive environment" policy of the IDEA?
    A. It is permissible to retain disabled students without passing them to the next grade level
    B. Students with disabilities need to be instructed in special classes
    C. Students with disabilities must be educated in an environment appropriate to them and their non-disabled peers, often a regular classroom
    D. Disabled students must be permitted to participate in the same classroom instruction as their non-disabled peers, even when it does not quite meet their needs

31. An IEP is a plan for
    A. Providing a tutor for an educationally handicapped student
    B. Providing counseling for an emotionally disturbed student
    C. Assisting parents in their problems handling a disabled student
    D. Assisting students in ways beyond what the classroom teacher can provide

32. A 504 differs from an IEP in that the 504
    A. Focuses on helping emotionally or physically disabled students within the classroom
    B. Is a legal document and requires formal assessment of the disability
    C. Requires the student to be referred for help by a parent or family member
    D. Requires regular monitoring and may be adjusted during the school year

33. Which of the following is NOT a reason for having a parent conference?
    A. The teacher wants to share information about the child's behavior and progress with the parents
    B. The teacher wants to receive information about the child from the parents
    C. The teacher wants to ask for parent support or involvement in specific activities
    D. The child's behavior is so difficult that the teacher wants the parents to withdraw the child from school

Copyright © Mometrix Media. You have been licensed one copy of this document for personal use only. Any other reproduction or redistribution is strictly prohibited. All rights reserved.

34. What is the advantage of placing students in community organizations like the ASB (Associated Student Body) or the PTSA (Parent Teacher Student Association)?
    A. These organizations help students to become politically savvy and be able to manipulate the rules of their school
    B. These organizations help students who are falling behind in school with tutoring and mentoring
    C. These organizations provide opportunities for students to develop leadership skills and learn to appreciate the value of collaborative processes
    D. Membership in these organizations can be listed on a student resume when the student is applying to colleges or universities

35. Which of the following genres is most important for children just beginning to become readers in grades K, 1, and 2?
    A. Alphabet books, wordless picture books, and easy-to-read books
    B. Legends and tall tales
    C. Biographies and informational books
    D. Chapter books and fantasy books

36. Which of the following is NOT a goal of children's literature?
    A. Focus on choices, morals, and values
    B. Instruct students through entertaining stories
    C. Promote an interest in reading itself
    D. Instruct students in the sciences, such as mathematics and biology

37. In which genre does the literature rely on the reader's suspension of disbelief about magical and mythical creatures?
    A. Science fiction
    B. Fantasy
    C. Action and adventure
    D. Historical fiction

38. A story about a young detective who solves mysteries using mental and physical skills would be classified as
    A. Action and adventure
    B. Historical fiction
    C. Horror and ghost stories
    D. Biography

39. The statement, "He ran as fast as a startled rabbit," is an example of
    A. Analogy
    B. Metaphor
    C. Symbolism
    D. Repetition

Copyright © Mometrix Media. You have been licensed one copy of this document for personal use only. Any other reproduction or redistribution is strictly prohibited. All rights reserved.

40. Young children are more likely to respond to analogies in stories than to metaphors because
    A. They are old enough to understand the abstract thinking and symbolism that analogies express
    B. The ability to understand the kinds of abstraction expressed in metaphors is not developed until later in childhood
    C. They can apply the concepts expressed in analogies to their own daily lives, but metaphors do not compare things that children are familiar with
    D. Metaphors and symbols are usually found only in books that children find boring because of their abstractions

41. When students compare nonfiction literature to fictional literature, what differences will they find?
    A. Nonfiction stories will be told in logical order and will relate only the facts, while fictional stories are never told in logical order
    B. Fictional stories deal with plot, characters, setting, and themes, and nonfiction does not
    C. In addition to plot, character, setting, and theme, a nonfiction work will also introduce interpretations, theory, and research
    D. Students will find few, if any, differences between these two types of literature because they are essentially the same

42. Which of the following would you expect children in grades k–2 to learn by being exposed to both fictional and nonfictional literature?
    A. How to tell fiction from nonfiction
    B. How to do research to find information
    C. How to tell if a nonfiction writer is writing from a biased viewpoint
    D. How to understand themes, theories, and settings

43. In selecting literature for children, the most important first step a teacher should perform is to evaluate
    A. Whether the characters are interesting
    B. Whether the plots are appealing
    C. Class composition and preferences
    D. The reading level of the material

44. What is the best way for a teacher to make sure that books in the classroom are at an appropriate reading level, neither too easy nor so difficult that beginning readers will become frustrated?
    A. Administer a reading pretest to the class before selecting suitable books
    B. Purchase books that are easy enough for even the most beginning of readers
    C. Make sure that all the books are just slightly above students' reading level, so they will grow
    D. Provide a wide variety of reading materials for children to choose from

45. One of the most important elements in children's literature that captures children's interest is
    A. Character
    B. Accuracy
    C. Information
    D. Vocabulary

Copyright © Mometrix Media. You have been licensed one copy of this document for personal use only. Any other reproduction or redistribution is strictly prohibited. All rights reserved.

46. If a teacher does not have time to pre-read all the books she selects for her classroom, what is a good alternative?
    A. Look at children's book reviews in professional materials
    B. Seek input from children themselves about their favorite books
    C. Seek the assistance of the school librarian
    D. All of the above

47. The adaptation of language in a piece of writing to meet the author's purpose or audience is called
    A. Theme
    B. Point of view
    C. Style
    D. Voice

48. The perspective from which a story is told is called
    A. Theme
    B. Point of view
    C. Style
    D. Voice

49. In Mr. Booker's first grade classroom, students are studying marine animals in science. Mr. Booker wants to select a book to read to the class that will enhance their understanding of this subject while at the same time capturing their interest in a story. Which of the following would be the best choice?
    A. *The Wild Whale Watch*, part of the Magic School bus series, a chapter book about whales
    B. *The Whale Watchers Guide*, a book designed to help plan a whale-watching trip
    C. M*oby Dick*, a famous 19th century novel about a man and a white whale
    D. *The Pacific Ocean*, a book describing the ocean floor, tides, wave formation, and currents

50. Which of the following describes one difference between role-play writing and early writing?
    A. In role-play writing, the child writes in scribbles that are only meaningful to him or her. In early writing, the child uses real letters
    B. In early writing, the child writes in scribbles that are only meaningful to him or her. In role-play writing, the child writes in groups of words with a period at the end
    C. In role-play writing, the child writes in simple forms of language, usually the way the word sounds. In early writing, the child starts to use sight words and familiar text
    D. In early writing, the child has a sense of audience and a purpose for writing. In role-play writing, the child writes from the point of view of an imaginary character

51. Which of the following is a developmental skill a child should have before beginning to write?
    A. Large muscle control
    B. Ability to speak coherently
    C. Small muscle control
    D. Ability to hold a pencil correctly

52. A child using the prewriting strategy called "free writing" will
    A. Make a list of all ideas connected with the chosen topic
    B. Create a visual map on paper to connect ideas
    C. Ask the questions "Who?," "What?," "When?," and "Where?"
    D. Write thoughts and ideas without stopping to edit them

Copyright © Mometrix Media. You have been licensed one copy of this document for personal use only. Any other reproduction or redistribution is strictly prohibited. All rights reserved.

53. Which of the following is NOT a prewriting strategy?
   A. Brainstorming
   B. Visual mapping of ideas
   C. Asking questions
   D. Organizing writing into paragraphs

54. In the organization stage of writing, the writer
   A. Determines the purpose, thesis, and supporting details of the written work
   B. Brainstorms ideas for items to include in the written work
   C. Submits the writing to a classmate for editing
   D. Writes the introduction and conclusion

55. Maria's topic sentence is "My family prepares for holidays in a big way." Which of the following would be the best supporting detail to follow that sentence?
   A. Holidays are just a waste of everyone's time and money
   B. First, we decide who is going to host the holiday dinner
   C. In my family are me, my brother, my sister, and our parents
   D. Afterwards we all help clean up and then relax

56. Which of the following is true of the introduction to a written piece?
   A. It should be written first
   B. It should be written last
   C. It should reinforce the points made in the piece
   D. It is the least important part of a piece of writing

57. Which of the following is not a method of peer editing?
   A. Pairs of students analyze each others' sentences for variety
   B. Groups of students ask questions of the author to make the writing more clear
   C. Students work together to perform a final edit
   D. Students decide whether another student's essay is good writing or poor writing

58. Which of the following should not be capitalized?
   A. State names
   B. Small words like "of" in titles
   C. Proper names
   D. Main words in titles of written work

Copyright © Mometrix Media. You have been licensed one copy of this document for personal use only. Any other reproduction or redistribution is strictly prohibited. All rights reserved.

59. Elena wrote the following paragraph:

> I believe that everyone should try to care for our planet. The best ways to do this are through recycling and using natural energy instead of fossil fuels. The supply of fossil fuels such as oil and coal will be used up some day, so we should try now to use less. Solar panels can reduce the use of fossil fuels. Windmills can be used to make electricity. Hybrid cars also use less fuel. If we do not try to be "green," our planet will soon be in trouble from global warming and the absence of fossil fuels. What kind of world would that be?

The purpose of Elena's paragraph was
    A. Narration
    B. Entertainment
    C. Persuasion
    D. Description

60. Students should learn to write for a variety of audiences because
    A. Writing everything just for the teacher is boring
    B. Their classmates are also a potential audience
    C. Students are more involved in their writing if the audience varies
    D. Students can make political statements with letters to the editor

61. Which of the following genres takes an opinion and defends it?
    A. Essays
    B. Biographies
    C. Memoirs
    D. Informational texts

62. The final resolution of a fictional plot is called
    A. Exposition
    B. Rising Action
    C. Falling Action
    D. Denouement

63. Assonance means that two or more words
    A. Start with the same sound
    B. End with the same sound
    C. Have the same vowel sound
    D. Sound like an item they portray

64. The basics of writing to a particular audience do NOT include
    A. Precise vocabulary
    B. Correct facts
    C. Figurative language
    D. Illustrations or examples

Copyright © Mometrix Media. You have been licensed one copy of this document for personal use only. Any other reproduction or redistribution is strictly prohibited. All rights reserved.

65. The direct instruction model for teaching students to recognize numbers includes
    A. Showing newly introduced numbers more often than other numbers
    B. Having students count the number of dots and match them to a number
    C. Using manipulatives to count and then write a number
    D. Showing students the different ways a number can be written

66. Which of the following is an example of an ordinal number?
    A. 13
    B. One-half
    C. Second
    D. Ten

67. The property of numbers that states that 1 + 3 is the same as 3 + 1 is called
    A. Associative
    B. Distributive
    C. Inverse
    D. Commutative

68. A number system in which the position of a digit in a number determines its value is called a
    A. Relationship system
    B. Place value system
    C. Regrouping system
    D. Tens and hundreds system

69. Paper strips and Cuisenaire rods are manipulatives used to teach
    A. Place value
    B. Fractions
    C. Addition of whole numbers
    D. Percents

70. A decimal can be converted to a percent by
    A. Moving the decimal point two places to the right
    B. Dividing by 100
    C. Doubling the number
    D. Moving the decimal point one place to the left

71. By rewriting 5 times 9 as 9 + 9 +9 + 9 + 9, students will learn
    A. The commutative property of numbers
    B. The relationship between multiplication and addition
    C. The relationship between addition and division
    D. The associative property of numbers

72. Although there are 100 addition facts, if students understand commutativity, they actually need to learn
    A. 95 facts
    B. 75 facts
    C. 65 facts
    D. 55 facts

Copyright © Mometrix Media. You have been licensed one copy of this document for personal use only. Any other reproduction or redistribution is strictly prohibited. All rights reserved.

73. Which of the following is NOT a model that helps students understand subtraction?
    A. Take away
    B. Missing addend
    C. Number line
    D. Adding zero

74. Which of the following is NOT a way to teach young children to recognize patterns?
    A. Count by twos beginning with 5
    B. Comparing geometric shapes
    C. Solving for x in an equation
    D. Analyzing the results of a class survey

75. Geometric figures can be classified by
    A. The number of sides
    B. The angles where sides meet
    C. Whether they are polygons or solids
    D. All of the above

76. John drew two triangles on a piece of paper, like this:

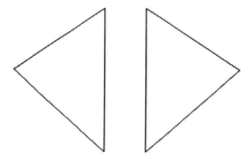

They were facing away from each other, but had the exact same size and shape. This is best described as an example of which geometrical concept?
    A. Rotation
    B. Reflection
    C. Translation
    D. Magnification

77. A missing object problem like the one below is one way of helping students learn what concept?
Truck car bike train truck car bike _____ truck car bike train
    A. Counting
    B. Problem solving
    C. Manipulation of objects
    D. Basic addition

78. When deciding to measure the sides of a two-dimensional object, what attributes of that object should be considered?
    A. Volume and liquid measurement
    B. Length and width
    C. Weight and mass
    D. Perimeter and area

Copyright © Mometrix Media. You have been licensed one copy of this document for personal use only. Any other reproduction or redistribution is strictly prohibited. All rights reserved.

79. What is the educational purpose of having students measure the length of an object, such as their desk or table, with non-standard measuring units smaller than the object, such as crayons?
    A. Measuring with small units is easier for young children
    B. Children cannot read the markings on a standard ruler or yard stick
    C. Students learn to measure something larger than a unit with repetitive use of that unit
    D. Students will later be able to transfer measurements from meters to yards

80. For three days, Mr. Hanson had his students keep track of how many times each of them used a pencil during the school day. What is the best kind of graph to use to display these data?
    A. Bar graph
    B. Circle graph
    C. Pictograph
    D. Line graph

81. Katrina wanted to solve this math problem: "If there are 30 days in a month and today is the 12th, how many days until the end of the month?" What should be her first problem-solving step?
    A. Devise a plan for solving the problem
    B. Carry out the plan she created
    C. Look back to check that her answer is correct
    D. Understand what the problem is asking

82. A third-grade teacher decides to introduce new vocabulary words using a word association game. What is required in order for the students to succeed with word associations?
    A. The definition of the new words.
    B. Prior knowledge.
    C. The spelling of the word.
    D. Synonyms of the new words.

83. Which teaching strategy would be best for teaching multiplication tables to a second-grade class?
    A. Priming.
    B. Discussion.
    C. Repetition.
    D. Listening.

84. What is a primary contribution of the Israelites to civilization?
    A. Secularism
    B. Democracy
    C. Monarchism
    D. Monotheism

85. A major scientific development that began near the beginning of the 17th century was
    A. The development of scientific theories
    B. The use of experiments to verify theories
    C. The concept of an attraction between bodies called gravity
    D. The theory of relativity

Copyright © Mometrix Media. You have been licensed one copy of this document for personal use only. Any other reproduction or redistribution is strictly prohibited. All rights reserved.

86. The results of increased production of crops and a managed approach to agriculture is called
    A. The industrial revolution
    B. The information revolution
    C. The agricultural revolution
    D. The scientific revolution

87. Which of these refers to the oceans and water areas of earth?
    A. Atmosphere
    B. Hydrosphere
    C. Exosphere
    D. Lithosphere

88. What is one benefit of a cooperative learning group?
    A. Increased engagement.
    B. Socialization.
    C. Down time for the teacher.
    D. Assistance for struggling students.

89. Due process means
    A. It's important for every citizen to follow the laws of their state and country
    B. Any accused person may confront the accuser and provide a defense
    C. Capital punishment is appropriate if a person is convicted of murder
    D. An accused person is considered guilty until proven to be innocent

90. In the Constitution of the United States, which of the following powers are reserved for the states?
    A. Taxation
    B. Declaring war
    C. Regulation of intrastate trade
    D. Granting patents and copyrights

91. A law proposed in Congress but not yet passed is called
    A. A bill
    B. A proposal
    C. An introduced law
    D. A debate

92. It is snack time in your kindergarten class, and you pour two children equal amounts of water; however, one child's cup is bigger. The child with the bigger cup complains that he has less water. In terms of cognitive development, what can you determine by this complaint?
    A. The child has a developmental delay because he does not understand conservation.
    B. The child has not reached the concrete operational stage and does not understand conservation; this is normal for a child of this age.
    C. The child is displaying a delay in intuitive processes commonly acquired during the pre-operational stage of cognitive development.
    D. The child is displaying a preconceptual process that is common among this age group.

Copyright © Mometrix Media. You have been licensed one copy of this document for personal use only. Any other reproduction or redistribution is strictly prohibited. All rights reserved.

93. A belief or opinion in opposition to certain beliefs is called
    A. Respect
    B. Obedience
    C. Dissent
    D. Rights

94. Repetition is important to scientific inquiry because
    A. It is the only way to prove that an experiment is valid
    B. It adds to the number of statistics supporting the concept
    C. It assists the scientist in determining which data to consider
    D. It requires many groups of investigators working on a project

95. The father of microscopy was
    A. Pasteur
    B. Koch
    C. Leeuwenhoek
    D. Watson

96. What effect does science have on technology?
    A. Science verifies what technology discovers
    B. Technology often results from scientific discoveries
    C. Science has no effect on technology; each is independent of the other
    D. Scientific progress is dependent on technology

97. Which of the following are required by all organisms in order to survive?
    A. Water, cells, shelter, and space
    B. Food, water, cellular growth, nurturing
    C. Food, water, sunlight, and air
    D. Air, shelter, space, and companionship

98. What is the difference between mass and weight?
    A. There is no difference; they are the same
    B. Mass is the amount of matter in an object; weight is the pull of gravity on the object
    C. Mass determines the amount of volume of an object; weight does not
    D. Mass is the amount of cubic space that an object occupies. Cubic space is not related to weight

99. World weather patterns are very much influenced by
    A. Wind belts
    B. The Earth's orbit
    C. Ocean currents
    D. Atmospheric conditions

100. In the technological design process, after the problem has been identified and a possible solution selected, what is the next step?
    A. Propose designs
    B. Evaluate the solution
    C. Try out the proposed solution
    D. Report results

Copyright © Mometrix Media. You have been licensed one copy of this document for personal use only. Any other reproduction or redistribution is strictly prohibited. All rights reserved.

Answers and Explanations

1. D: Analysis. Compare and Contrast is a higher level of thinking and requires analysis.

2. C: Concrete operational stage. The manipulation of objects in the learning process involves using concrete materials to bridge understanding of abstract concepts.

3. B: Conventional. There is actually a hint to this answer in its name. According to Kohlberg, the stage of development during which children learn conventional behavior—e.g., good behavior—is the Conventional Stage.

4. D: Late childhood. This is not one of Erikson's levels of development.

5. B: Microsystem. The family unit and the classroom unit constitute a small social system, a microsystem.

6. C: The importance of play as a learning activity. Vygotsky pointed out that play is the way children learn cooperation and coordination, among other things.

7. A: Students, teachers, and classmates establish knowledge cooperatively every day. In the Constructivist learning theory, the interactions among students, classmates, and teachers were an important contributor to learning.

8. B: The social interaction of students that aid or inhibit learning. According to these theories, students do not just learn in isolation or in a one-on-one relationship with a teacher. They also learn attitudes toward education from their peers, sometimes positive and sometimes negative.

9. C: Report the crisis situation to school or civil authorities. The situation cannot be ignored, but it needs to be dealt with officially and not by the teacher.

10. B: Cooperate with school administrators and public officials to provide assistance, such as a free lunch program and/or academic assistance. Hungry students are not in a position to learn. The family with limited income may not have introduced their child to as many preschool experiences as other children have had, and placement in a special program may be needed to support the child's progress.

11. D: All of the above. There are many possible explanations for a child having decreased attention in class. All should be analyzed to discover the actual problem.

12. B: Acts of jealousy or aggression toward other children. The emotionally-neglected child often behaves negatively toward other children. He or she may not know another way of gaining attention from classmates.

13. B: Play teaches children cooperation and sharing. Play is one way a child learns to relate to other children in a positive way.

Copyright © Mometrix Media. You have been licensed one copy of this document for personal use only. Any other reproduction or redistribution is strictly prohibited. All rights reserved.

14. D: All of the above. Play provides the child with opportunities to develop hand-eye coordination, develop personal interests, and learn to amuse him or herself when alone.

15. D: All areas of development—physical, social, and cognitive—are interrelated. A teacher who is aware of this may be able to emphasize the most appropriate method of instruction for this particular child.

16. D: Developing skills may give clues for the next stage of instruction a student will need. For example, the teacher may observe a child developing skill with manipulative materials and introduce the child to the next step, moving from manipulative to written materials.

17. C: Schizophrenia. The schizophrenic child often has a flat or agitated expression and may speak incoherently or repetitively.

18. D: All of the above. Students with disabilities are best served by a child-centered approach, help in identifying their own learning needs, and need learning experiences that are structured to be appropriate to their needs.

19. B: Sign of emotional difficulties. When children are upset or disturbed, they often manifest their feelings non-verbally in angry outbursts.

20. D: May be abusing drugs. Children using drugs withdraw from social contact and academic activities.

21. B: Having a diagnosed physical or emotional disability that has been professionally evaluated. The child can then be placed in a program that will meet his or her needs. This process often begins with a recommendation by a teacher or parent, but to receive special education services, the child must first be professionally evaluated.

22. A: Lack of sleep or nutrition. Lacking either of these, a child is unable to focus on classroom instruction and may become agitated easily.

23. C: Four years. One hundred percent language development is not achieved until age five.

24. B: Use in-depth evaluation and early intervention to assist the child with language delays. Research shows that early intervention is highly successful, while a wait-and-see approach just prolongs the delayed language development. Common developmental problems like saying "w" instead of "r" disappear on their own as the child matures and do not need intervention.

25. D: Exaggerated efforts to make friends. The child with emotional problems is likely to withdraw from social interactions and exhibit lower academic performance and aggressive behavior.

26. B: Assign the student an appealing task related to the subject area that requires creativity, research, or in-depth study, such as making a collage or creating a play. Assigning the student to tutor classmates does not assist in the intellectual growth of an academically talented student, and the student is apt to resent such an assignment. The teacher needs to be aware that academically talented students also have special academic needs and continue to challenge them with meaningful assignments.

Copyright © Mometrix Media. You have been licensed one copy of this document for personal use only. Any other reproduction or redistribution is strictly prohibited. All rights reserved.

27. A: Vary instructional pace and content to meet the specific needs of disabled students. Answers B, C, and D would stigmatize the disabled student and probably not result in a proper pace and content level.

28. D: The students' classroom teacher. Often, disabilities are not apparent in the home setting, and community agencies will not discover disabled children until informed about them, usually by the teacher.

29. B: Parents know their children's needs, and an IEP must be tailored to meet those needs. The classroom teacher will also be aware of some of those needs, but the child spends more time at home than at school, and the parents may be aware of a disability that is not evident in the classroom but needs to be addressed. Also, the implementation of an IEP is most successful when parents, the school, and the community work together as a team.

30. C: Students with disabilities must be educated in an environment appropriate to them and their non-disabled peers, often a regular classroom. Students with disabilities were formerly segregated into special classes, but the least restrictive environment frequently turns out to be a regular classroom, sometimes with additional assistance for the teacher and the student.

31. D: Assisting students in ways beyond what the classroom teacher can provide. This may include any or all of the assistance suggested in the other answers, such as tutoring, counseling, and assisting or advising parents.

32. A: Focuses on helping emotionally or physically disabled students within the classroom. This is the focus of a 504. An IEP has broader applications to other disabilities or special needs.

33. D: The child's behavior is so difficult that the teacher wants the parents to withdraw the child from school. The teacher may desire this, but has no authority to request it from parents. Sometimes a student will attend school for a limited part of the day, but the decision to limit the day or exclude the child will be made by a team, not by the teacher alone in the process of a teacher-parent conference. Conferences are beneficial for sharing information between a teacher and parents and for enlisting parental support for planned activities involving the child.

34. C: These organizations provide opportunities for children to develop leadership skills and learn to appreciate the value of collaborative processes. Not all community resources are directed toward the disabled child. These organizations, ASB and PTSA, are designed to teach leadership skills to students who show leadership potential. Sometimes a student representative is assigned to the school board for the same reasons.

35. A: Alphabet books, wordless picture books, and easy-to-read books. The other genres are more suitable for older children with well-developed reading skills.

36. D: Instruct students in sciences, such as mathematics and biology. Textbooks have that goal. Children's literature is designed to enhance moral values, instruct through entertaining stories, and promote a life-long interest in reading.

37. B: Fantasy. Fantasy stories and books revolve around magical or supernatural creatures. The Harry Potter books are one example of this genre. Science fiction is a similar genre, but relies on the portrayal of a future world, creatures from other planets or galaxies, etc. Action and Adventure

Copyright © Mometrix Media. You have been licensed one copy of this document for personal use only. Any other reproduction or redistribution is strictly prohibited. All rights reserved.

involves solving mysteries. Historical fiction stories are set sometime in the past and are usually accurate in their historical information.

38. A: Action and Adventure. One example of this genre is Nancy Drew. Action and Adventure stories do not rely on magical or supernatural events as do Fantasy, Horror, and Ghost stories. They are not biographical unless telling the life of a real person.

39. A: Analogy. The statement is not a metaphor because it contains the word "like." A metaphor does not. An example of a metaphor would be "He was a frozen statue, motionless beside the door." There is no symbolism in the statement, "He ran as fast as a rabbit," nor is there any repetition.

40. B: The ability to understand the abstract concept expressed in metaphors is not developed until later in childhood. Analogies are easier for children to understand because they compare known items, whereas metaphors require abstract thinking.

41. C: In addition to plot, character, setting, and theme, a nonfictional work will also introduce interpretations, theories, and research. For example, a biography is a type of nonfiction that may have plot, character, setting, and theme, and in addition it will introduce interpretations and theories (of the person's life and actions) as well as evidence of the author's research.

42. A: How to tell fiction from nonfiction. This is a skill that children learn by following clues within the literature that point out whether the story is true or not. Young children are not yet ready to distinguish bias in an author's writing or understand themes and theories.

43. C: Class composition and preferences. Before selecting literature for the classroom, the teacher needs to assess the class, considering where they are with their reading skills and what their current interests are. After determining these things, the teacher would next evaluate books that seem appropriate for this particular group of children in terms of plot, character, and reading level.

44. D: Provide a wide variety of reading materials for children to choose from. Each classroom will have students who are just beginning to read and some that are reading fluently above grade level. Providing reading materials with an appealing variety of subject matter and broad distribution of reading levels will ensure that every child in the class can select an appropriate book to read.

45. A: Characters. Children enjoy identifying with a character and experiencing life from that character's point of view. If readers do not bond with a character, they will not enjoy the story.

46. D: All of the above. It is not realistic to expect a teacher to preview every book selected for the classroom, and fortunately there are alternatives, such as asking for help from the school librarian, reading professional reviews, and discussing favorite books with children.

47. C: Style. An author writing a humorous book will use a different style than an author writing a biography.

48. B: Point of view. The point of view is generally first or third person. Stories in the second person exist, but these are rare.

49. A: The *Wild Whale Watch*, part of the Magic School bus series, a chapter book about whales. First graders love to listen to chapter books, but most first graders are not quite able to read chapter books on their own. The undersea fictional adventures in this book will impart a great deal of

Copyright © Mometrix Media. You have been licensed one copy of this document for personal use only. Any other reproduction or redistribution is strictly prohibited. All rights reserved.

marine information while simultaneously capturing students' attention with the story. The *Whale Watchers Guide* is not a good choice since the class is not planning a whale watching trip. *Moby Dick* is a well-known adult book, which first graders would not understand. *The Pacific Ocean* will probably offer a lot of marine information, but may not capture first graders' interests.

50. A: In role playing writing, the child writes in scribbles that are only meaningful to him or her. In early writing, the child begins to use real letters.

51. C: Small muscle control. Small muscles are those that enable us to make precise motions, such as gripping a pencil and writing letters with it. Large muscle control involves activities such as running or jumping. The ability to speak is not a developmental skill leading to the ability to write.

52. D: Write thoughts and ideas without stopping to edit them. Freewriting is a prewriting strategy that asks the writer to simply write without any internal editing or concern about formalities, such as spelling or punctuation. The purpose of freewriting is to get the flow of ideas going.

53. D: Organizing writing into paragraphs is done either during the writing process or afterwards in the revision stage. It is not a prewriting strategy.

54. A: In the organization stage of writing, the writer determines the purpose, thesis, and supporting details of the written work. In other words, the organization stage is the part of the writing process where the writer decides on the structure of the proposed written work. In this stage, the writer organizes the ideas already decided upon in the prewriting stage.

55. B: "First we decide who is going to host the holiday dinner." A clue is found in the word "first." A list of actions or ideas often follows a topic sentence.

56. B: It should be written last. Although it is the first part of the written piece, the introduction needs to discuss what is in the entire piece. Until the writing is complete, the writer cannot do that. Writing the introduction first runs the risk that what follows may not completely conform to the ideas expressed in the introduction.

57. D: Students decide whether another student's essay is good writing or poor writing. Peer editing should consist of suggestions for improvement and never involve judgmental decisions about quality.

58. B: Small words in titles like "the" and "of." State names, proper names, and main words in titles should all be capitalized.

59. C: Persuasion. Elena's paragraph was written to persuade. Clues to her purpose can be found in the first and last sentences, which clearly try to influence the reader.

60. C: Students are more involved in their writing if the audience varies. Examples of varied audiences include letters to the editor, letters to a friend, an essay written for a community group, and a story written for younger children or beginning readers.

61. A: Essays. In an essay, the writer defends an opinion, giving reasons for that opinion. Biographies are written to narrate the life of a person. Memoirs detail a person's own life and do not defend opinions. Informational texts are factual.

Copyright © Mometrix Media. You have been licensed one copy of this document for personal use only. Any other reproduction or redistribution is strictly prohibited. All rights reserved.

62. D: Denouement. The denouement is the end of the story. The other choices are intermediate steps in writing a story.

63. C: Have the same vowel sound. Words with assonance have the same vowel sound. An example would be cow and loud.

64. B: Correct and accurate facts are not part of the basics of writing to a particular audience. Some writing for some audiences will not be factual at all, for example, a fairy tale written for young children. The basics of writing to a particular audience include precise vocabulary, figurative language, and illustrations or examples.

65. A: Showing newly introduced numbers more often than other numbers. The direct instruction method depends on repetition of newly introduced numbers. Other methods involve counting dots, using manipulatives, and examining different ways of writing a number.

66. C: Second. Ordinal numbers are first, second, third, fourth, etc.

67. D: Commutative. The property that states that the order in which numbers are added does not change the answer is called the commutative property.

68. B: A place value system. That is the system that requires the position of a digit in a number to determine the digit's value. For example, in the number 123, the digit two is in ten's place, and its value is 20.

69. B: Fractions. Students can manipulate the different lengths of materials like paper strips and Cuisenaire rods, in order to determine that one rod is one half the length of the other, for example.

70. A: Moving the decimal point two places to the right. For example, the decimal 3.42 stands for 342.0 percent of something.

71. B: The relationship between multiplication and addition. By performing these activities, students will see that multiplication is just the repetitive addition of a number a certain number of times.

72. D: 55 facts. When students learn that 3 + 8 is 11, they are also learning that 8 + 3 is 11, so they do not need to memorize 100 facts, just 55.

73. D: Adding zero. Adding zero does not assist students in understanding subtraction. Physically taking some objects away from an array of objects, working a problem with a missing addend like 7 + __ = 13 helps students learn that 13-7 = 6. Moving to the left on a number line is another way of helping students understand subtraction.

74. C: Solving for x in an equation. Young children are not ready for algebraic equations, but they can learn to recognize patterns by counting by twos, comparing geometric shapes, and analyzing data they have collected.

75. D: All of the above. Geometric figures can be classified in a number of ways, including the number of sides, the angles where sides meet, and as polygons or solids.

Copyright © Mometrix Media. You have been licensed one copy of this document for personal use only. Any other reproduction or redistribution is strictly prohibited. All rights reserved.

76. B: Reflection. One triangle faces the other. They are alike in all other ways. In a rotation, two like figures are rotated about a central point. A translation is a change in the position of a geometric figure. Magnification refers to a change in size of the figure.

77. B: Problem solving. Because an item is missing in the middle of the pattern, the process asked for cannot be counting or addition. Solving this puzzle does not involve manipulation of objects.

78. B: Length and width. Since the object is not a solid, no other dimensions are needed.

79. C: Students learn to measure something larger than a unit by repetitive use of that unit.

80. A: Bar graph. A bar graph is used to compare quantities. A circle is used to compare parts of a whole. A pictograph shows comparison of quantities using symbols. A line graph shows trends over a period of time.

81. D: Understand what the problem is asking. Before you can solve a problem, you must decide what it is about.

82. B: Word associations require a student to pull from previous knowledge or experience. For example, if the student is presented with the word "aardvark" but has never seen or heard of an aardvark, he or she will not be able to make associations. While word association may be a good activity for students after they have reviewed the vocabulary words, it may be counterproductive if the students are unfamiliar with the words. Teachers should also be mindful of cultural differences that may account for a variation in previous knowledge.

83. C: Learning multiplication tables is best accomplished with repetition. As the students repeat the problems and their solutions, connections are made in the brain, and learning is enhanced. While there are many newer methods of teaching and learning, repetition is still useful for a number of tasks. This strategy is also typically used with students learning the alphabet or their phone number and address. Teachers should be aware that young children have short attention spans and can easily become distracted. Therefore, when using repetition as a teaching strategy, the sessions should be relatively short.

84. D: Monotheism. Before the Israelites, almost all civilizations, including the Egyptian, Greek, and Roman civilizations, believed in many gods.

85. B: The use of experiments to verify theories. Before the idea of experimenting was developed, many scientists had theories, often in conflict with each other, but these ideas were never verified scientifically to demonstrate which one was correct. Experiments provided a way to prove ideas.

86. C: The agricultural revolution. A dependable food supply is essential to all populations. The agricultural revolution, an organized, almost scientific approach to agriculture, increased the food supply necessary for a growing world population.

87. B: Hydrosphere. The earth's environment consists of the atmosphere, (the air we breathe), the hydrosphere (water), and the lithosphere (the land).

88. A: In the classroom setting, some students may be hesitant to openly participate. This may be due to a number of reasons, including the fear of being wrong or shyness. Utilizing cooperative learning groups is one way to increase student participation in class. Creating smaller groups

Copyright © Mometrix Media. You have been licensed one copy of this document for personal use only. Any other reproduction or redistribution is strictly prohibited. All rights reserved.

within the class allows students to participate in a less threatening environment. Additionally, motivation and overall outcomes have also been shown to improve in these environments. Using these learning groups in conjunction with other teaching methods keeps students interested and engaged.

89. B: The right of a defendant to confront accusers and to provide a defense.

90. C: Regulate intrastate trade. Intrastate trade is solely within a state, so the state has jurisdiction over it. Taxation is a right granted to both federal and state authorities. Declaring war is a national decision. Patents and copyrights apply to goods made and/or sold throughout the country; therefore, they are a federal responsibility.

91. A: A bill. A bill is a proposed law.

92. B: The child is developing normally; typical of his age group, he is in the preoperational stage of development and has not yet mastered conservation. Conservation is the ability to use logical reasoning to determine quantity. In this case, the child thinks one glass has more water simply because the glass is bigger. As this child enters into the concrete operational stage of development, he will understand that two amounts can be equal despite the size or shape of the container they are in. However, since this skill is not yet developed, the child will continue to believe one has more. If the teacher pours the water from the bigger glass into a glass that equals the size of his classmate's, the child will have a different reaction and possibly think the two are now equal.

93. C: Dissent. Dissent occurs when a citizen disagrees with a certain concept or law.

94. A: It is the only way to prove that an experiment is valid. If an experiment can't be successfully repeated with the same outcome, one cannot determine that the experimental results are valid. Repetition is the key to scientific progress.

95. C: Leeuwenhoek. Pasteur discovered the role of micro-organisms in disease. Koch determined that each disease has a specific pathogen. James Watson developed the science of genetics.

96. B: Technology often results from scientific discoveries. The relationship between science and technology is evident when scientific discoveries prompt technologic advances.

97. C: Food, water, sunlight, and air. All living organisms need food, water, sunlight and air. Shelter, space, and nurturing are nice to have but not crucial to sustaining life.

98. B: Mass. Mass is the amount of matter in an object. Weight is the measure of the pull of gravity on an object.

99. C: Ocean currents. Wind belts, the Earth's orbit, and atmospheric conditions have some effect on weather, but ocean currents have the greatest influence.

100. C: Try out the proposed solution. The first step is to identify a problem and propose a solution. Trying the solution comes next, followed by evaluation and reporting the results.

Copyright © Mometrix Media. You have been licensed one copy of this document for personal use only. Any other reproduction or redistribution is strictly prohibited. All rights reserved.

Secret Key #1 - Time is Your Greatest Enemy

Pace Yourself

Wear a watch. At the beginning of the test, check the time (or start a chronometer on your watch to count the minutes), and check the time after every few questions to make sure you are "on schedule."

If you are forced to speed up, do it efficiently. Usually one or more answer choices can be eliminated without too much difficulty. Above all, don't panic. Don't speed up and just begin guessing at random choices. By pacing yourself, and continually monitoring your progress against your watch, you will always know exactly how far ahead or behind you are with your available time. If you find that you are one minute behind on the test, don't skip one question without spending any time on it, just to catch back up. Take 15 fewer seconds on the next four questions, and after four questions you'll have caught back up. Once you catch back up, you can continue working each problem at your normal pace.

Furthermore, don't dwell on the problems that you were rushed on. If a problem was taking up too much time and you made a hurried guess, it must be difficult. The difficult questions are the ones you are most likely to miss anyway, so it isn't a big loss. It is better to end with more time than you need than to run out of time.

Lastly, sometimes it is beneficial to slow down if you are constantly getting ahead of time. You are always more likely to catch a careless mistake by working more slowly than quickly, and among very high-scoring test takers (those who are likely to have lots of time left over), careless errors affect the score more than mastery of material.

Copyright © Mometrix Media. You have been licensed one copy of this document for personal use only. Any other reproduction or redistribution is strictly prohibited. All rights reserved.

Secret Key #2 - Guessing is not Guesswork

You probably know that guessing is a good idea. Unlike other standardized tests, there is no penalty for getting a wrong answer. Even if you have no idea about a question, you still have a 20-25% chance of getting it right.

Most test takers do not understand the impact that proper guessing can have on their score. Unless you score extremely high, guessing will significantly contribute to your final score.

Monkeys Take the Test

What most test takers don't realize is that to insure that 20-25% chance, you have to guess randomly. If you put 20 monkeys in a room to take this test, assuming they answered once per question and behaved themselves, on average they would get 20-25% of the questions correct.

Put 20 test takers in the room, and the average will be much lower among guessed questions. Why?
1. The test writers intentionally write deceptive answer choices that "look" right. A test taker has no idea about a question, so he picks the "best looking" answer, which is often wrong. The monkey has no idea what looks good and what doesn't, so it will consistently be right about 20-25% of the time.
2. Test takers will eliminate answer choices from the guessing pool based on a hunch or intuition. Simple but correct answers often get excluded, leaving a 0% chance of being correct. The monkey has no clue, and often gets lucky with the best choice.

This is why the process of elimination endorsed by most test courses is flawed and detrimental to your performance. Test takers don't guess; they make an ignorant stab in the dark that is usually worse than random.

Copyright © Mometrix Media. You have been licensed one copy of this document for personal use only. Any other reproduction or redistribution is strictly prohibited. All rights reserved.

$5 Challenge

Let me introduce one of the most valuable ideas of this course—the $5 challenge:

You only mark your "best guess" if you are willing to bet $5 on it.
You only eliminate choices from guessing if you are willing to bet $5 on it.

Why $5? Five dollars is an amount of money that is small yet not insignificant, and can really add up fast (20 questions could cost you $100). Likewise, each answer choice on one question of the test will have a small impact on your overall score, but it can really add up to a lot of points in the end.

The process of elimination IS valuable. The following shows your chance of guessing it right:

If you eliminate wrong answer choices until only this many remain:	Chance of getting it correct:
1	100%
2	50%
3	33%

However, if you accidentally eliminate the right answer or go on a hunch for an incorrect answer, your chances drop dramatically—to 0%. By guessing among all the answer choices, you are GUARANTEED to have a shot at the right answer.

That's why the $5 test is so valuable. If you give up the advantage and safety of a pure guess, it had better be worth the risk.

What we still haven't covered is how to be sure that whatever guess you make is truly random. Here's the easiest way:

Always pick the first answer choice among those remaining.

Such a technique means that you have decided, **before you see a single test question**, exactly how you are going to guess, and since the order of choices tells you nothing about which one is correct, this guessing technique is perfectly random.

This section is not meant to scare you away from making educated guesses or eliminating choices; you just need to define when a choice is worth eliminating. The $5 test, along with a pre-defined random guessing strategy, is the best way to make sure you reap all of the benefits of guessing.

Copyright © Mometrix Media. You have been licensed one copy of this document for personal use only. Any other reproduction or redistribution is strictly prohibited. All rights reserved.

Secret Key #3 - Practice Smarter, Not Harder

Many test takers delay the test preparation process because they dread the awful amounts of practice time they think necessary to succeed on the test. We have refined an effective method that will take you only a fraction of the time.

There are a number of "obstacles" in the path to success. Among these are answering questions, finishing in time, and mastering test-taking strategies. All must be executed on the day of the test at peak performance, or your score will suffer. The test is a mental marathon that has a large impact on your future.

Just like a marathon runner, it is important to work your way up to the full challenge. So first you just worry about questions, and then time, and finally strategy:

Success Strategy

1. Find a good source for practice tests.
2. If you are willing to make a larger time investment, consider using more than one study guide. Often the different approaches of multiple authors will help you "get" difficult concepts.
3. Take a practice test with no time constraints, with all study helps, "open book." Take your time with questions and focus on applying strategies.
4. Take a practice test with time constraints, with all guides, "open book."
5. Take a final practice test without open material and with time limits.

If you have time to take more practice tests, just repeat step 5. By gradually exposing yourself to the full rigors of the test environment, you will condition your mind to the stress of test day and maximize your success.

Copyright © Mometrix Media. You have been licensed one copy of this document for personal use only. Any other reproduction or redistribution is strictly prohibited. All rights reserved.

Secret Key #4 - Prepare, Don't Procrastinate

Let me state an obvious fact: if you take the test three times, you will probably get three different scores. This is due to the way you feel on test day, the level of preparedness you have, and the version of the test you see. Despite the test writers' claims to the contrary, some versions of the test WILL be easier for you than others.

Since your future depends so much on your score, you should maximize your chances of success. In order to maximize the likelihood of success, you've got to prepare in advance. This means taking practice tests and spending time learning the information and test taking strategies you will need to succeed.

Never go take the actual test as a "practice" test, expecting that you can just take it again if you need to. Take all the practice tests you can on your own, but when you go to take the official test, be prepared, be focused, and do your best the first time!

Copyright © Mometrix Media. You have been licensed one copy of this document for personal use only. Any other reproduction or redistribution is strictly prohibited. All rights reserved.

Secret Key #5 - Test Yourself

Everyone knows that time is money. There is no need to spend too much of your time or too little of your time preparing for the test. You should only spend as much of your precious time preparing as is necessary for you to get the score you need.

Once you have taken a practice test under real conditions of time constraints, then you will know if you are ready for the test or not.

If you have scored extremely high the first time that you take the practice test, then there is not much point in spending countless hours studying. You are already there.

Benchmark your abilities by retaking practice tests and seeing how much you have improved. Once you consistently score high enough to guarantee success, then you are ready.

If you have scored well below where you need, then knuckle down and begin studying in earnest. Check your improvement regularly through the use of practice tests under real conditions. Above all, don't worry, panic, or give up. The key is perseverance!

Then, when you go to take the test, remain confident and remember how well you did on the practice tests. If you can score high enough on a practice test, then you can do the same on the real thing.

Copyright © Mometrix Media. You have been licensed one copy of this document for personal use only. Any other reproduction or redistribution is strictly prohibited. All rights reserved.

General Strategies

The most important thing you can do is to ignore your fears and jump into the test immediately. Do not be overwhelmed by any strange-sounding terms. You have to jump into the test like jumping into a pool—all at once is the easiest way.

Make Predictions

As you read and understand the question, try to guess what the answer will be. Remember that several of the answer choices are wrong, and once you begin reading them, your mind will immediately become cluttered with answer choices designed to throw you off. Your mind is typically the most focused immediately after you have read the question and digested its contents. If you can, try to predict what the correct answer will be. You may be surprised at what you can predict.

Quickly scan the choices and see if your prediction is in the listed answer choices. If it is, then you can be quite confident that you have the right answer. It still won't hurt to check the other answer choices, but most of the time, you've got it!

Answer the Question

It may seem obvious to only pick answer choices that answer the question, but the test writers can create some excellent answer choices that are wrong. Don't pick an answer just because it sounds right, or you believe it to be true. It MUST answer the question. Once you've made your selection, always go back and check it against the question and make sure that you didn't misread the question and that the answer choice does answer the question posed.

Benchmark

After you read the first answer choice, decide if you think it sounds correct or not. If it doesn't, move on to the next answer choice. If it does, mentally mark that answer choice. This doesn't mean that you've definitely selected it as your answer choice, it just means that it's the best you've seen thus far. Go ahead and read the next choice. If the next choice is worse than the one you've already selected, keep going to the next answer choice. If the next choice is better than the choice you've already selected, mentally mark the new answer choice as your best guess.

The first answer choice that you select becomes your standard. Every other answer choice must be benchmarked against that standard. That choice is correct until proven otherwise by another answer choice beating it out. Once you've decided that no other answer choice seems as good, do one final check to ensure that your answer choice answers the question posed.

Valid Information

Don't discount any of the information provided in the question. Every piece of information may be necessary to determine the correct answer. None of the information in the question is there to throw you off (while the answer choices will certainly have information to throw you off). If two seemingly unrelated topics are discussed, don't ignore either. You can be confident there is a relationship, or it wouldn't be included in the question, and you are probably going to have to determine what is that relationship to find the answer.

Copyright © Mometrix Media. You have been licensed one copy of this document for personal use only. Any other reproduction or redistribution is strictly prohibited. All rights reserved.

Avoid "Fact Traps"

Don't get distracted by a choice that is factually true. Your search is for the answer that answers the question. Stay focused and don't fall for an answer that is true but irrelevant. Always go back to the question and make sure you're choosing an answer that actually answers the question and is not just a true statement. An answer can be factually correct, but it MUST answer the question asked. Additionally, two answers can both be seemingly correct, so be sure to read all of the answer choices, and make sure that you get the one that BEST answers the question.

Milk the Question

Some of the questions may throw you completely off. They might deal with a subject you have not been exposed to, or one that you haven't reviewed in years. While your lack of knowledge about the subject will be a hindrance, the question itself can give you many clues that will help you find the correct answer. Read the question carefully and look for clues. Watch particularly for adjectives and nouns describing difficult terms or words that you don't recognize. Regardless of whether you completely understand a word or not, replacing it with a synonym, either provided or one you more familiar with, may help you to understand what the questions are asking. Rather than wracking your mind about specific detailed information concerning a difficult term or word, try to use mental substitutes that are easier to understand.

The Trap of Familiarity

Don't just choose a word because you recognize it. On difficult questions, you may not recognize a number of words in the answer choices. The test writers don't put "make-believe" words on the test, so don't think that just because you only recognize all the words in one answer choice that that answer choice must be correct. If you only recognize words in one answer choice, then focus on that one. Is it correct? Try your best to determine if it is correct. If it is, that's great. If not, eliminate it. Each word and answer choice you eliminate increases your chances of getting the question correct, even if you then have to guess among the unfamiliar choices.

Eliminate Answers

Eliminate choices as soon as you realize they are wrong. But be careful! Make sure you consider all of the possible answer choices. Just because one appears right, doesn't mean that the next one won't be even better! The test writers will usually put more than one good answer choice for every question, so read all of them. Don't worry if you are stuck between two that seem right. By getting down to just two remaining possible choices, your odds are now 50/50. Rather than wasting too much time, play the odds. You are guessing, but guessing wisely because you've been able to knock out some of the answer choices that you know are wrong. If you are eliminating choices and realize that the last answer choice you are left with is also obviously wrong, don't panic. Start over and consider each choice again. There may easily be something that you missed the first time and will realize on the second pass.

Tough Questions

If you are stumped on a problem or it appears too hard or too difficult, don't waste time. Move on! Remember though, if you can quickly check for obviously incorrect answer choices, your chances of guessing correctly are greatly improved. Before you completely give up, at least try to knock out a couple of possible answers. Eliminate what you can and then guess at the remaining answer choices before moving on.

Brainstorm

If you get stuck on a difficult question, spend a few seconds quickly brainstorming. Run through the complete list of possible answer choices. Look at each choice and ask yourself, "Could this answer

Copyright © Mometrix Media. You have been licensed one copy of this document for personal use only. Any other reproduction or redistribution is strictly prohibited. All rights reserved.

the question satisfactorily?" Go through each answer choice and consider it independently of the others. By systematically going through all possibilities, you may find something that you would otherwise overlook. Remember though that when you get stuck, it's important to try to keep moving.

Read Carefully

Understand the problem. Read the question and answer choices carefully. Don't miss the question because you misread the terms. You have plenty of time to read each question thoroughly and make sure you understand what is being asked. Yet a happy medium must be attained, so don't waste too much time. You must read carefully, but efficiently.

Face Value

When in doubt, use common sense. Always accept the situation in the problem at face value. Don't read too much into it. These problems will not require you to make huge leaps of logic. The test writers aren't trying to throw you off with a cheap trick. If you have to go beyond creativity and make a leap of logic in order to have an answer choice answer the question, then you should look at the other answer choices. Don't overcomplicate the problem by creating theoretical relationships or explanations that will warp time or space. These are normal problems rooted in reality. It's just that the applicable relationship or explanation may not be readily apparent and you have to figure things out. Use your common sense to interpret anything that isn't clear.

Prefixes

If you're having trouble with a word in the question or answer choices, try dissecting it. Take advantage of every clue that the word might include. Prefixes and suffixes can be a huge help. Usually they allow you to determine a basic meaning. Pre- means before, post- means after, pro - is positive, de- is negative. From these prefixes and suffixes, you can get an idea of the general meaning of the word and try to put it into context. Beware though of any traps. Just because con- is the opposite of pro-, doesn't necessarily mean congress is the opposite of progress!

Hedge Phrases

Watch out for critical hedge phrases, led off with words such as "likely," "may," "can," "sometimes," "often," "almost," "mostly," "usually," "generally," "rarely," and "sometimes." Question writers insert these hedge phrases to cover every possibility. Often an answer choice will be wrong simply because it leaves no room for exception. Unless the situation calls for them, avoid answer choices that have definitive words like "exactly," and "always."

Switchback Words

Stay alert for "switchbacks." These are the words and phrases frequently used to alert you to shifts in thought. The most common switchback word is "but." Others include "although," "however," "nevertheless," "on the other hand," "even though," "while," "in spite of," "despite," and "regardless of."

New Information

Correct answer choices will rarely have completely new information included. Answer choices typically are straightforward reflections of the material asked about and will directly relate to the question. If a new piece of information is included in an answer choice that doesn't even seem to relate to the topic being asked about, then that answer choice is likely incorrect. All of the information needed to answer the question is usually provided for you in the question. You should not have to make guesses that are unsupported or choose answer choices that require unknown information that cannot be reasoned from what is given.

Copyright © Mometrix Media. You have been licensed one copy of this document for personal use only. Any other reproduction or redistribution is strictly prohibited. All rights reserved.

Time Management

On technical questions, don't get lost on the technical terms. Don't spend too much time on any one question. If you don't know what a term means, then odds are you aren't going to get much further since you don't have a dictionary. You should be able to immediately recognize whether or not you know a term. If you don't, work with the other clues that you have—the other answer choices and terms provided—but don't waste too much time trying to figure out a difficult term that you don't know.

Contextual Clues

Look for contextual clues. An answer can be right but not the correct answer. The contextual clues will help you find the answer that is most right and is correct. Understand the context in which a phrase or statement is made. This will help you make important distinctions.

Don't Panic

Panicking will not answer any questions for you; therefore, it isn't helpful. When you first see the question, if your mind goes blank, take a deep breath. Force yourself to mechanically go through the steps of solving the problem using the strategies you've learned.

Pace Yourself

Don't get clock fever. It's easy to be overwhelmed when you're looking at a page full of questions, your mind is full of random thoughts and feeling confused, and the clock is ticking down faster than you would like. Calm down and maintain the pace that you have set for yourself. As long as you are on track by monitoring your pace, you are guaranteed to have enough time for yourself. When you get to the last few minutes of the test, it may seem like you won't have enough time left, but if you only have as many questions as you should have left at that point, then you're right on track!

Answer Selection

The best way to pick an answer choice is to eliminate all of those that are wrong, until only one is left and confirm that is the correct answer. Sometimes though, an answer choice may immediately look right. Be careful! Take a second to make sure that the other choices are not equally obvious. Don't make a hasty mistake. There are only two times that you should stop before checking other answers. First is when you are positive that the answer choice you have selected is correct. Second is when time is almost out and you have to make a quick guess!

Check Your Work

Since you will probably not know every term listed and the answer to every question, it is important that you get credit for the ones that you do know. Don't miss any questions through careless mistakes. If at all possible, try to take a second to look back over your answer selection and make sure you've selected the correct answer choice and haven't made a costly careless mistake (such as marking an answer choice that you didn't mean to mark). The time it takes for this quick double check should more than pay for itself in caught mistakes.

Beware of Directly Quoted Answers

Sometimes an answer choice will repeat word for word a portion of the question or reference section. However, beware of such exact duplication. It may be a trap! More than likely, the correct choice will paraphrase or summarize a point, rather than being exactly the same wording.

Copyright © Mometrix Media. You have been licensed one copy of this document for personal use only. Any other reproduction or redistribution is strictly prohibited. All rights reserved.

Slang

Scientific sounding answers are better than slang ones. An answer choice that begins "To compare the outcomes…" is much more likely to be correct than one that begins "Because some people insisted…"

Extreme Statements

Avoid wild answers that throw out highly controversial ideas that are proclaimed as established fact. An answer choice that states the "process should used in certain situations, if…" is much more likely to be correct than one that states the "process should be discontinued completely." The first is a calm rational statement and doesn't even make a definitive, uncompromising stance, using a hedge word "if" to provide wiggle room, whereas the second choice is a radical idea and far more extreme.

Answer Choice Families

When you have two or more answer choices that are direct opposites or parallels, one of them is usually the correct answer. For instance, if one answer choice states "x increases" and another answer choice states "x decreases" or "y increases," then those two or three answer choices are very similar in construction and fall into the same family of answer choices. A family of answer choices consists of two or three answer choices, very similar in construction, but often with directly opposite meanings. Usually the correct answer choice will be in that family of answer choices. The "odd man out" or answer choice that doesn't seem to fit the parallel construction of the other answer choices is more likely to be incorrect.

Copyright © Mometrix Media. You have been licensed one copy of this document for personal use only. Any other reproduction or redistribution is strictly prohibited. All rights reserved.

Additional Bonus Material

Due to our efforts to try to keep this book to a manageable length, we've created a link that will give you access to all of your additional bonus material.

Please visit http://www.mometrix.com/bonus948/ftceprekinprim to access the information.

Copyright © Mometrix Media. You have been licensed one copy of this document for personal use only. Any other reproduction or redistribution is strictly prohibited. All rights reserved.

65242892R00114

Made in the USA
Lexington, KY
05 July 2017